Global History in China

Xin Fan

Global History in China

palgrave
macmillan

Xin Fan
Faculty of Asian and Middle Eastern
Studies
University of Cambridge
Cambridge, Cambridgeshire, UK

ISBN 978-981-97-3380-4   ISBN 978-981-97-3381-1   (eBook)
https://doi.org/10.1007/978-981-97-3381-1

PREFACE

On September 28, 1980, Xiao Qian 蕭乾 (1910–1999) wrote to the British economist Joan Robinson (1903–1983). In this letter, this septuagenarian Chinese journalist and writer, who had studied and worked in Cambridge and London during the Second World War, expressed optimism for his country's future. After a decade-long Cultural Revolution and years of chaos caused by political movements and ideological campaigns, he celebrated the prospect that "China at long last is on the right track." He noted that intellectuals were "mobilised" and "received much better treatment," and writers like himself also enjoyed "much more freedom" to publish and to travel around the world. He expressed a desire to reconnect with his friends in Cambridge, promising in China "[overseas] relations are no longer taboo." China had ceased treating Western countries as enemies. Drawing on the example of America, he observed a shift in discourse. Only one out of the recent ten articles published in *The People's Daily*, he counted, was critical, while the rest were "about their merits." "No one dare do so in the past," but now people in China knew, as he reflected, "America had nothing to lose by our distortions." He sighed, "We are the losers."[1]

---

[1] "Xiao Qian's Letter to Joan Robinson on September 28, 1980," Joan Robinson Collection, King's College Archive Centre, Cambridge, vii/214/1.

Reading this letter in a chilly early autumn morning at a Cambridge college archive, I was deeply moved by the energy radiating from it— a spirit that captures the vigor of Chinese intellectuals in the 1980s rejecting past isolationist policies, reconnecting with the outside world, and embracing the new opportunities brought by the budding movement of globalization. To some extent, writing this book on global history in China is my way of paying tribute to several generations of Chinese scholars who exerted tremendous efforts to integrate the study of China's past within the globalized world from the 1980s to the present day.

This is a book about historiography. Global history is an emerging field of scholarly studies in China. Despite a growing number of scholars claiming it as their research interest in recent decades, challenges persist in its development. One major challenge lies in the lack of a designated place in the Chinese classification of academic disciplines. In other words, it is an intellectual movement without its own "discipline." But the movement itself remains significant.

In this book, I invite the reader to trace the origin of global history in China and to examine its current state. I argue, rooted in a warm appreciation of globalization during the era of Opening-up and Reform and presented as a trendy transnational intellectual movement at the beginning of the twenty-first century, global history, on the one hand, claims the identity of the "new," eager to criticize the Eurocentric bias inherent in narratives of the "old," such as those found in world history; on the other hand, as an emerging field, it faces competition from national histories and area studies, both of which are supported by the latest state initiatives with explicit political agendas. Thus, I contend that global history, as a whole, reflects Chinese scholars' tenacious interest in studying globalization through the lens of history.

Transitioning from theory to practice, Chinese historians have also embraced global history to explore China's place in world-historical time and space. In this book, I present case studies on three promising approaches, including conceptual history, global history as a critique of Eurocentrism, and studies of global moments. Global history is still under developing in China, and the future of global history is contingent on a critical examination of temporal and spatial aspects of historical inquiries, as well as a reconsideration of the relationship between secondary scholarship and primary sources in historiography.

Written for a wider audience with an interest in global history extending beyond the China field, *Global History in China* provides a succinct narrative accessible to non-Chinese readers. I am actively working to synthesize both Chinese and non-Chinese language scholarship, aiming to facilitate a viable exchange of knowledge between scholars in China and their international counterparts in the post-pandemic era. Moreover, this book serves as an ideal reference for graduate seminars on world history and global history at research universities in East Asia, North America, and Western Europe.

Writing a book on global history in China in English poses a challenging task in transcultural and translingual practice. It requires researchers not only to introduce a body of non-English scholarship to an English-speaking audience but also to contextualize the significance of these works within both Chinese and global historiographies. This challenge is particularly pronounced as global history remains a fluid intellectual movement, yet to find its place in China's national system of disciplinary classification. If studying historiography is akin to "nailing jelly to the wall," studying global history in China involves the preliminary task of determining what this elusive "jelly" actually encompasses.[2]

To surmount these cultural barriers in studying global history in China, access to Chinese-language scholarship proves pivotal. As someone who has studied, worked, and lived outside the country for nearly two decades, I am especially grateful for my friends, colleagues, and mentors in China, including Cao Shengsheng, Cao Yin, Chu Zhuwu, Fan Shitao, Ge Zhaoguang, Geng Yuanli, Huang Jiangjun, Jin Qianwen, Li Danhui, Li Xuetao, Li Yongbin, Liu Jiahe, Liu Xian'ge, Ni Tengda, Niu Dayong, Shen Zhihua, Yang Gongle, Zhang Ke, Zhang Xupeng, Zhang Yang, and others. Some of them helped me to acquire publications and sources for this research project, while others shared their experiences as world/global historians through enlightening conversations and dialogues. Without their invaluable contributions, writing such a book is an insurmountable task. Special thanks also go to Tan Shengguang at Tsinghua University, Yao Baihui at Capital Normal University, and Marc Matten at the University of Erlangen-Nuremberg for their assistance in obtaining permissions to include valuable images in this book. At Palgrave, my editor Jacob Dreyer has been an outstanding cheerleader,

---

[2] Peter Novak compares writing historiography to "nailing jelly to the wall" in *That Noble Dream: The "Objectivity Question" and the American Historical Profession* (Cambridge: Cambridge University Press, 1988).

demonstrating exceptional patience with my multiple requests for deadline extensions and generously providing unwavering support. It has been a great honor to collaborate with him and with Palgrave.

On multiple occasions, both in person and online, I had the privilege of presenting chapters from this manuscript. At Peking University, my dear mentor and esteemed colleague in Cambridge, Hans van de Ven, organized an excellent panel on "China in a Global WWII" in November 2023, during which I presented the chapter covering "global moments." Questions and feedback from Joseph Esherick, Niu Dayong, and other panelists inspired me to delve deeper into the examination of the national versus the global in Chinese historiography. I also presented two chapters at online conferences organized by scholars from Beijing Normal University and Capital Normal University. Engaging with scholars in China was truly a blessing, providing invaluable assistance in navigating research beyond Eurocentric academic settings.

While completing the book manuscript at Cambridge, I am immensely grateful for the help provided by a group of scholars. Tom Barrett shared his insightful perspectives on Japanese scholarship, enabling me to incorporate this significant dimension into my study of global historiography. Adam Yuet Chau chaired a workshop where I presented the chapter on the rise of area studies, and the daily conversations with him contributed to a source of inspiration throughout the book project. Toshihiko Aono provided valuable comments on several chapters and offered excellent suggestions on framing the introduction. Lynn Zhang, Lang Chen, and several others read certain chapters, and their feedback proved to be instrumental. I also gained tremendous benefits from the scholarly discussions with Roel Sterckx, John Nilsson-Wright, Bill Hurst, Mary Brazelton, Dan Knorr, Rachel Leow, Jeremy Adelman, Tom McBride, Sam Meston, and others. Barak Kushner, the energic chair of the Department of East Asian Studies, is always there to help with all my urgent requests for assistance and support. Elena Fulgheri and Miki Jacobs at both the University Library and the Faculty of Asian and Middle Eastern Studies also offered enormous help. Last but not least, I am truly grateful to Lucy Cavendish College for offering me a fellowship. Many of the great ideas for this book project were first tested at the dinner table of Lucy's extraordinary formal halls.

In Europe, Dominic Sachsenmaier hosted me during my multiple visits to Göttingen where the idea of this book was first conceived through conversations, seminars, and debates. He also provided constructive feedback on several chapters of the manuscript. So did Marc Matten at Erlangen. I appreciate Marc's continuous interest in this project. I feel privileged and grateful to be invited by him to visit the SASS Collection. It was during his workshop I first planned to write about the rise of area studies. The chapter on global conceptual history is a product of a working group coordinated by Margrit Pernau and Alp Eren Topal in Berlin, and I appreciate insightful comments from Lisa Mitchell and Martin Plot during our several online meetings. In Barcelona, Carles Brasó Broggi showed great hospitality when I presented this book project at Universitat Oberta de Catalunya. David Martínez-Robles, Xavier Ortells-Nicolau, Maria Iñigo, Andrés Burbano, Enrique Mora, Ferran de Vargas, Javier Borrás, Carles Prado, and others offered useful feedback and helpful suggestions. It was my first time presenting the project as a book manuscript, and the positive response encouraged me to pursue it further.

Scholarship in world history and global history in North America continues to be a profound source of inspiration for my research. The Pittsburgh world history dissertation workshop in 2010 organized by Pat Manning, the late Adam McKeown, and Heather Streets marked the inception of my scholarly journey into writing on Chinese global historiography. As I send this draft to my mentor, I hope that Pat enjoys reading it. I have also had the privilege of collaboration with Kristin Stapleton and Els van Dongen, thanks to another project on historiography. Their extensive knowledge of Chinese history has significantly broadened my understanding of the field. The long walks and late summer dinners with Rebecca Karl have been enjoyable, and her kindness in encouraging me to appreciate both my strengths and weaknesses in both life and work is invaluable. Q. Edward Wang remains my dear mentor and intimate friend, a towering figure in historiography whose support justifies all the hard work. The same sentiment holds for my dear friend Chen Huaiyu, whose prolific publications on nearly every subject in history establish him as a true "global historian" of our generation.

Some of the ideas presented in this book were initially introduced in other publications or will be featured in upcoming works. A section of Chapter 2 was originally published as "'International Law in Ancient China': Eurocentrism and the Rethinking of Case Studies in Chinese Intellectual History" in *Global Intellectual History* 7, no. 2 (2022): 265–281. I express my sincere gratitude to Taylor & Francis Group for granting permission to republish it in this volume, and I appreciate the chief editor of the journal Rosario López's support. Chapter 1 is a commissioned contribution to Q. Edward Wang's edited volume on East Asian historiography. However, it is important to note that all these prior publications have undergone careful revisions to ensure consistency within the context of this book.

Global History in China was completed during the time my family transitioned from the United States to the United Kingdom. I am truly grateful for my wife Yan He's intellectual companionship. She now oversees one of the most prestigious Chinese studies collections in the world. Her tireless pursuit of knowledge in history and great devotion to the profession of librarianship continue to serve as a tremendous inspiration to me. Without her encouragement, this project would be impossible. So, I dedicate the book to her. My son Eric is currently studying ancient Greek for his GCSE tests, a language I once dreamt of commanding. I hope that through him, the love for the shared legacy in humanity will persist in the next generation. Of course, both my parents Fan Songli and Chen Shuhua and my in-laws He Zhiqiang and Zhang Yujie always support our work. Any tiny little progress we make brings immense joy to them. Therefore, we will continue our family's global journey to pursue love, knowledge, and a genuine understanding of humanity.

Cambridge, UK   Xin Fan

CONTENTS

CONTENTS

LIST OF FIGURES

LIST OF TABLES

CHAPTER 1

Introduction

Abstract This chapter serves as an introduction to the book. It provides
the central argument, asserting that global history endeavors to incorporate China's historical narrative into the broader tapestry of human
experience while maintaining a dialogue with Chinese historiography.
Despite transcending national boundaries, the emergence of area studies
poses a challenge to the scholarly integrity of the field. This chapter critically assesses existing literature in the field while outlining the book's dual
methodology: an intellectual history of historiography and a sociological examination of disciplinary formation. Furthermore, it delineates key
personalities, events, and themes to be explored in subsequent chapters.

Keywords Global history · Intellectual history · Sociology of
knowledge · Critique of Eurocentrism · Historiography · Area studies

Global history is a subject of scholarly examination within contemporary
global historiography. Similar to its counterpart in North America and
Western Europe, the field of global history in China challenges Eurocentric biases, underscores global connections, and utilizes contextual

© The Author(s), under exclusive license to Springer Nature   1
Singapore Pte Ltd. 2024
X. Fan, *Global History in China*,
https://doi.org/10.1007/978-981-97-3381-1_1

comparisons.[1] Originating from the enthusiastic embrace of globalization by Chinese scholars in the 1980s, the concept of global history has evolved into a prominent topic among historians in the past four decades. In present-day China, global history signifies cutting-edge scholarship that aligns with scholarly trends in the West. Yet its relationship with world history remains an open-ended question. As *Global History in China* traces the development of this field, it attempts to define global history in China by contextualizing its entangled relationship with world history.

"World history," referred to as "shijie shi" (世界史), stands as a well-defined scholarly discipline in China. According to the most recent state classification, world history holds the status as "a first-level discipline" (*yiji xueke*, 一級學科) within the broader field of historical studies, running parallel with disciplines such as "Chinese history," "Museum studies," and "Archaeology." As of now, world history is further categorized into five "second-level" disciplines (*erji xueke*, 二級學科),—historical theory and foreign historiography, ancient and medieval world history, modern and contemporary world history, world regional and country histories, and specialized topics in world history. Despite the absence of a clear definition in official documentation, world historians in China seldom incorporate Chinese history into their studies due to the distinct disciplinary division between "Chinese History" and "World History." In other words, world history in China is effectively regarded as the study of "foreign history."[2]

In contrast, global history, known as "quanqiu shi" (全球史), remains an intellectual movement without a clearly defined place within the state-sanctioned disciplinary structure. Most historians who claim global history as their research interest hold their primary disciplinary affiliations with either "World History" or "Chinese History." Additionally, individuals from backgrounds in language education, foreign culture studies, and international studies also contribute to the field. As a result, global history

---

[1] For recent English-language scholarship on global history, see Sebastian Conrad, *What Is Global History?* (Princeton: Princeton University Press, 2017); Patrick Manning, *Navigating World History: Historians Create a Global Past* (New York: Palgrave Macmillan, 2003); Pamela Crossley, *What Is Global History?* (Cambridge: Polity, 2008).

[2] Q. Edward Wang, "World History on a Par with Chinese History? China's Search for World Power in Three Stages," *Global Intellectual History* 7, no. 2 (2022): 303–324; Xin Fan, *World History and National Identity in China: The Twentieth Century* (Cambridge: Cambridge University Press, 2021).

in China lacks standardized educational curricula, unified professional assessment standards, and dedicated funding sources. Students interested in studying global history often navigate through curricula that may not prioritize global historical education. Scholars pursuing global historical research face evaluations from colleagues who may even be resistant to global history's research agendas. This sociological void within the knowledge production system poses a significant challenge to the development of global history in China.

Yet while China's world history discipline continues to maintain a separation between "Chinese history" and "the world," global history in China emerges as a commendable intellectual endeavor to bridge this cultural dichotomy. The concept of incorporating global perspectives into historical studies took root in the 1980s when Chinese intellectuals enthusiastically embraced the era of "opening-up" (開放) to the world. Scholars characterize globalization as the defining spirit of the contemporary world. Since then, global history has welcomed both world historians and Chinese historians, emphasizing the importance of embracing global interconnectedness in historical studies. As underscored in this book, the inclusion of the Chinese perspective has been a prominent feature of global history in China.

This study particularly concentrates on two essential aspects to comprehend global history as an evolving scholarly discipline in China: intellectual history and the sociology of knowledge. By "intellectual history," I mean an examination of evolving concepts, ideas, and thoughts concerning China's relationship with the world and China's existence in the world. Its component provides a narrative that traces the rise of global perspectives in historical thinking throughout the twentieth century and even into the late Qing dynasty. Over this period, a prevailing trend emerged among Chinese historians, aiming to construct a global narrative of the collective community of humanity. In contrast, by "sociology of knowledge," I mean studies of the social dimensions in the production of knowledge concerning interpersonal relations, institutional structures, and state–society dynamics. This study particularly highlights the institutional development that facilitates the rise of global historical research in China. As a scholarly approach, it adds a unique dimension to the understanding of how global history has taken shape within the expansive academic landscape in China and within the world.[3]

Positioned as an intellectual history project, *Global History in China* contends that, for numerous scholars, global history signifies a profound acknowledgment of China's integrated place both within the global space and world-historical time. This book examines diverse dynamics within modern Chinese intellectual thought that propel the rise of global history in Chinese historiography. First and foremost is the Chinese historians' quest for a common humanity in the collective past of human beings.

Historically, mainstream scholarship has emphasized the discourse of cultural differences between China and the rest of the world. As well documented the debates on Hua-Yi differences (華夷之分), some scholars once strongly argued that Chinese scholar-officials perceived a fundamental distinction between Confucianism tradition and Western modernity.[4] Many Chinese scholars in the May Fourth and during the 1980s held a similar view criticizing China's cultural tradition for its lack of dynamics and isolationist tendencies attributing them to its decline in the modern world order. Throughout this book, I challenge this assumption and document how certain Chinese historians are embracing shared values among cultures. They are actively working to bridge the gaps between China and the wider world through the promotion of global history. These scholars sometimes might be the minority within the Chinese intellectual community, but their perspective represents a persistent trend in modern Chinese thought.

In my previous work, *World History and National Identity in China*, I examined the resistance exhibited by certain world historians against cultural nationalism. The rise of global history presents new prospects for connecting Chinese history with broader world history narratives, as scholars from both realms actively contribute to this burgeoning field.

---

[3] Dominic Sachsenmaier also underscores this sociological aspect in his comparative studies on the rise of global historical views in China, America, and Germany. Dominic Sachsenmaier, *Global Perspectives on Global History: Theories and Approaches in a Connected World* (Cambridge: Cambridge University Press, 2011).

[4] Scholars have widely discussed this tension. To just cite one post-colonial critique as an example, see Lydia Liu, *The Clash of Empires: The Invention of China in Modern World Making* (Cambridge, MA: Harvard University Press, 2004).

Among them, those scholars specializing in Chinese history are particularly bold in asserting that China is an integrated part of global historical analysis.

As articulated by Fudan historian Ge Zhaoguang 葛兆光 (1950–), a distinction exists between "telling global history from China" (從中國出發) and "telling global history with China being at the center" (以中國為中心). Scholars like him reject a Sinocentric perspective and boldly embrace their positionality in advocating for global history from China. Ge argues that, on the one hand, global history is not all-encompassing, necessitating scholars to acknowledge the inherent limitations in their knowledge and experiences. On the other hand, recognizing that each country occupies a unique geographical vantage point, Chinese perspectives, when combined with those from other parts of the world, contribute to a more comprehensive global understanding.

The impact of this school of thought has extended beyond the confines of academic research. Global historians such as Ge actively engage in global history education through social media, emphasizing the importance of avoiding alienation of popular audiences. Ge in collaboration with a team of scholars successfully organized a lecture series on global history, making significant strides in popularizing the subject in China.[5] Over the course of two and a half years, the series has captured the attention of more than 100,000 audiences, who have accumulatively engaged with the program millions of times.[6] This collective effort has transformed global history into a dynamic movement that not only connects professional historians with broader audiences but also strives to instill a global perspective on human history among the Chinese public.

The second aspect delves into Chinese intellectuals' ambivalent stance toward Eurocentrism. Deeply entrenched in a self-perceived tradition of

[5] Ge Zhaoguang collaborated with public intellectual and journalist Liang Wendao 梁文道 launched a 200-episode podcast series *Cong Zhongguo chufa de quanqiu* [Global History Starting from China]. The series includes six seasons including, the first on the common beginning of human civilization, the second on war and migration, the third on merchandise, trade, and material exchanges, the fourth on religions and beliefs, the fifth on disease, climate, and environment, and the last one on the age after the Great Geographical Discovery. https://zt.vistopia.com.cn/page/?page_id=bVlRr.

[6] Li Jing, "Ge Zhaoguang: Quanqiushi shi bici lianxi de lishi" [Ge Zhaoguang: Global History Is a History of Connectedness], *Nanfang renwu zhoukan* [People in the South Weekly], no. 12 (April 28, 2023): https://www.infzm.com/contents/248149?source=131.

cultural continuity, Chinese scholars in the twentieth century developed a strong conviction that understanding the strength of Western modernity required grasping its cultural roots in classical antiquity. Some prominent voices like Chen Duxiu 陳獨秀 (1879–1942) during the New Culture Movement advocated for total Westernization.[7] Chinese students also traveled to Europe and North America for education, and some of them became political elites and actively promoted the discourse of modernity in China, including senior members of the Communist Party such as Deng Xiaoping 鄧小平 (1904–1997) and Zhou Enlai 周恩來 (1898–1976) as well as renowned world historians such as Lei Haizong 雷海宗 (1902–1962) and Qi Sihe 齊思和 (1907–1980). Despite the upheavals of the Cultural Revolution and radical communist movements, Chinese scholars in the humanities retained a sense of admiration for Western culture. As a result, studies of Western culture, particularly Greek and Roman antiquity, experience a revival in China in stark contrast to their decline in other parts of the world.[8]

At the same time, as Chinese scholars engage in the study of the West, they encounter the deep-seated bias of European and American scholarship toward the non-Western world, including China. This sentiment significantly influences Chinese scholarship on global history. From its inception, global historians in China have diligently followed developments in global history in the West, actively translating works from English, German, Japanese, and French into Chinese while remaining acutely aware of the Eurocentric bias present in much of this literature. They have consistently provided critiques of Eurocentrism through their narratives of global history.

In 1980, when Chinese historians re-engaged with the global academic community at the International Congress of Historical Sciences in Bucharest, they posed questions about the neglect of China's contributions to World War II scholarship. They sought to integrate China's War of Resistance into a more comprehensive global narrative of WWII. Similarly, a new generation of global historians in China is actively contributing to global historiography today by emphasizing angles

[7] Charlotte Furth, "Intellectual Change: From the Reform Movement to the May Fourth Movement, 1895–1920," in *An Intellectual History of Modern China*, eds. Merle Goldman and Leo Ou-fan Lee (Cambridge: Cambridge University Press, 2002), 79.

[8] Shadi Bartsch, *Plato Goes to China: The Greek Classics and Chinese Nationalism* (Princeton: Princeton University Press, 2023), 6.

and perspectives previously overlooked in Eurocentric scholarship. This includes a renewed focus on regions such as the Indian Ocean, Southeast Asia, and South Asia, highlighting their significance in the broader global historical context and decentralizing the role of nation-states. Unlike previous-generation world historians, they do not hesitate to incorporate China within these global, transnational, and regional connections.[9]

However, the critiques of Eurocentrism have not invariably led to a more "global" perspective on global history. Despite the positive strides made in global history, there is a concerning trend where some scholars are replacing Eurocentrism with Sino-centrism. The third aspect shaping global history in China is the rise of nationalism. Viewing history as a tool to advance specific ideological agendas, an increasing number of historians advocate for the writing of a "global history with Chinese characteristics." This trend, particularly evident in the recent surge of the history of "Great Powers" (*daguo shi*, 大國史), is troubling, as it has the potential to glorify power politics and legitimize colonial and imperial aggressions.

Furthermore, as demonstrated in this book, the recent rise of area studies appears to be a more overt attempt to politicize academic research. In *Global History in China*, I align with Ge Zhaoguang's perspective, emphasizing that a global history from China should not be a history centered on China. Instead, global history should fundamentally be a collaborative effort to construct a global narrative of humanity's collective past. In essence, global history serves as a powerful critique of the nationalist framework within existing world history scholarship.

In addition to these three themes, *Global History in China* explores the critical question of anti-colonialism and anti-imperialism in modern Chinese thought. In the Republican period, as detailed in this book, figures such as Sun Yat-sen 孫中山 (1866–1925), Chiang Kai-shek 蔣介石 (1887–1975), and the Nationalist Party actively advocated for China's

[9] In recent years, some young historians based in China have published interesting works on South Asia, Southeast Asia, maritime history, and environmental history both in Chinese and English. Often trained outside China, they are an impactful force promoting global history in China today. Just to name a few examples: on South Asia, see Yin Cao, *Chinese Sojourners in Wartime Raj, 1942–45* (Oxford: Oxford University Press, 2022); on maritime history, Guang Ma, *Rupture, Evolution, and Continuity: The Shandong Peninsular in East Asian Maritime History During the Yuan-Ming Transition* (Wiesbaden: Harrassowitz, 2021), and Chen Boyi, *Yinghuan zhilue: Quanqiushi zhong de haiyangshi* [Seeing Across the Oceans: Maritime History in Global History] (Guilin: Lijiang chubanshe, 2024).

recognition as a semi-colonial nation in a world dominated by colonialism and imperialism. By emphasizing China's classification as a "weak and small" country, the Nationalists celebrated the solidarity of China with other nations in the colonial world, seeking to draw imperial Japan into a global conflict involving empires and colonies. Similarly, the Communist Party adopted an anti-imperial rhetoric during the War with Japan, viewing China's resistance efforts as integral to global anti-fascist movements. This strong sense of anti-imperial sentiment persisted in the early years of the People's Republic, laying the emotional foundation for the surge in international studies and foreign histories in the 1960s and 1970s. To a certain degree, this anti-imperial legacy serves as the ideological justification for anti-global movements among conservative scholars in present-day China, as illustrated in this book's concluding chapter.

While *Global History in China* can be interpreted as a book on modern Chinese intellectual history, it equally emphasizes the institutional aspects contributing to the rise of global history in China. Employing a sociology of knowledge approach, I would like to draw the reader's attention to the significant challenge faced by global history, both in China and worldwide—the struggle to secure a distinct place within the existing framework of academic disciplines and classifications.

As discussed in the opening of this book, professionalization emerges as a dominant theme shaping the evolution of historiography in China throughout the twentieth century. This movement was initiated with the reforms by Cai Yuanpei 蔡元培 (1868–1940) at Peking University in 1916, rooted in the late Qing New Policies reform, and continued to unfold during both the Republican and People's Republic periods. This process encompassed the establishment of research centers, the launch of scholarly journals, and the separation of professional historians from amateur scholars through specialized research. Three key institutional aspects are crucial for comprehending the ascendancy of global history in China.

The first crucial aspect is the enduring influence of the Maoist legacy in shaping the contemporary knowledge production system in China. While the history profession in Republican-era China mirrored Western trends, the communist government diverged in the 1950s by forging a unique academic structure combining Soviet influence with local elements. The introduction of the teaching and research unit (*jiaoyanshi*, 教研室) system heightened specialization in historical teaching and research, creating a distinct separation between world history and Chinese history.

The establishment of the Chinese Academy of Social Sciences (abbreviated as "CASS"), functioning as a conglomerate of state-sponsored think tanks, empowered the party state to coordinate nationwide research projects in social sciences and humanities, exerting influence over university historians. A noteworthy development was the creation of the "Philosophy and Social Sciences" (*zhexue shehui kexue*, 哲學社會科學) division, running in parallel with Engineering and Natural Sciences. This unique structure elevated Marxist ideology as a philosophy within the contemporary Chinese knowledge hierarchy. Despite the shift from radical ideology to pragmatic politics after 1989, these institutional structures persist in China today.

The second aspect concerns the absence of representation of global history within China's national system of historical teaching and research. Thanks to the enduring impact of the Maoist legacy, the teaching and research of scholarly disciplines are highly centralized today. In 1992, the General Administration of Quality Supervision, Inspection and Quarantine of the People's Republic of China (abbreviated as "AQSIQ") introduced a national classification system to regulate various academic disciplines. As indicated in this classification, "world history" and "Chinese history" are delineated as separate secondary disciplines.[10] World history is further segmented into seven tertiary disciplines, including the history of primitive society, ancient world history, medieval world history, modern world history, contemporary world history, history of international relations, and general world history, among other subjects. In parallel to world history, there are five tertiary disciplines representing area studies, including Asian history, African history, history of the Americas, European history, and history of Australia and Oceania. Currently, global history has yet to secure a distinct place within this established system.

As global history lacks a well-defined position within the sociological structure of knowledge, it draws influences from various secondary and tertiary disciplines. This diversity in origin forms the third aspect that impacts the development of global history in China. Many global historians are typically classified either as world historians or Chinese historians, based on existing disciplinary classifications. In this book,

---

[10] *Classification and Code of Disciplines*, issued by AQSIQ on May 5, 2009, and implemented starting on November 1, 2009. https://openstd.samr.gov.cn/bzgk/gb/newGbInfo?hcno=4C13F521FD6ECB6E5EC026FCD779986E.

we introduce world historian Qi Shirong 齊世榮 (1926–2015), whose pioneering work places globalization at the center of historical studies, establishing him as a renowned scholar in contemporary world history and the history of international relations. Similarly, Liu Jiahe 劉家和 (1928–), a significant contributor to the theoretical reflections on historical comparison, is primarily a historian of ancient Chinese history, ancient world historiography, and history theory. Ge Zhaoguang, cited in this introduction, is widely acknowledged as a leading figure in Chinese history. These scholars represent aspects from Chinese history, world history, and comparison, and engaging with their works provides us with a comprehensive bird's-eye view of the evolution of the field.

From an institutional standpoint, university history departments typically serve as the primary home institutions for most global historians. However, noteworthy figures advocating for global history, such as Yu Pei 于沛 and Zhang Xupeng 張旭鵬, are also affiliated with research centers under the CASS system, particularly the newly founded Institute of History Theory and Historiography. While these institutions primarily focus on history teaching and research, the 1960s witnessed the emergence of several global history-related institutions. These functioned as centers for foreign studies, area studies, international studies, international relations, and international politics, reflecting the context of radical politics at the time. The recent resurgence of area/national-specific studies (*quyu guobie yanjiu*, 區域國別研究) seems to revive the strong connection between non-Chinese studies in history and international relations in politics. In this book, I argue that this ambivalent link from history to politics has the potential to compromise the scholarly nature of global history in China.

While the relationship between politics and history is not the central theme in *Global History in China*, it is an aspect that cannot be overlooked when reflecting upon the rise of global history. As discussed in this book, the concept of politics has taken on a distinct meaning in contemporary Chinese discourse. Instead of emphasizing participatory democracy, it underscores order and governance supervised by the party and state. The critical question explored in this book is to what extent global historians in China can avoid politicization and pursue a more independent agenda that celebrates the shared nature of common humanity. This question holds significance not only for scholars within China but also for global historians worldwide.

A significant challenge for the field is that, unlike other emerging sub-fields out of world history, such as area studies and national histories, global history in China has rarely received substantial state funding support and has not developed into a stand-alone sub-field within the country's academic structure. However, due to its limited attachment to specific political agendas, global historians have the flexibility to pursue topics that are more scholarly in nature. At the same time, as global historians eagerly introduce the works of Western historians on global history and world history, there is a risk of occasionally falling back into the old Eurocentric trap.

Global History in China is structured into seven chapters across three parts, each addressing essential aspects of global history in China—its theory, practice, and future opportunities and challenges. After this introductory chapter, the focus in Part I is on the origins and fundamental theoretical orientations of global history, consisting of two chapters. Chapter 2, titled "World History in China," provides a comprehensive survey of the evolution of world history in China throughout the twentieth century. Recognizing the entangled relationship between global history and world history, this chapter establishes the contextual framework for understanding the genesis of global history in China. Notably, global history originated within the world history discipline and continues to be considered one of its subdivisions. The chapter delves into key theoretical issues surrounding the study of world history in China, including debates on whether it is a foreign import, whether it only commenced after the founding of the People's Republic in 1949, and whether world history in China is inherently distinct from its Western counterpart. Furthermore, the chapter traces the progression of world history from being a teaching field to evolving into a research field, spanning the Republican period to contemporary China. Special attention is given to the institutional aspects shaping this development.

Despite its significance, the rise of global history in China remains inadequately addressed in current historiography, often perceived as a "runaway child" of world history. In Chapter 3, titled "Origins of Global History," I provide a succinct introduction to the emergence of global history and global perspectives in Chinese historiography. Unlike other sub-fields in world history, such as modern-and-contemporary world history (*shijie jinxiandai shi*, 世界近现代史), global historians in China face challenges in organizing national associations, and their expertise is not fully recognized within the existing academic structure. In this chapter, I propose a novel perspective on its origin. Instead of following intellectual trends and surveying scholarly networks, I begin with a pivotal scholar who played a crucial role in advancing global perspectives in Chinese historical scholarship during the last few decades of the twentieth century—historian Qi Shirong. Qi, who taught at Capital Normal University in Beijing and served as the university's president, emerged as a leading figure. In the 1990s, he served as one of the chief editors of national textbook projects on modern-and-contemporary world history. Qi defined globalization as the zeitgeist of the contemporaneous period and positioned it at the center of his world-historical research. According to his view, globalization marks the commencement of the "present" in China. His advocacy for studying globalization through a world-historical lens influenced a new generation of Chinese historians who increasingly focused on global history at the turn of the twenty-first century. Capital Normal University, under his influence, became a key institution supporting global history initiatives, culminating in the establishment of the Center for Studies of Global History in 2004.

In addition to its great potential, global history in China encounters a significant challenge: unlike other subfields in world history, it has yet to produce foundational textbooks and celebrated masterpieces that definitively define the field. In "Part II: Critical Approaches to Global History," I introduce a novel perspective on historical practice, prompting readers to contemplate three major approaches to global history.

Concepts serve as the cornerstone for cross-cultural knowledge exchange. However, the translation of a concept from one cultural context to another has proven to be a contentious process, as demonstrated by global historians. Presently, global conceptual history stands out as a dynamic approach among Chinese scholars. In Chapter 4, I delve into the practice of global conceptual history within the field of China studies. Through a case study focusing on the translation of the term "republic" from English into Chinese via Japan, I aim to illustrate the dynamic relationship between the local, the regional, and the global.

Chinese global historians have not hesitated to voice sharp criticism against Eurocentrism through their works. The second chapter, Chapter 5 on world-historical analogy, in Part II, serves as an example of how global history can effectively serve as a tool for re-examining the Eurocentric bias embedded in the system of international law. By tracing the assertion of the existence of international law in ancient China, I argue that the extensive Chinese historical records provide rich references to expose the short-term thinking behind the discourse of modernity.

An additional case study involves the exploration of global moments, particularly in the context of the ongoing discourse among historical theorists and world historians in China regarding the role of the national in shaping global history. Some scholars advocate for the composition of global history with distinctive Chinese characteristics, emphasizing the inherent national character essential to historical practice. In Chapter 6 on "global moments," I diverge from this perspective to scrutinize a pivotal moment that significantly influenced modern Chinese identities— the War of Resistance. My contention is that even during the initial stage of the conflict, before the outbreak of the Pacific War, when the Nationalist government in China purportedly confronted Japanese aggressions without substantial foreign aid, a global conceptual framework remains crucial for comprehending the motives behind the resistance. Despite the Nationalist leaders' profound concerns for the nation's survival, diverse political forces within China proposed various interpretations of China's struggle with Japan within a global context. These ranged from anti-colonial rhetoric and anti-imperial aspirations to anti-fascist alliances and anti-Western racial discourse. By uncovering the global dimensions within the national narrative, this chapter encourages a departure from the simplistic binary distinctions prevailing in current historiography in China.

If, by this point, global history is more negatively defined in relation to its connection with world history, what does its future hold? Part III concludes with Chapter 7, focusing on the rise of area studies and its potential impact on global history. In this concluding chapter, I revisit the political radicalism embodied by the ascent of international studies and foreign studies in the 1960s and 1970s. With a strong anti-imperial sentiment, early world historians and international studies scholars utilized history to advance the ideological agenda of world revolution, leaving behind a legacy that scholars in area studies in China are now willing to embrace.

In recent years, the increasing funding opportunities accompanying the rise of area studies have significantly facilitated new research initiatives for historians in China engaged in global history. However, global historians are simultaneously encountering both opportunities and challenges as they seek to reconcile the intricate relationship between history and politics at the outset of the second decade of the twenty-first century.

Part I

Theory

CHAPTER 2

World History in China

Abstract This chapter belongs to the first part of the book on the origins
and fundamental theoretical orientations of global history. It provides
a comprehensive survey of the evolution of world history in China
throughout the twentieth century. Recognizing the entangled relationship between global history and world history, this chapter establishes the
contextual framework for understanding the genesis of global history in
China. Notably, global history originated within the world history discipline and continues to be considered one of its subdivisions. The chapter
delves into key theoretical issues surrounding the study of world history
in China, including debates on whether it is a foreign import, whether
it only commenced after the founding of the People's Republic in 1949,
and whether world history in China is inherently distinct from its Western
counterpart. Furthermore, the chapter traces the progression of world
history from being a teaching field to evolving into a research field, spanning the Republican period to contemporary China. Special attention is
given to the institutional aspects shaping this development.

Keywords World history · Historiography · Intellectual history ·
Sociology of knowledge · Professionalization · World history-Chinese
history divide

© The Author(s), under exclusive license to Springer Nature   17
Singapore Pte Ltd. 2024
X. Fan, *Global History in China*,
https://doi.org/10.1007/978-981-97-3381-1_2

Navigating the study of world history in China within a transnational and transcultural framework poses significant challenges. The term "history" in English encompasses a spectrum of meanings that both align with and diverge from the diverse interpretations of the Chinese term (歷史). History may refer to past events, the documentation of those events, or an academic discipline dedicated to scholarly investigation. At the same time, when scholars refer to world history in China, they often address issues running in parallel with limited overlapping interests. For instance, Elke Papelitzky's recent work on world history in late Ming China and maritime Asia differs substantially from Luo Xu's seminal essay on world history in the People's Republic.[1] Both approaches are valid, with Papelitzky focusing on a narrative linking Ming China to the maritime world and Xu emphasizing the transformation of a scholarly discipline. In this chapter, while acknowledging the scholarly merit of the former approach, I opt to concentrate solely on the disciplinary dimension of world history in China due to the project's constrained scope and the collective focus of this edited volume, primarily centered on historiography. This serves as the initial disclaimer in the introduction.

Furthermore, in contemporary China, there is a growing interest in crafting world history with distinctively Chinese characteristics. Scholars, supported by generous state funding, are enthusiastic about composing " 中國的世界史" [China's world history or Chinese world history]. While acknowledging the considerable influence of this approach, it is a deliberate decision in this chapter to conceptualize world history as a knowledge domain transcending national boundaries. I firmly believe that "world history" is not the exclusive possession of any single nation; thus, there should be no America's world history, Germany's world history, or China's world history. Instead, world history emerges through the collaborative endeavors of scholars across the globe to construct a comprehensive narrative of humanity's shared past.[2] Rooted in this conviction, I often refrain from using the term "Chinese world history"

---

[1] Luo Xu, "Reconstructing World History in the People's Republic of China Since the 1980s," *Journal of World History* 18, no. 3 (September 2007): 325–350. Elke Papelitzky, *Writing World History in Late Ming China and the Perception of Maritime Asia* (Wiesbaden: Harrassowitz, 2020).

[2] As a global effort to rewrite a global history of the world, see Sven Beckert and Dominic Sachsenmaier, eds., *Global History, Globally: Research and Practice Around the World* (London: Bloomsbury, 2018).

in this chapter and, instead, prefer to characterize it as "world history in China."

Thirdly, our examination of "world history in China" will unfold as a narrative detailing the ascent and evolution of a modern academic discipline dedicated to scholarly inquiry. I posit that the overarching theme characterizing this trajectory is professionalization. In my previous work, I defined the "professionalization" of world history as a multi-faceted process, encompassing, though not confined to, three key aspects: the introduction and translation of world-historical works from, Japan, Western Europe, North America, and the Soviet Union into China, the integration of world history courses into national school curricula, and the emergence of a national market for world history textbooks. By embracing this concept, I aim to assert that the development of the world history discipline is an ongoing continuum that transcends the transitions between the Republican period and the early People's Republic. At the same time, I acknowledge the impact of political events on the conceptualization of world history in China, such as the rise of cultural nationalism in the War against Japanese aggression in the 1930s and 1940s and the radicalization of political ideology in the early 1960s, as I will address these topics later in this chapter.

Adhering to these three principles, this chapter takes the form of a historiographical essay, offering readers a comprehensive overview of the evolution of the field of world history in China throughout the twentieth century. Additionally, I contend that the shift in the sociology of knowledge resulting from the professionalization process has, reciprocally, influenced the perception of China's place in the world among the country's educated elites. As a result, this topic holds substantial significance not only in historiography but also in the realm of modern Chinese thought.

For scholars intrigued by the study of world history in China, three debates have significantly influenced the discourse on the state of knowledge. These debates center around three key questions: (1) Is world history in China a foreign import? (2) Did the scholarly exploration of world history in China commence only after the establishment of the People's Republic of China? (3) Should Chinese scholars approach the composition of world history in a manner fundamentally distinct from their foreign counterparts? This chapter aims to address these inquiries while providing an overview of the general development of world history as an academic discipline.

First, many scholars from earlier generations held a mechanical view of China's relationship with the world. To put it simply, and perhaps oversimplifying, they perceived China as a living yet stagnant tradition, seemingly incapable of instigating positive changes when confronted with a dynamic and ever-progressing Western world characterized by modernity. European thinkers from Hegel and Marx to Max Weber heavily influenced Western scholarly studies on China, shaping perceptions of both its historical narrative and its modern presence.

Contemporary Chinese studies scholars now often view this tradition versus modernity dichotomy as Eurocentric.[3] A growing number of scholars are exploring internal trends of change within Chinese society, recognizing these as driving forces behind this country's ongoing integration into the globalized world.[4] This scholarly trend extends to studies on world history in China. For example, Dominic Sachsenmaier in his recent work illustrates how a Han Chinese scholar in late Ming, who "never traveled," developed an entangled view on the world that synthesized Confucian canons with translated missionary sources from Europe.[5]

Similarly, drawing from maritime travel experiences, one could make a convincing case that Ming China produced works related to world history, especially concerning the South China Sea and Southeast Asia.[6] However, the classification of these works as world history remains uncertain. Even in the early stages of Chinese historiography, historians like Sima Qian 司馬遷 extensively covered foreign-related topics. Despite the limited travel experiences of individuals during that period, their works encompassed the entire world known to them. This ambiguity resonates with other

---

[3] The most pertinent critique of this Eurocentric bias remains Paul Cohen's classic, *Discovering History in China: American Writing on the Recent Chinese Past* (New York: Columbia University Press, 1984).

[4] For example, Eugenia Lean has convincingly demonstrated the continued influence of traditional business practice in China's industrial globalization in the late Qing and Republican periods. Lean, *Vernacular Industrialism in China: Local Innovation and Translated Technologies in the Making of a Cosmetics Empire, 1900–1940* (New York: Columbia University Press, 2020).

[5] Dominic Sachsenmaier, *Global Entanglements of a Man Who Never Traveled: A Seventeenth-Century Chinese Christian and His Conflicted Worlds* (New York: Columbia University Press, 2018).

[6] In addition to Elke Papelitzky, a more prominent example is Timothy Brook, *Mr. Selden's Map of China: The Spice Trade, a Lost Chart & the South China Sea* (London: Profile Books, 2013).

pre-modern writers like Herodotus, Polybius, and Ibn Battuta, who could all be considered "world historians." Chinese historian Ge Zhaoguang convincingly argues that most of these pre-modern writers were still deeply influenced by a strong sense of native identity against foreign others, perceiving themselves as the center of the world.[7] There were world-historical writers before the establishment of professional studies of world history.

While we can engage in a debate about whether pre-modern writers could conceptualize a world history akin to ours, a crucial distinction lies in the disciplinary aspect. Modern historians are professionalized and specialized researchers equipped with cutting-edge resources, such as state-of-the-art libraries, access to extensive archival collections, and the privilege of utilizing museum curation. Additionally, they benefit from the rigorous scrutiny provided by peer-reviewed feedback. These factors collectively differentiate the scholarly practices of contemporary historians from those of their pre-modern counterparts.[8]

Within the dichotomy of tradition versus modernity, scholars once presumed that world history, as a product of the "modern knowledge system," was an entirely foreign import, carried in on the cultural "wind" from the West.[9] This assumption has been increasingly challenged by several scholars, myself included. We argue that the transformation of the Confucian classical tradition in the late Qing period equipped scholars to embrace world-historical knowledge more effectively. The forerunners of world-historical writers, while not yet professional world historians, often drew on frames and ideas from China's ancient past to comprehend their foreign counterparts.[10]

---

[7] Ge Zhaoguang, "The Evolution of a World Consciousness in Traditional Chinese Historiography," *Global Intellectual History 7*, no. 2 (2022): 207–225.

[8] Manning, *Navigating World History*, 18.

[9] For example, Xing Ke, "Wan Qing zhi Minguo shiqi Zhonguo 'Shijieshi' shuxie" [The Writing of 'World History' from Late Qing to the Republican Period], *Xueshu yanjiu* [Academic Research], no. 5 (2015): 113–120.

[10] Leigh Jenco, *Changing Referents: Learning Across Space and Time in China and the West* (Oxford University Press, 2015); Fan, *World History and National Identity*, especially in Chapter 1. Outside history and political theory, Theodore Huters' work in Chinese receptions of world literature remain stimulating, see Theodore Huters, *Bringing the World Home: Appropriating the West in Late Qing and Early Republican China* (Honolulu: University of Hawai'i Press, 2005).

The second debate revolves around the establishment of world-historical studies. A conventional perspective suggests that it all began after the founding of the People's Republic when the newly established party state, eager to learn from the Soviet Union, introduced a Marxist framework for the teaching and research of world history in the early 1950s. Many historians in today's China still adhere to this viewpoint, influencing the perspective reflected in the first English-language monograph on world history in China by Dorothea Martin.[11] By examining contemporary world events through the Marxist lens of historical materialism, Martin portrayed world history in China as heavily influenced by state ideology, describing it as "a handmaiden of political ideology."[12]

In recent years, alongside my own research, several scholars have explored how historians during the Republican period approached the teaching and writing of world history in the Chinese language. Moreover, numerous scholars have dedicated their work to individuals whose contributions laid the foundation for the future development of the world history discipline. Additionally, several Ph.D. projects have investigated the origins of world history in China before the establishment of the People's Republic.[13]

Thirdly, a more contemporary debate revolves around whether historians in China should craft a world history with Chinese characteristics. Scholars in the West might have recognized the unique tradition of world history in China. In 1988, Danish historian Leif Litrrup visited China,

[11] For a recent statement on this, see Xu Lan, "Xin Zhongguo 70 nian shijieshi xueke de huigu yu zhanwang" [Retrospect and Outlook on the 70 Years of World History in New China], *Guangming ribao* (August 26, 2019), http://www.qstheory.cn/llwx/2019-08/26/c_1124922041.htm; Dorothea Martin, *The Making of a Sino-Marxist World View: Perceptions and Interpretations of World History in the People's Republic of China* (Armonk, NY: M. E. Sharpe, 1990).

[12] Martin, *The Making of a Sino-Marxist World View*, 15; Fan, *World History and National Identity*, 8.

[13] Just to list a few examples,—Robert Culp, "'Weak and Small Peoples' in a 'Europeanizing World': World History Textbooks and Chinese Intellectuals' Perspectives on Global Modernity," in *The Politics of Historical Production in Late Qing and Republican China*, eds. Tze-ki Hon and Rebert Culp (Leiden: Brill, 2007), 211–247; Marc A. Matten and Yang Zhao, *Chinese Students and Their PhD Education in the United States (1919–1945)* (Erlangen: FAU University Press, 2023), https://open.fau.de/handle/openfau/30267; Sally Chengji Xing, "Pacific Crossings: The China Foundation and the Negotiated Translation of American Science to China, 1913–1949," PhD diss. (Columbia University, 2023).

conducting an investigation into the state of the world history discipline. Subsequently, in 1989, he published an article in Denmark, which was soon translated into Chinese and published in 1993, garnering attention from scholars in the West.[14] In his work, Litrrup introduced Chinese historians, such as Wu Yujin 吳于廑 (1913–1993), and highlighted their pioneering efforts that embraced an interactive approach, combining horizontal connections among world regions and vertical movements of economic productivity. Despite Chinese historians making significant strides in breaking away from a Eurocentric framework of world-historical studies, the divide between world history and Chinese history persisted as a barrier to fully integrating Chinese history into the global narrative.[15]

From an external perspective, the notion of crafting world history with Chinese characteristics has evolved into a state-sponsored movement in contemporary China. As part of the broader initiative to forge "a Chinese path to modernity," as promoted by the state, some historians contend that world history in China should present distinctive national characteristics. Their works often find space in state-sponsored publications such as *People's Daily* and *Guangming Daily*. While these three debates continue to unfold today, scholars interested in world history in China must be mindful of their role in shaping the discourse within this evolving field.

Taking these considerations into account, the following sections will survey the key issues and conceptual debates in the development of world history as a discipline in China, spanning from the late Qing and the Republican period to the People's Republic.

The period from 1895 to 1911 is conceptualized as a moment of critical change in Chinese historiography.[16] Not only did it witness the collapse of the Manchu empire and the rise of what is deemed Asia's "first republic," but it also marked a profound shift in China's political culture. As described by Peter Zarrow, this era brought an end to the

---

[14] Li Laifu [Leif Littrup], "Juyou Zhongguo tese de shijieshi" [The World History with Chinese Characteristics], trans. Li Jianrong, *Wuhan daxue xuebao* [Journal of Wuhan University (Philosophy and Social Sciences Edition)], no. 4 (1993); the original article was published as Leif Littrup, "World History with Chinese Characteristics," *Culture and History* 5. Suppl. (1989): 39–63.

[15] Li Laifu, "Juyou Zhongguo tese de shijieshi," 26.

[16] Rebecca Karl, *Staging the World: Chinese Nationalism at the Turn of the Twentieth Century* (Durham: Duke University Press, 2002), 3.

monarchy, not only as a tangible reality but also as a conceptual framework. Following the downfall of the Qing, Chinese intellectuals could no longer envision a monarchy as a viable political system for the country.[17] The introduction of world history knowledge, one would argue, played a role in precipitating the end of monarchy in Chinese political culture.

World history, admittedly, did not exist as a scholarly discipline during this period. Confucian canons maintained their centrality in the Civil Examination system, and knowledge related to world history was not widely shared by mainstream intellectuals.[18] Several intellectual movements contributed to the emergence of world-historical consciousness in the years leading up to the revolution. The first significant factor was translation. Despite the interruption of active interaction between Jesuit missionaries and Chinese scholar-officials due to the Controversy of the Rite, by the middle nineteenth century, Protestant missionaries resumed this interaction. Through translation, often with the assistance of their Chinese friends, they introduced knowledge about world history, geography, and international law to China. Thanks to the meticulous work with primary sources by scholars in China, there is now a better understanding of the scope and depth of these translation projects.[19]

Meanwhile, and especially after the First Sino-Japanese War, books related to world history published in Japan were swiftly introduced,— sometimes translated, and sometimes republished if the original version was in classical Chinese,—further spreading knowledge of world history

---

[17] Peter Zarrow, *After Empire: The Conceptual Transformation of the Chinese State, 1885–1924* (Stanford: Stanford University Press, 2012), 3.

[18] But this does not mean a total ignorance of world history in China. Jesuit missionaries had already translated some works related to world history in the late Ming and the early Qing period, to be sure. Regarding their influence on conceptualization of the globe among Chinese Christian scholars, see Sachsenmaier, *Global Entanglements of a Man Who Never Traveled*.

[19] Just to name two foundational monographs out of a number of works on this topic, Li Xiaoqian, *Xifang shixue zai Zhongguo de chuanbo, 1882–1949* [The Spread of Western Historiography in China, 1882–1949] (Shanghai: Huadong shifan daxue chubanshe, 2007); Zou Zhenhuan, *Xifang chuanjiaoshi yu wanqing xishi dongjian: yi 1815 zhi 1900 nian xifang lishii yizhu de chuanbo yu yingxiang wei zhongxin* [Western Missionaries and the Eastern Spread of Western Historiography: The Spread and Impact of the Translated Historical Works from the West from 1815 to 1900 as the Center] (Shanghai: Shanghai guji chubanshe, 2008).

among educated elites.[20] As documented in my own work, by 1901, the availability of knowledge about world history had reached a point where scholars such as Zhou Weihan 周維翰 (1870–1910), who did not know any foreign languages, were able to produce extensive works on ancient world history relying solely on translated sources.[21]

In contrast to translation, a more radical change that played a pivotal role in the rise of world history in the late Qing was education. Following the Qing's defeat in the Sino-Japanese War, political and societal forces called for a more radical reform to modernize China's education system. After various early attempts, the Qing government finally introduced a national system of standardized education in late 1903 and implemented it in early 1904 until the fall of the Qing. Known as the "Gui-Mao School System," it, for first time, recognized the significance of world history and stipulated that foreign history should be included in history curricula, starting from the Middle School level.[22] While scholars like Klaus Mühlhahn criticized the New Policies Reform for being too late to rescue the downfall of the Qing, they generally agreed upon its lasting impact on the Chinese education system.[23] With inclusion in national curricula, world history (often referred to as foreign history by this time) almost immediately became a prominent subject in the textbook market, marking the third factor driving the rise of world history in China.

Scholars specializing in print culture have explored the emergence of print capitalism in urban centers, particularly in treaty ports like Shanghai.

---

[20] For example, Okamoto Kansuke 岡本監輔 (1839–1904)'s *Wanguo shiji* [History of myriad nations] gained wide influence and lasting impact in China, and the book was written in classical Chinese. For a recent study, see Shen Wanying, "Jiawuzhan qian *Wanguo shiji* zai Zhongguo de chuanbo yu liubian" [The Spread and Evolution of *Wanguo shiji* in China Before the Sino-Japanese War], in *Yazhou yu shijie* [Asia and the World], eds. Li Xuetao and Shen Guowei, vol. 4 (Beijing: Shehui kexue wenxian chubanshe, December 2021), 198–208.

[21] Fan, *World History and National Identity*, Chapter 1.

[22] Robert Culp, *Articulating Citizenship: Civic Education and Student Politics in Southern China, 1921–1940* (Cambridge, MA: Harvard Asia Center, 2007), 29; Fan, *World History and National Identity*, 25.

[23] Klaus Mülhahn, *Making China Modern: From the Great Qing to Xi Jinping* (Cambridge, MA: Harvard University Press, 2019), 12, 214–218, Peng Xiaopu, "Xilun *Zouding xuetang zhangcheng* zhong youguan waiguo wenshi jiaoxue de fangce" [On the Rules Regarding Foreign History and Literature Education in the *Memorial on Regulations on School Curricula*], *Guoli Taiwan shifan daxue lishi xuebao* [History Journal of National Taiwan Normal University] 17 (June 1989): 241–285.

Despite their ambivalence toward profit, owners of printing houses from the late Qing to the early Republican period grew progressively competitive in the expanding textbook market, a significant source of their profits.[24]

To some extent, the prevailing trends of the late Qing continued to shape the development of world history in the early Republican period,— translation of Western works on world history, inclusion in national education curricula, and competition in the textbook market. A noteworthy change, however, was the emergence of academic professionals including university professors and experts, following Cai Yuanpei's higher education reform at Peking University. Returning from an extensive study journey in Europe, Cai aimed to establish a research and teaching institution that shielded scholars from external influences and fostered intellectual tolerance (Fig. 2.1).[25]

The first generation of academic professionals included university professors and publishing editors who often received foreign education and had a keen interest in world history. Some of them taught courses related to world history at Chinese universities, translated world history books into Chinese, and a select few embarked on compiling world history textbooks for Chinese audiences. An exemplary figure is Chen Hengzhe 陳衡哲 (1890–1976), recognized as the first female professor in Chinese higher education history. Chen was educated in history at Vassar College in the United States. After a brief stint of teaching at Peking University, she shifted her focus to writing. In 1924, she published *Xiyang shi* [History of the West], a senior high school history textbook. Her friend and colleague Hu Shi 胡適 (1891–1962; also known as Hu Shih) praised this work for being "the first of its kind written for Chinese readers interested in Western history, establishing a new tradition." During the same period, He Bingsong 何炳松 (1890–1946), a Princeton graduate, also published several books on European and world history. The first generation of Chinese world history textbook writers,

---

[24] Christopher Reed, *Gutenberg in Shanghai: Chinese Print Capitalism, 1876–1937* (Vancouver: University of British Columbia Press, 2004), 212.

[25] Tse-Tsung Chow, *The May 4th Movement: Intellectual Revolution in Modern China* (Cambridge, MA: Harvard University Press, 1960), 50–51; Timothy Weston, *The Power of Position: Beijing University, Intellectuals, and Chinese Political Culture, 1898–1929* (Berkeley: University of California Press, 2004), 123.

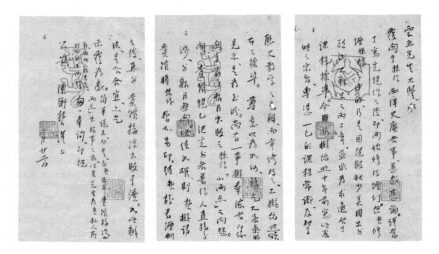

Fig. 2.1 Chen Hengzhe's letter to Commercial Press manager Wang Yunwu (Courtesy of Tsinghua University Museum)

exemplified in Chen Hengzhe's work, held a liberal view of the world, promoting internationalism and anti-imperialism.[26]

These foreign-educated professors continued to drive the development of world history in China during the early Republican years. Although world history did not exist as *shijie shi* in its modern translation, courses with content related to world history, such as foreign history, history of the West, and history of Asia, were integrated both in China's higher and secondary education curricula. This trend persisted after the founding of the Nanjing government after the Northern Expedition. The new Nationalist government endorsed the anti-imperialist sentiments among China's educated elites and issued new national education standards that further promoted foreign history education. Amid China's struggle in the colonial world dominated by imperial powers, the Nationalist government

[26] Fan, *World History and National Identity*, 50–52.

sought to foster a discourse of solidarity with other "weak and small countries" through history education.[27]

Meanwhile, Chinese readers continued to show interest in world history books translated from the West. H. G. Wells's *Outline of History*, for example, became a sensation in the market. A team of ten scholars with stellar education backgrounds including Liang Sicheng 梁思成 (1901–1972), the son of the public intellectual Liang Qichao 梁啓超 (1873–1929) and a graduate from the University of Pennsylvania, participated in the translation, and the press managed to secure endorsements from some of the most reputable scholars in China. In such cases, we can clearly observe the entangled relationship between world history knowledge, public interest, and commercial interests.

Despite these positive signs, scholars argue that world history in China during this period remained primarily a commercial interest, a textbook topic, and a teaching subject rather than a robust research field. This is why some insist on the assertion that world history as a scholarly field only existed in the People's Republic. This is a legitimate claim. But this chapter invites the reader to pay more attention to two significant aspects that are crucial for its future developments.

The first aspect is that world history as a teaching field, one may argue, had already developed in this period. With the introduction of mandatory world history-related courses, history students at Chinese universities had opportunities to study a broad range of topics beyond Chinese history. To the extent that Chinese historians such as Lei Haizong complained that students at elite universities in China had studied too many history topics compared to their counterparts in the United States.[28] Through this education exposure, these students began to develop a world-historical consciousness, laying the groundwork for their future engagement in world history research.

In turn, educators focusing on world history in the Republican period developed a "macroscopic" view to position Chinese culture within a world-historical perspective. They engaged in comparing and contrasting civilizational differences between the East and the West, critiqued Eurocentric biases embedded in the world history narratives in the West, and,

---

[27] Culp, "'Weak and Small Peoples' in a 'Europeanizing World'"; for general opinion atmosphere, see Craig Smith, *Chinese Asianism: 1894–1945* (Cambridge, MA: Harvard Asia Center, 2021), 199–201.

[28] Fan, *World History and National Identity*, 59n35.

particularly during the War with Japan, cultivated a culturalist under-standing of the Chinese nation. They adopted Oswald Spengler's cultural morphology as a scholarly approach to foster wartime solidarity among the Chinese nation, justifying the Chinese nation's struggle within the world-historical context. Scholars like Lei Haizong and Lin Tongji 林同济 (1906–1980) argued that world history was fundamentally a combina-tion of histories of different cultures and that cultures like living organisms had cycles of life. To them, the war with Japan was a symbolic moment for Chinese culture's rejuvenation. Despite all the suffering and destruction, they welcome the prospect that a strong and centralized China would reemerge after it. This cultural history approach would also go on to have a great impact on world historians after the war.[29]

The founding of the People's Republic of China had a transformative impact on Chinese historiography. Not only did the Communist state launch a nationwide effort to instill Marxist ideology among the people through education, but it also underwent an overhaul of China's educa-tion system in the early 1950s, including a restructuring of the higher education system. Following the Soviet model, the state officially estab-lished the discipline of world history, known as "shijie shi," as a teaching and research institution.

Three prominent themes have dominated the intellectual history of the People's Republic period, each providing insights into the evolution of the world history discipline. The first theme is featured in the works of scholars such as Yu Ying-shih 余英時 (1930–2021), Timothy Cheek, and Merle Goodman, who investigate the changing relations between state and society through Chinese intellectual life. While some offer a nuanced analysis of Chinese intellectuals' position vis-à-vis the Communist state, others tend to provide moral judgments—either praising those who stood up against the state totality or criticizing those who did not.[30] Scholars holding on to such a view, including Dorothea Martin, have questioned the historiographical value of world history in China, suggesting that the field grew out of ideological influences.

---

[29] Fan, *World History and National Identity*, 73–80.

[30] Such a view is reflected in one of the most influential intellectual biographies in recent years in China, see Lu Jiandong, *Chen Yinke de zuihou ershi nian* [The Last Twenty Years in Chen Yinke's Life] (Beijing: Sanlian shudian, 1995).

Second, a more recent trend adopts a sociology of knowledge approach to re-examining the social and organizational aspects of the transformation of Chinese intellectuals in the early 1950s. Global historians like Dominic Sachsenmaier remind us of the significance of the sociology of knowledge in identifying patterns of global changes in the rise of global history in China, comparing it with its counterparts in Germany and the United States.[31] To delve into local experiences, Eddy U examines how the Party adopted "the intellectual" (*zhishifenzi*, 知識分子) as a category of social classification, questioning the identity formations and transformations of educated Chinese from the 1920s to the end of 1964. U argues that this process of "objectification" had a profound impact on educated Chinese, and we believe that world historians were both its product and its victims.[32] On the one hand, the newly established teaching and research unit system (*jiaoyan shi*, 教研室) recognized the significance of world history teaching and research, establishing ancient and medieval, modern, and contemporary units under the umbrella of this discipline. On the other hand, Chinese historians were often assigned to these world history units against their own will and expertise, leading to resentment and resistance against this transition.[33]

The third theme revolves around ideas. While intellectual historians of modern China today are increasingly aware of the challenges and opportunities presented by new approaches to studying history, society, and culture, their interest remains focused on how ideas have shaped the world. Given the complex changes in China's modern transformation, they explore a wide range of topics, from the dichotomy of tradition vs. modernity to "Chinese worldviews," resulting in a lack of shared interests in the field. Chinese intellectual history is becoming increasingly fragmented. At the same time, two issues are crucial for scholars seeking to understand the evolution of world history during this period, one inside China and the other outside. As China transitions into the "New Era" under Xi Jinping's leadership, inside the country, the state actively promotes studies of the "Sinicization of Marxism" in support

[31] Sachsenmaier, *Global Perspectives on Global History*, 3.

[32] Eddy U, *Creating the Intellectual: Chinese Communism and the Rise of a Classification* (Berkeley: University of California Press, 2019), 16.

[33] Fan, *World History and National Identity*, Chapter 3.

of new nation-building agendas.[34] Outside the country, China watchers observe the rise of "new" nationalism in the post-Mao period, prompting a reconsideration of the age-old question of Marxism versus Nationalism.[35] For scholars interested in world history in China, a central question intertwines both themes: to what extent is world history in China a handmaiden of state ideology? While some, like Martin, reject its intellectual and historiographical value, others recognize the dynamic interaction between Marxism and nationalism in the rise of world history in the People's Republic era.[36]

Studies of world history in the People's Republic era have increasingly become a topic that attracts scholarly attention. As current research is still unfolding, this chapter outlines several landmark events in the development of the field within the context of national and international politics. First and foremost, the restructuring of the higher education system from 1949 to 1952 was the most significant social and political change framing the development of the discipline. Although the government strategically allocated more resources to natural science and engineering sectors, claiming to serve the needs of China's industrialization, it also initiated some profound changes in humanities and social sciences.[37] For example, it reorganized the old history departments and divided the new ones into subdivisions known as "the Teaching and Research Unit" (jiaoyan shi). Within the area of "world history," ancient and medieval world history (shijie gudai he zhongshiji shi) unit, modern world history (shijie jindai shi) unit, and contemporary world history (shijie xiandai shi) unit were established. World history officially occupied a position both separated from and in parallel to Chinese history. Despite the changes in the post-Mao era, the system largely remains in place in China today, resulting

---

[34] For Xi's promotion of the Sinicization thesis, see Xi Jiping, "Kaipi Makesi zhuyi Zhongguohua shidaihua xin jingjie" [To Explore the New Horizon for Sinicization and Modernization of Marxism], *Qiushi* [Seeking Truth] (October 15, 2023). https://www.gov.cn/yaowen/liebiao/202310/content_6909263.htm.

[35] Peter Gries, *China's New Nationalism: Pride, Politics, and Diplomacy* (Berkeley: University of California Press, 2004).

[36] Q. Edward Wang, "Between Marxism and Nationalism: Chinese Historiography and the Soviet Influence, 1949–1963," *Journal of Contemporary China* 9, issue 23 (August 2000): 95–111; Fan, *World History and National Identity*, chapter 4.

[37] Chu Zhuwu, *Dangdai Zhongguo zhexue shehui kexue fazhan shi (1949–1966)* [History of Contemporary Chinese Philosophy and Social Sciences, 1949–1966] (Beijing: Shehui kexue wenxian chubanshe, 2023), 171.

in a large percentage of historians in China self-identifying as "world historians." Additionally, courses on world history, such as the surveys on ancient and modern world histories, became mandatory subjects for all history students in the country. At the same time, as in the late Qing and Republican periods, world history-related courses continued to constitute a significant portion of secondary education curricula after the Communist takeover.

Second, in addition to the inclusion of world history in higher education, a recent trend among scholars in China is to study the establishment of the national system of research, especially focused on the national think tank in social sciences and humanities, the Chinese Academy of Social Sciences (abbreviated as "CASS"). Scholars like Chu Zhuwu have pointed out that this process was not simply a copy of the Soviet system; the long-term development within the party's ideological branches back in the Yan'an era gave birth to a new and unique categorization, the Philosophy and Social Sciences sector (Zhexue shehui kexue) in the mid and late 1950s.[38] This system dismantles the general framework of humanities, elevating philosophy (and thus Marxist ideology) to a unique position equal to the entire weight of other social science subjects in the system of knowledge production in the People's Republic of China (abbreviated as "PRC" thereafter) and excluding literature from social sciences. It created a unique legacy in China today, as state funding structures and disciplinary evaluation systems still follow its framework. Within this umbrella of Philosophy-Social Sciences, world history was required to better serve the needs of the socialist state, leading to the third important development of world history in the People's Republic, the state-initiated projects of textbook editing and research institution buildup.

In the early 1960s, the Party Central called the Ministries of Education and Propaganda to compile new textbooks that were more suitable for the educational needs in socialist China. With strong state support, by the mid-1960s, scholars had published more than seventy titles and over 140 volumes of humanities textbooks with another twenty-four titles and thirty-three volumes in sight.[39] During this period, led by Zhou Yiliang 周一良 (1913–2001) and Wu Yujin, a team of China's new world historians published a four-volume college textbook on the general

---

[38] Chu, *Dangdai Zhongguo zhexue shehui kexue fazhan shi*, 2–18.

[39] Chu, *Dangdai Zhongguo zhexue shehui kexue fazhan shi*, 325.

history of the world (*Shijie tongshi*, 世界通史), followed by additional editions on reference materials on ancient world history chief edited by Zhou Yiliang; medieval world history by Guo Shoutian 郭守田 (1910–1993); and modern world history (two volumes) by Jiang Xiangze 蒋相泽 (1916–2006), published respectively in December 1962, September 1964, and April 1964.[40] These textbooks laid the foundation for world history education in China in the decades to follow.

The split of Sino-Soviet relations in the early 1960s radicalized Chinese international stance, leading the government to adopt stronger rhetoric against Eurocentrism and anti-imperialism. As CCP leaders became increasingly interested in international affairs, a cluster of research centers and institutes for international and area studies were established by both government branches and universities by 1964. To just list a few, CCP's International Liaison Department founded the Center for Soviet and Eastern European Studies and the Institute for Southeast Asian Studies, the Foreign Ministry established the Center for Indian Studies, and CASS (by then, still called "the Chinese Academy of Sciences") established the Center for World Economy and Politics. Meanwhile, international studies and world politics were introduced into the curricula at leading Chinese universities such as the Center for Afro-Asian Studies at Peking University, the Center for Iranian Studies (now as the Institute for Middle Eastern Studies) at Northwest University, and the Center for Southwestern Asian Studies at Yunnan University.[41] The interest in world affairs further widened the basis for world history in China during this period.

While scholars today recognize the significant institutional development of world history as a discipline in the 1950s and early 1960s, they tend to dismiss the scholarly quality of works done during this period. This makes sense, as the world history of this period was indeed heavily influenced by political ideology, much like other sub-disciplines in history.[42] However, five issues dominated the history field and inspired world historians' work. Known as the "Five Golden Flowers," they include "periodization in ancient history," "feudalism in China," "the

[40] Yu Pei and Zhou Rongyao, "Qianyan" [preface], in *Zhongguo shijie lishi xue 30 nian* [The Thirty Years of Chinese World History Studies (sic)], eds. Yu Pei and Zhou Rongyao (Beijing: Zhongguo shehui kexue chubanshe, 2008), 11.

[41] Chu, *Dangdai Zhongguo zhexue shehui kexue fazhan shi*, 330; Xu, "Xin Zhongguo 70 nian shijieshi xueke de huigui."

[42] Fan, *World History and National Identity*, esp. Chapter 4.

role of peasant wars in history," "the sprouts of capitalism in traditional China," and "the formation of the Han Chinese nationality."
As my work has demonstrated, world historians in China during this
period were particularly interested in debating the periodization in world
history, questioning whether China's past fit into the teleological schema
proposed by Marxist historical materialists.[43]

Few scholars have written extensively about world history in China
during the Cultural Revolution (1966 to 1976). For most, it was a decade
of "chaos" when the regular development of world history was put on
pause. Some evidence suggests that a small minority of world historians in
China were still able to conduct translation projects during these unusual
times.[44] More careful research about this period is still in order.

More scholars, however, would agree that the period after the end of
the Cultural Revolution and the death of Mao Zedong 毛澤東 (1893–
1976) witnessed a speedy recovery of world history teaching and research
agendas. In the 1980s, several major developments further shaped the
institutional aspects of world history in China as well as defined theoretical
awareness.

First, the institutional developments were arguably the most significant
structural change in world history in the early 1980s. In higher education,
a postgraduate education system was introduced for the first time in PRC
history. This change had a great impact on world history. By the mid-
1980s, sixteen centers for world history PhD education were established
nationwide, with twenty-three scholars serving as supervisors, in addition
to sixty world history MA programs. By 1986, a total of 410 students
received MA degrees in world history.[45] This new generation of world
historians would lead future developments in the field until today.

The organizing of national scholarly associations and the launching
of specialized academic journals on world history-related subjects were

[43] Wang, "Between Marxism and Nationalism," 69; Fan, *World History and National
Identity*, Chapter 4 on the Asiatic Mode of Production debate.

[44] To name just one example, the textbooks and sourcebook series on world history
edited by Zhou Yiliang and Wu Yujin released revised editions in 1974 in the middle
of the Cultural Revolution. Li Laifu, "Juyou Zhongguo tese de shijie shi," 21; Yu and
Zhou, "Qianyan," 11.

[45] Chen Qineng, *Jianguo yilai shijieshi yanjiu gaishu* [An Overview of World-Historical
Studies After the Founding of the People's Republic] (Beijing: Shehui wenxian chubanshe,
1991), 6; Yu and Zhou, "Qianyan," 4.

other significant aspects in the institutional development after the end of the Cultural Revolution. These associations cover each major aspect of world history research in China, including ancient (also medieval) world history, modern world history, contemporary world history, African history, Latin American history, British history, French history, German history, American history, Korean history, Japanese history, Soviet and Eastern European history, Sino-Japanese history, International Communist Movements history, WWII history, and more.[46] During the same period, the flagship journal for world-historical studies *Shijie lishi* 世界歷史 [World History] was also established.[47] As a result, world history became further professionalized and specialized.

Second, with strong institutional support both at local research centers and national scholarly organizations, world historians in China continued developing their research agendas. As it was in the early PRC period, national textbook editing projects again mobilized the best scholars in the field across the country. On the one hand, they continued editing the existing textbook and sourcebook series originally published in the 1960s, adding volumes to new topics such as "contemporary world history" and "world history map series"[48]; on the one hand, they published new editions, and the one in the 1990s edited by Wu Yujin and Qi Shirong marked a major achievement in world-historical teaching and research in the PRC. Known as the "Wu-Qi Edition," this six-volume series offers a general history of the world from primitive society through ancient and medieval periods to the modern and contemporary world. Unlike other works that separate Chinese history from the world, it offers an organic narrative of the history of the world, including the one from China.[49] The theoretical foundation of this series is what Chinese historian Wu Yujin proposed "an integrated view on world history." First proposed in the 1980s, Wu argued that world history was a double process that integrated both a horizontal movement connecting various regions and

---

[46] Yu and Zhou, "Qianyan," 3.

[47] Yu and Zhou, "Qianyan," 4.

[48] Yu and Zhou, "Qianyan," 11–14.

[49] Li Laifu, "Juyou Zhongguo tese de shijie shi," 22.

peoples across the globe and a vertical movement manifesting in the materialistic progress of human productivity.[50]

Like the earlier Republican period, translation remains an important way for Chinese scholars to engage in world-historical research and study. In the early years of the People's Republic, due to the "leaning on one side" policy, the primary works in world history translated into Chinese were from the Soviet Union. After the Cultural Revolution, scholars in China diversified their interests and translated world history-related texts not just from English and Russian but also German, French, Japanese, and other languages. The most impressive achievement is the Commercial Press's "World Academic Classics in Chinese Translation Series" (Hanyi shijie xueshu mingzhu congshu). From 1951 until today, this series has released twenty series with a total of 900 titles, covering works in philosophy, history, geography, politics, law, sociology, economics, and linguistics written by authors from ancient Greece and Rome to the contemporary world. To some extent, it laid the epistemological foundation for PRC Chinese scholars' understanding of global scholarship.[51] Book series such as *Shijie wuqian nian* 世界五千年 [The world in five thousand years] also gained wide circulation among common readers, including middle school students.[52]

The 1980s witnessed the "Cultural Fever" and the "New Enlightenment" in Chinese society.[53] Young scholars, university students, and amateur historians passionately debated culture-related issues such as nature of humanity, cross-cultural comparisons, general characteristics of Chinese culture, and modernity. In many aspects, works written for these debates lack scholarly value when judged by the professional standards of specialized researchers today; yet these debates have framed the problematic for future scholarly studies from the 1990s and event today. Scholars

---

[50] Yu and Zhou, "Qianyan," 6–7; Xu, "Reconstructing World History in the People's Republic of China," 329–334; Fan, *World History and National Identity*, 160–161.

[51] "Hanyi shijie xueshu mingzhu congshu" [World Academic Classics in Chinese Translation Series], Commercial Press webpage, https://www.cp.com.cn/hanyi40/.

[52] Duan Wanhan, Gu Hansong, and Chen Bixiang, eds., *Shijie wuqian nian* [The World in Five Thousand Years] (Beijing: Shaonian ertong chubanshe, 1991).

[53] Jing Wang, *High Culture Fever: Politics, Aesthetics, and Ideology in Deng's China* (Berkeley: University of California Press, 1996); Huaiyin Li, *Reinventing Modern China: Imagination and Authenticity in Chinese Historical Writing* (Honolulu: University of Hawaii, 2013), 170–172.

have discussed several aspects regarding the intellectual history of the 1980s and 1990s. For example, Wang Hui 汪暉 discusses the decline of political consciousness among Chinese scholars after 1989, and Els van Dongen further historicizes this period and proposes calling it a "Realistic Revolution."[54] In contrast, Sebastian Veg and Ian Johnson help us appreciate the resistance against state authority from non-professional scholars.[55] However, more careful research on this period is still in order.

While this is occurring, this chapter tentatively outlines several issues that engaged the attention of world historians during this period, focusing on the questions of modernity, civilizational discourse, and historical periodization. While I have discussed the question of historical periodization in ancient world history and addressed the question of civilizational discourse in *World History and National Identity in China*, other scholars such as Huaiyin Li have written on the modernity debate.[56] In the 1980s, historian Luo Rongqu 羅榮渠 (1927–1996) was a pioneer who introduced the modernization theory into China. His article on "Modernization Theory and Historical Research" marked the beginning of Chinese scholars' exploration of this topic in the post-Mao era.[57] Operating within the existing framework of historical materialism, Luo questioned whether the historical development of modernization followed a unilinear process dominated by a Eurocentric story, such as the five stages of development outlined by Soviet scholars. Instead, he argued for a process of "one direction with multiple paths" (*yiyuan duoxian*, 一元多線).[58] On the one hand, he insisted on the deterministic role of economic relations in social development; on the other hand, he rejected the "paradigmatic order of

---

[54] Wang Hui, "Dangdai Zhongguo de sixiang zhuangkuang yu xiandaixing wenti," *Tianya* 5 (1997): 133–150, and the English translation, "Contemporary Chinese Thought and the Question of Modernity," trans. Rebecca Karl, *Social Text* 55 (1998): 9–44; Els van Dongen, *Realistic Revolution: Contesting Chinese History, Culture, and Politics after 1989* (Cambridge: Cambridge University Press, 2019).

[55] Sebastian Veg, *Minjian: The Rise of China's Grassroots Intellectuals* (New York: Columbia University, 2019); Ian Johnson, *Sparks: China's Underground Historians and Their Battle for the Future* (Oxford: Oxford University Press, 2023).

[56] Li, *Reinventing Modern China*, especially Chapter 7.

[57] Li, *Reinvention Modern China*, 207; Sachsenmaier, *Global Perspectives on Global History*, 209–211.

[58] Luo Rongqu, "New Perspectives on Historical Development and the Course of Modernization in East Asia," trans. Guo Wu, *Chinese Studies in History* 43, no.1 (Fall 2009): 18. (original in Chinese).

ancient commune–slavery–feudalism–capitalism" derived from European history, advocating for recognizing divergent paths to modernization in East Asian region or other world regions.[59] Luo established a center for modernization studies at Peking University and educated a generation of promising young scholars who were primarily working in the field of world history.[60] However, by the time Luo passed away in 1996, world historians were grappling with the interplay between Europeanization, Westernization, and Modernization, and Luo's initiative went awry.[61]

Entering the twenty-first century, world history in China experiences unprecedented opportunities for development. With a thriving economy and substantial government funding support, world historians in China have gained increasingly more opportunities to conduct field research abroad, to study at foreign research centers, and to publish works both in Chinese and other foreign languages. Since 1996, the Chinese Ministry of Education established the China Scholarship Council (CSC), providing both funding for Chinese citizens to study abroad and for foreign students to study in China.[62] Many of these scholarships have sponsored Chinese students pursuing advanced degrees at world-leading universities, with some choosing to focus on world history-related subjects. Together with the returnees who studied with private funds, a new generation of young scholars is actively engaged in world-historical research with foreign degrees at Chinese universities, fostering intense interaction between world historians in China and their counterparts worldwide.

With the internationalization of the young talent pool in world-historical studies, research topics in this field have become increasingly diverse in recent years. Some researchers continue to operate within the framework of historical materialism, choosing topics that align with state agendas and national interests, such as the history of great nations and the promotion of China's unique path to modernity. Others are

---

[59] Luo, "New Perspectives on Historical Development," 19–23.

[60] Luo Rongquan, "Huiyi Luo Rongqu dage" [Remembering My Big Bother Luo Rongqu], *Zhuanji wenxue* [Biography] 88, no. 1 (2006): 93.

[61] This does not mean that scholars in China stopped engaging with topics related to modernity and modernization. However, the study of modernization and modernity in the context of world history has not been as vigorous as in Luo's years.

[62] Ryan Fedasiuk, "The China Scholarship Council: An Overview," *CSET Issue Brief* (Washington, DC: Center for Security and Emerging Technology at Georgetown University, July 2020), 3.

more interested in specialized topics, attempting to steer clear of political issues—examples include studies on rabies in ancient Mesopotamia and buffalos as an energy regime in Southeast Asia. Notably, the field has witnessed the emergence of global history, a spin-off of world-historical studies originating in Europe and America. This new approach attracts scholars seeking to place China within a global context and provide a connected history of the human past.[63] In contrast, a growing concern is the ongoing separation of Chinese history from world history—a long-standing issue manifesting in new ways through academic evaluation systems and other forms in the sociology of knowledge.[64] Equally disconcerting is the recent call by the party state to establish "China's own world history system," signaling a potential divergence of world-historical practice in China from the international scholarly community.

Studying world history in China inevitably raises the moral question of defining good scholarship. Scholars in the past grappled with the realization that the genesis of this discipline was deeply rooted in the Communist state's endeavor to shape political ideology. They harbored resentment, particularly toward world historians who appeared to be "collaborating" with the state's agenda, compromising their individual "free will" as historians. According to their perspective, without agency, the pursuit of good history would be compromised. However, contemporary scholars, influenced by social theories on power and knowledge relations, have embraced a more nuanced view of the intricate relationship between state control and intellectual resistance during the early socialist period. Some researchers are increasingly drawn to the study of world history in China precisely because of its inherent ambiguity.[65]

---

[63] Dominic Sachsenmaier has touched upon the rise of global history in China, Sachsenmaier, *Global Perspectives on Global History*. For recent discussions, see Zhang Xupeng, "Quanqiu shiguan yu minzu xushi: Zhongguo tese de quanqiushi heyi keneng" [Global History and National Narrative: The Possibility of a Global History with Chinese Characteristics], *Lishi yanjiu*, no. 1 (2020): 156. A German translation of this article from Chinese is available in *Globalgeschten aus China*, 245–284. Also, see the next chapter in this book on the rise of global history in China.

[64] Wang, "World History on a Par with Chinese History?": 303–324.

[65] Wang, "Between Marxism and Nationalism"; for a study on Chinese scholars' relationship with the state in the field of archaeology, see Erika Evasdottir, *Obedient Autonomy: Chinese Intellectuals and the Achievement of Orderly Life* (Vancouver: University of British Columbia, 2004).

Acknowledging the intricate nature of world history in China, it is essential to recognize its major contributions to global historiography throughout the twentieth century. First and foremost, Chinese historians, including those identified as world historians, have displayed a keen sensitivity to the Eurocentric bias prevalent in historical narratives. Over the course of the century, they have generated compelling and noteworthy works challenging this Eurocentric framework in historical writing. Oft-times, though admittedly, they seem to replace Eurocentric frameworks with Sinocentric ones. However their approach to questioning Eurocentrism continues to offer valuable insights to historians today.

At the same time, world history in China serves as a reservoir that holds a wealth of data, providing scholars with the means to comprehend "Chinese worldviews."[66] Beyond the realm of historians, scholars from diverse fields also find this subject intriguing. For example, published in the early 1990s, David Shambaugh's survey of American studies in China still offers valuable insights for reevaluating China's ambivalent view of America.[67] Debates surrounding concepts such as the "Clash of Civilizations," the "End of History," and the "Thucydides Trap" remain pivotal in shaping Chinese International Relations scholars' visions for China's future place in the world. Thus, world history in China is both a significant and timely topic, warranting thorough examination.

[66] See the special issue, Q. Edward Wang, "Worldviews in Twentieth-Century Chinese Historiography," *Global Intellectual History* 7, no. 2 (2022): 201–206.

[67] David Shambaugh, *Beautiful Imperialist: China Perceives America, 1972–1990* (Princeton: Princeton University Press, 1993).

CHAPTER 3

Origins of Global History

Abstract This chapter provides a succinct introduction to the emergence
of global history and global perspectives in Chinese historiography. Unlike
other sub-fields in world history, global historians in China face challenges in organizing national associations, and their expertise is not fully
recognized within the existing academic structure. Instead of following
intellectual trends and surveying scholarly networks, this chapter begins
with a pivotal scholar who played a crucial role in advancing global
perspectives in Chinese historical scholarship during the last few decades
of the twentieth century—historian Qi Shirong. Qi defined globalization
as the zeitgeist of the contemporaneous period and positioned it at the
center of his world-historical research. According to his view, globalization marks the commencement of the "present" in China. His advocacy
for studying globalization through a world-historical lens influenced a
new generation of Chinese historians who increasingly focused on global
history at the turn of the twenty-first century. In addition to its great
potential, this chapter also argues that global history in China encounters a significant challenge: unlike other subfields in world history, it has
yet to produce foundational textbooks and celebrated masterpieces that
definitively define the field.

Keywords Global history · Intellectual history · Historiography · Qi
Shirong · History textbook · Global perspectives in history ·
Globalization

In 2011, historian Liu Xincheng 劉新城 discussed the emergence of *Quanqiu shiguan* (全球史觀) in an influential essay published by *Historical Research* (Lishi yanjiu, 歷史研究), the flagship journal for historical studies in China.[1] As a leading advocate for global historical studies, he provides an authoritative overview of the debates on the "global view of history" in China during the first decade of the twenty-first century.[2] Half a year later, its English-language version appeared in the *Journal of World History*, the official journal of the worldwide World History Association. In this early attempt to introduce China's global history to foreign audiences, Liu reminds his readers through translation that, although originating in the West, global history "has been variously interpreted in China, and some of these interpretations may sound totally surprising to Western global historians." Thus, "global history" in China has been "a very interesting phenomenon that we cannot afford to ignore." Liu promises that "when placed in different contexts, global history can stimulate serious thinking on some of the same essential issues."[3]

There are indeed convergent interests and divergent concerns regarding global history in China and abroad. Like their counterparts in Europe and America, Chinese historians have divided views on both its theory and practice. Some welcome its development, considering it "an urgent task for China's world historians" to "employ the global view of history to replace the old mosaics of nation-states."[4] On the other hand, others doubt its practicality, raising the question of whether China truly needs global history.[5] Beyond the country, a widening divide is

---

[1] Liu Xincheng, "Quanqiu shiguan zai Zhongguo" [The Global View of History in China], *Lishi yanjiu* [Historical Research], no. 6 (Dec. 2011): 180–187.

[2] From 2007 to 2013, Liu Xincheng was president of Capital Normal University in Beijing. After his thriving success in academia, he later embarked on an even more impressive political career. Not being a CCP party member himself, he has been serving as deputy chair of the Chinese People's Political Consultative Conference since 2018.

[3] Liu Xincheng, "The Global View of History in China," *Journal of World History* 23, no. (Sept. 2012): 507–508.

[4] Li Longqing, "Yingjie xinshiji chonggou shijie lishi xinkuangjia" [Embracing a New Framework for Reconstructing World History], *Huazhong shifan daxue xuebao* [Journal of Central China Normal University (Humanities and Social Sciences edition)] 39, no. 4 (2000): 118. Also, cited in Liu, "The Global View of History in China," 492–493.

[5] Wu Xiaoqun, "Women zhen de xuyao 'quanqiu shiguan' ma?" [Do We Really Need a "Global View of History"?], *Xueshu yanjiu* [Academic Research] 1 (2005): 22–25. Also cited in Liu, "The Global View of History in China," 493.

growing between Chinese scholars and "Western global historians" on how to establish "universal human values" through historical studies. Liu observes that, as some Western "postmodernists" have given up on the effort, some Chinese scholars likewise return to a nationalistic root. He criticizes both the historical nihilism and nationalism embedded in these trends and insists on pursuing the fundamental issue in human history: the unity of human nature. To him, a shared concern for humanity was the driving force for the worldwide emergence of global history.[6]

Despite Liu's call for an appreciation of common humanity, a significant challenge arises in translation, or, to use cultural critic Lydia Liu's term, "translingual practice."[7] Specifically, the term "quanqiu shiguan" corresponds to multiple phrases in the English language. At the beginning of the essay, Liu notes that "quanqiu shiguan" first appeared in the Chinese language as a translation of the English phrase "a universal view of history" in Geoffrey Barraclough's *Main Trends in History* in 1987.[8] However, without much explanation, the translated term "quanqiu shiguan" shifts from "a universal view of history" to "a global view of history" throughout the rest of the essay. In Chinese, these two concepts appear synonymous to him, but in English, they are not. In this regard, one could argue that this linguistic difference might lead to Liu's assertion that global history originated in the late 1970s.[9] Is this anachronistic? Scholars may hold differing opinions on this matter. However, by examining this subtle difference as a case study, one can derive three general observations about the state of global history in China. As I argue in the opening of this chapter, these observations are essential for both understanding and appreciating its complicated origins in the context of global knowledge exchange and translingual practice.

First, what does global history mean in the Chinese language? As I contend here, the Chinese rendering of global history as *Quanqiu shi* (全球史) is not a perfect translation. It adds another layer of meaning to the original term in Western languages (whether it is "global history" in English, "gurobaru reikishi" in Japanese, "Globalgeschichte" in German,

---

[6] Liu, "The Global View of History in China," 511.

[7] Lydia Liu, *Translingual Practice: Literature, National Culture, and Translated Modernity—China, 1900–1937* (Stanford University Press, 1995).

[8] Liu, "The Global View of History in China," 491.

[9] Barraclough's book was first published in the late 1970s. Geoffrey Barraclough, *Main Trends in History* (New York: Holms & Meier Publishers, 1979).

or "Histoire globale" in French).[10] As a compound term, each of the three characters forming Quan-qiu-shi has a separate meaning: "Quan" means "whole," "qiu" means "globe," and "shi" means "history." Thus, put together, *quanqiu shi* literally means the "history of the entire globe." Because of this additional layer of meaning, Liu might have considered the "universal view of history" interchangeable with "global view of history." Yet, for contemporary global historians, few would accept global history as universal history. The latter is more conventionally translated as "pubian shi" (普遍史) in Chinese and has a distinct origin from a global history, tracing back to the Enlightenment period in Europe, if not earlier, as convincingly shown by scholars in China through recent case studies.[11]

Second, what is global history? Throughout the essay, Liu only discusses the "global view of history," and he never treats global history as a stand-alone subject. In other words, as a leading historian of global history, he still regarded global history as an intellectual trend rather than a scholarly field at the time he completed the essay. This cautious position reflects the context of the rise of global history. A decade later, as it is today, global historians would have established more scholarly forums and research centers. For example, in addition to the Global History Center at Capital Normal University, Beijing Foreign Languages University launched an Institute for Global History, and Fudan University in Shanghai is also planning to establish a new research center for global history. The *Global History Review* (Quanqiu shi pinglun), the Chinese flagship journal on global history, was also published in 2008, only two years after the release of the *Journal of Global History* in London.[12] Yet,

[10] Sachsenmaier, *Global Perspectives on Global History*, 2.

[11] Chin-shing Huang [Huang Jinxing], "Cong pubian shi dao shijie shi he quanqiu shi—yi Lanke shixue wei fenxi shidian" [From Universal History to World History and Global History–Ranke's Universal History as the Departure Point for Understanding the Current Issues of World History], *Beijing daxue xuebao (Zhexue shehui kexue ban)* [Journal of Peking University (Philosophy and Social Sciences)] 54, no. 2 (March 2017): 54–67; Zhang Yibo, "'Sa'er pubian shi' de Zhongguo lishi jiangou yu Ouzhou jindai xueshu zhuanxing" [Construction of Chinese History in Sale's *Universal History* and Modern Academic Transformation in Europe], *Jianghai xuekan* [Jianghai journal], no. 2 (2022): 172–184.

[12] Zhang, "Quanqiu shi yu minzu xushi: Zhongguo tese de quanqiu shi heyi keneng," 156. A German translation of this article from Chinese is available in *Globalgeschten aus China*, 245–284.

judged by its recent ascendancy, scholars often agree that global history remains an emerging field of scholarly studies in China.

Third, what is the boundary between global history and world history? Once again, throughout the essay, Liu did not clearly separate global history from world history. This is understandable because, at the time when he was writing the essay, global history, as one might argue, was considered part of world history. Yet, as global history is gradually gaining a separate identity, it has encountered resistance from world historians. Liu's essay documents some early and harsh criticism against global history in the early 2000s. Some scholars accused global history of being a tool for Western cultural hegemony, asserting that "the global view of history" emphasizes globality because it attempts to impose core values from Western culture, using economic methods to erase differences among various cultures and achieve uniformity in global culture.[13] Others contended that it was futile for historians to distance themselves from their national identities, and as a result, global history could only be national instead of truly global.[14] More scholars would join this debate later on.

Today, global history has gained even stronger momentum in China, with an increasing number of scholars claiming global history as their scholarly interest. According to a recent survey from 2004 to 2022, scholars in China published 464 articles that included "global history" in their titles. Additionally, scholars in various sub-fields of history have shown great interest in global history, spanning traditional areas such as economic history, Sino-foreign exchanges history, and historical geography, as well as emerging ones like the history of climate, environmental history, and maritime history.[15]

However, with the "global historical turn" unfolding, scholars in China today hold more divided opinions regarding the state of global historical studies. While Liu Xincheng called for a return to the fundamental question in world history—discussing the unity of human history—historians have become more outspoken about how to preserve national narratives

---

[13] Liu, "The Global View of History in China," 493–494. Wu Xaioqun, "Women zhen de xuyao 'quanqiu shiguan' ma?," 23; as for views from non-historians, see on Jiang Shigong's critique of globalization as a Western imperial project to dominate the world in Chapter 6.

[14] Liu, "The Global View of History in China," 493–494.

[15] Zhang Xupeng, "Quanqiu shi yu minzu xushi," 157.

within the context of global history, aiming to establish a "Chinese view of global history."[16] In addition to attempts to write "global history with Chinese characteristics," a recent movement aims to align global history with international relations studies.[17] Overall, the role of the state and the nation has become increasingly visible in China's global historical narratives.

Is this development positive, and what is the future of global history? To answer these questions, I invite the reader to revisit the origins of global history in China. In this chapter, I argue that to further promote global history in China as a field of scholarly studies (rather than as a tool of political ideology), we must return to its inception and understand the roots of this intellectual movement. Only by doing so can we comprehend other aspects of its evolution, such as institutional build-ups and its impact on popular culture.

By focusing on a case study centered on historian Qi Shirong, who advocated placing globalization at the center of contemporary history, I argue that a significant origin of global history is historians' efforts to conceptualize globalization through historiography. In other words, the ultimate drive to promote global views of history in China is an effort to historicize China's embrace of globalization, not a rejection of it.

Historians question whether biography should be at the center of historiography due to its "elite bias."[18] In the case of global history in China, however, Qi Shirong's life story encapsulates the subtle transition from world history to the pursuit of global views of history in the age of Opening-up and Reform. For, as a historian, he played a pivotal role in developing the field of world history and was a trailblazer in introducing the concept of globalization to world-historical studies, laying a necessary foundation for the later rise of global views of history.

Qi's intellectual upbringing bridged the Republican period and the early People's Republic. Born in Lianyungang 連雲港, Jiangsu 江蘇, his family later moved to Beiping [Beijing]. During the war with Japan,

---

[16] Zhang Xupeng, "Quanqiu shi yu minzu xushi," 172–173.

[17] Wang Lixin, "Quanqiu shi yanjiu yu guoji lilun chuangxin de keneng gongxian" [On Global Historical Studies' Possible Contribution to Innovations in IR Theories]; Zhang Xiaoming, "Quanqiu shi yu guoji guanxi yanjiu de rongtong yu hujian" [The Fusion of and Mutual Lessons between Global History and Studies of International Relations], *Zhongguo shehui kexue bao* [Chinese Social Sciences Newspaper], (November 10, 2022).

[18] Novak, *That Noble Dream*, 7–8.

he left the Japanese-occupied city and went to Chongqing, where he attended Qinghua Secondary School. In 1945, he continued his studies at Yenching University and, after two years, transferred to Tsinghua University, graduating with a degree in history in 1949. Following the Communist revolution's victory, he was assigned to teach world history and politics at Beijing Yuying Secondary School (now Beijing No. 25 Secondary School). In 1954, he joined Beijing Teachers' College (now Capital Normal University), where he taught history for forty years.[19] He also served as an administrator at the school, progressing from the chair of the Department of History and director of the Institute of Historical Research to eventually becoming the university's president.

Throughout the decades, Qi supervised and co-supervised thirteen PhD and twenty-two MA projects, and some of his students went on to become leading world historians, including Xu Lan 徐藍, an established figure in world history and a board member of the national world history textbook project, and Wu Yin 武寅, the former director of the World History Institute at the CASS.[20] Beyond the university, Qi was a leader of the scholarly association on contemporary world-historical studies in China. He was elected and served multiple terms as president of the Association of Contemporary World-Historical Studies, the national organization for contemporary world-historical studies. Thanks to his scholarly achievements, Qi is widely recognized as one of the founding fathers of world-historical studies in China.

Historians have engaged in debates regarding the origins of world history in China. As documented in Chapter 1 of this book, some scholars view world history as an import, but there is substantial evidence indicating that local intellectual traditions played a crucial role in shaping the field.[21] Qi's own intellectual trajectory serves as a compelling example of the connection between China's tradition and the rise of world history.

Qi entered the professional realm of history in the early 1950s. While teaching high school political science and world history shortly after the

---

[19] Zhang Hongyi, "Xiongzhong ziyou yibu shijie shi—Qi Shirong jiaoshou tan shijie shi yanjiu" [A World History from Heart: Professor Qi Shirong on World-Historical Studies], in *Qi Shirong xiansheng zhuisilu* [A Collection to Commemorate Mr. Qi Shirong; shortened as "*QSXZ*" thereafter], ed. Xu Lan (Beijing: Renmin chubanshe, 2018), 201–202.

[20] For a complete list of these projects, see *QSXZ*, 367–368.

[21] Fan, *World History and National Identity*, 16–49.

communist revolution's victory, he did not reject historical materialism, the prevailing political ideology at the time.[22] However, he acknowledged that the education he received before 1949 was pivotal in forming his views on history in later years. On numerous occasions, he addressed the significant concept of "shicheng" 師承, acknowledging the influence of his teachers during his college years at Yenching and Tsinghua before the political takeover.[23]

What is "shicheng"? This term can be translated as "intellectual genealogy" in English, emphasizing the interpersonal connection of knowledge transmission among scholars from one generation to another. In Qi's case, he particularly valued the way in which the Republican era combined knowledge from China's tradition with that from the West.[24] He recalled that his teacher at Yenching, Qi Sihe, offered courses on both the History of Warring States and the Modern History of the West. Weng Dujian 翁獨健 (1906–1986), a specialist in Yuan history, also taught the History of the Far East. After two years at Yenching, his teachers at Tsinghua University, Lei Haizong, Shao Xunzheng 邵循正 (1909–1972), and Zhou Yiliang, were also renowned for their broad scope of interest in teaching and research beyond a single field.

As he recalled, Lei Haizong taught not only the general history of China, the history of Shang-Zhou, and the history of Qin-Han, but also the modern history of the West and the cultural history of the West. Zhou Yiliang taught the history of Japan, even though his original research specialty was in the history of the Wei-Jin dynasties. The grand view of history endorsed by Tsinghua professors guided his later career as a world historian after 1949. Reflecting on this in later years, he stated:

---

[22] In his first published essay, Qi promoted patriotism in world-historical education. Qi Shirong, "Guanyu zai shijie shi jiaoxue zhong jinxing aiguo zhuyi sixiang jiaoyu de jidian yijian" [Several Suggestions on How to Implement Patriotic Education in World-Historical Pedagogy], *Guangming ribao* [Guangming Daily] (July 28, 1951); also, Qi Shirong, "Zhongshen congshi Zhongguo de shijie shi yanjiu—Fang Qi Shirong jiaoshou" [Lifelong Commitment to China's World-Historical Research: An Interview with Professor Qi Shirong], recorded by Zou Zhaochen and Jiang Mei, in *QSXZ*, 245.

[23] See Zou Zhaocheng's interview of Qi Shirong, Zou Zhaochen, "Ting xiansheng yixi hua, sheng du shinian shu" [To listen to master's one conversation is like ten years' reading], in *QSXZ*, 120–121.

[24] Ibid., 120.

The intellectual milieu at Tsinghua of the time was to seek a universal view of China and the West, which demanded not only to overcome the gap between Chinese and foreign but also past and present. Influenced by them [i.e., Tsinghua professors], I developed an interest in both Chinese and foreign histories at college, and I benefited from this scholarly approach throughout my life. Under such an academic atmosphere, in my youth I had believed that, although one needs to designate an area of expertise in scholarly research, he cannot know of nothing or very little outside this area. Those who study Chinese history must know some foreign history; those who study foreign history must know some Chinese history.[25]

He thus concluded that only by acquiring a universal view and a broad scope of thinking could one achieve greater progress in historical research.

World history in China was not merely a tradition inherited from scholars of the Republican period, as this case will demonstrate. Qi was not a blind follower of his teachers, showing a critical stance toward their viewpoints. For example, Lei Haizong, one of his beloved teachers, was highly praised by Qi for his achievements in historical pedagogy.[26] He recalled that Lei's courses were well-organized and highly memorable, with details still vivid in his memory even after fifty years. However, he did not hesitate to critique some of his teacher's fallacies, either. In the 1960s, Qi collaborated with colleagues to translate part of Oswald Spengler's *Der Untergang des Abendlandes* [The Decline of the West], a book endorsed by Lei.[27] Despite the rhetoric, Qi correctly pointed out that the book was essentially Eurocentric.[28] He was also puzzled by Lei's embrace of

[25] Ibid., 121. The academic discipline *shijie shi* was officially named after 1949. Both "foreign history" and "Western history" in the Republican period, as Qi mentioned here in this conversation, are its precursor.

[26] Qi, "Zhongshen congshi Zhongguo de shijie shi yanjiu," 243.

[27] Aosiwa'erde Sibingele [Oswald Spengler], *Xifang de moluo* [The Decline of the West], trans. Qi Shirong, et al. (Beijing: Shangwu yinshuguan, 1963). This is a limited translation of Spengler's three-volume work, only covering its second volume of the original work as well as the introduction to the first volume. Qi, "Zhongshen congshi Zhongguo de shijie shi yanjiu," 247.

[28] Ibid., 247; in his private correspondence with historian Zhang Guangzhi 張光直, Qi also mentioned his view of Spengler as Eurocentric, see Zhang Guangzhi, "Gaoshan yangzhi, jingxing xingzhi—mianhuai Qi Shirong xiansheng" [We May Gaze up to the Mountain's Brow; We May Travel along the Greater Road: Commemorating Mr. Qi Shirong], in *QSXZ*, 50.

cultural morphology, a rather idealist construct not grounded in historical reality.[29]

Nevertheless, the "Tsinghua tradition" played a crucial role in nurturing Qi's universal view of history. Historian Luo Zhitian 羅志田, on the ninetieth anniversary of the founding of the Tsinghua History Department (2016), remarked on the differences between the Departments of History at Tsinghua University ("Tsinghua") and Peking University ("Beida") in the years before and after the Northern Expedition period (ca. 1926/27). According to Luo, each department represented a distinctive trend of historical inquiry. Beida focused on historical philology and text criticism, while Tsinghua was renowned for its balanced approach to historical studies between foreign and national histories. Tsinghua offered a historical curriculum promoting various social science methods and encouraging macroscopic views in historical studies.[30] More work has to be done on the contrast and comparison between these two departments, to be sure. Qi, in particular, was a product of Tsinghua's all-round education on both Chinese and foreign histories. Despite being recognized as a leading authority in world history, Qi never lost interest in Chinese history. In his later works, he made various attempts to discuss the nature of historical research with reference to both Chinese and non-Chinese sources.[31]

[29] Ibid., 247. As for a critique of Lei Haizong's cultural fascist tendency embedded in his embrace of Spengler's cultural morphology, see Xin Fan, "The Making of the Zhanguo Ce Clique: The Politicization of History Knowledge in Wartime China," in *The Engaged Historian: Perspectives on the Intersections of Politics, Activism and the Historical Profession*, ed. Stefan Berger (New York: Berghahn Books, 2019), 136–150.

[30] Luo Zhitian, "Beifa qianhou Qinghua yu Beida de shixue" [Historical Studies at Tsinghua (University) and Peking University Around the Period of the Northern Expedition], *Qinghua daxue xuebao (zhexue shehui kexue ban)* [Journal of Tsinghua University (philosophy and social sciences edition)] 31, no. 6 (2016): 11. Luo's observation is based on historian He Bingdi's recollection. As a review of He's work, see Xin Fan, "The Anger of Ping-Ti Ho: The Chinese Nationalism of a Double Exile," *Storia Della Storiografia* (History of Historiography) 69, no. 1 (2016): 147–160. For an excellent study on the development of Tsinghua University during the Great War period, see Chen Huaiyu, *Qinghua yu "yizhan": Meiji jiaoshou de Zhongguo jingyan* [Tsinghua and the "First War": American professors' China experiences] (Hangzhou: Zhejiang chubanshe, 2021).

[31] For example, in his later work, Qi discussed the nature of historical sources where he widely referenced works both in Chinese and world historiography. Qi Shirong, *Shixue wujiang* [Five lectures on historiography] (Beijing: Renmin chubanshe, 2017).

Qi's decision to study the history of international relations also reflects the influence of Tsinghua, where Jiang Tingfu 蒋廷黻 (1895–1965) might have been another source of inspiration. Jiang later became a successful politician, serving as Republican China's ambassador to the United States and the United Nations. In 1929, he became the chair of the history department at Tsinghua. Educated at Columbia University in the United States as a diplomatic historian himself, Jiang initiated a series of reforms to professionalize history education, emphasizing the study of diplomatic history. He also placed archival research at the center of historical education. Although Jiang left Tsinghua for governmental posts in the early 1930s, the tradition he established continued when Qi studied there. Qi's choice to delve into the history of international relations aligns with the legacy of Jiang Tingfu and the emphasis on diplomatic history and archival research at Tsinghua.[32]

World historians in China, particularly in teaching, frequently encounter a critical challenge: how to strike a balance between the limited scope of research expertise and the expansive scale of world-historical narratives. The increasing tensions between professionalization and specialization in the field have further underscored the significance of addressing this challenge. As a leader in the field, Qi provided his insights on this matter and encouraged historians to venture beyond their comfort zones. In an interview, he stated:

> No matter whether it is in China or in the scope of the world, historians have paid little attention to the academic subject of world history surveys (or so-called "global history") for a long time. They think that their content is too "broad and superficial" to be handled as an academic subject. Only by picking one country's history or choosing a part of it or even a few questions with regard to it could they conduct focused research, producing "elegant, refined, and top-notched" stuff. As a matter of fact, what scares them is that due to the grand scale of world history surveys, one must utilize the outcome of someone else's research. It is hard to avoid producing something with many "mistakes," amusing specialists.[33]

---

[32] Zou Zhaochen, "Ting xiansheng yixi hua, sheng du shinian shu," 131; Luo Zhitian, "Beifa qianhou Qinghua yu Beida de shixue," 11; Qi Shirong, "Zhongshen congshi Zhongguo de shijie shi yanjiu," 243.

[33] Zhang Hongyi, "Xiongzhong ziyou yibu shijie shi," 203.

Indeed, the tension between the limited scholarly expertise and the unlimited scope of world history is an issue that troubles world historians around the world.[34] Scholars in the West often adopt two approaches to tackling the problem. On the one hand, they are seeking to command as much as possible as historians, to develop language skills, acquire primary sources, and conduct field research[35]; on the other hand, they rely on the existing literature of scholarly research and critically examine the pattern of world-historical connections through theoretical lenses.[36] Recently with the rise of digital humanities, a number of historians have collaborated with data scientists and developed mega datasets by which to gather a more meaningful look into the grand patterns of historical changes.[37] Admittedly world historians in China have to yet catch up with these trends of development. However, in contrast to their foreign counterparts, they have developed a unique tradition of collaboration, especially through textbook projects at national levels, and Qi played a leadership role in these efforts.

One could perhaps argue that, as a world historian, Qi Shirong's greatest contribution to the field was the editing of textbooks. Indeed, since the Self-Strengthening Movement in the late nineteenth century, Chinese scholars and public intellectuals have been keenly following the works on world history from North America, Western Europe, and Japan and translated a great number of them in a timely manner as documented in the previous chapter. From the contemporary works of research to the collections from classical antiquity, Chinese publishers such as the Commercial Press have also organized massive translation projects

[34] Manning, *Navigating World History*, 265–267.

[35] The recent rise of frontier studies in Central Eurasian Studies is an example. One can see that historians often command multiple language skills as well as utilized archives from various countries.

[36] For example, C. A. Bayly's masterpiece *The Birth of the Modern World* emerges from the traditional scholarly field of British Imperial history with a critical view of the contribution of peripherals in shaping the modern world. It grows out of the recent critique of Eurocentrism. Bayly, *The Birth of the Modern World* (Oxford: Wiley-Blackwell, 2003).

[37] As a growing trend, several research centers in North America have organized innovative digital resource reservoirs such as the Collaborative for Historical Information and Analysis at the University of Pittsburgh (http://www.chia.pitt.edu/) as well as the China Biographical Database Project at Harvard University (https://projects.iq.harvard.edu/cbdb/home).

such as the World Classics Series and introduced the most crucial texts in world-historical studies to the Chinese audience. As a result, world-historical knowledge has constantly served as powerful references to China's modernization movement.

Yet it is education that further spreads the knowledge of world history among the ordinary people in China at a much deeper and perhaps more effective level. Historians have paid attention to the significant role of textbooks in shaping public awareness and citizenship in China through education.[38] In terms of world history education, the most significant achievement of the past century, one may argue, is the six-volume world history textbook. After its first release from 1992 to 1994, the textbook series sold over one million copies by 2017.[39] Generations of young scholars grew up reading this book. Qi Shirong was one of two chief editors of this textbook project along with historian Wu Yujin.

Commonly known as "Wu-Qi Edition," the six-volume world history textbook series is targeted at an audience of undergraduates, graduates, and junior researchers.[40] Funded by the Ministry of Education, the project convened the leading scholars of world-historical studies in various sub-fields, starting from primitive society through tracing human development all the way to the present. The series contains three parts. The first part covers the ancient world starting from primitive society to the end of the fifteenth century. The second part covers the modern world starting from the sixteenth century to the end of the nineteenth century. The last part covers the contemporary world starting from the early twentieth century to the present. Each part contains two volumes, and each volume has one or two chief editors. Liu Jiahe and Wang Dunshu 王敦書 served as editors of the first volume of Part I, and Zhu Huan 朱寰 and Ma Keyao 馬克垚 the second volume; Liu Zuochang 劉祚昌 and Wang Juefei 王覺非 co-edited both volumes in Part II. Qi Shirong edited the first volume

[38] See Peter Zarrow, *Educating China: Knowledge, Society, and Textbooks in a Modernizing World, 1902–1937* (Cambridge: Cambridge University Press, 2015); Culp, *Articulating Citizenship*; Jenny Day, "The War of Textbooks: Educating Children during the Second Sino-Japanese War, 1937–1945," *Twentieth-Century China* 46, no. 2 (2021): 105–129.

[39] Xu Lan, "Qi Shirong xiansheng shixue sixiang pingshu" [On Mr. Qi Shitong's View of History], in *QSXZ*, 299.

[40] *Shijie shi* [World History], ed. Wu Yujin and Qi Shirong (Beijing: Gaodeng jiaoyu chubanshe, 1992–1994) (abbreviated as *shijie shi* thereafter).

of Part III, and Peng Shuzhi 彭樹智 the second volume. This textbook series is known for its integrated approach to including Chinese history as part of the organic narrative of the global past, and many sections on China's position in the world contain high scholarly value.

It was massive work. The "Wu-Qi Edition" contains more than one and a half million Chinese characters, and it took a team of forty-five scholars nearly a decade for its completion.[41] It became even more challenging when Wu Yujin, the chief editor of the entire project, passed away in 1993, one year before its final completion. How to coordinate such a massive project with more than forty scholars all over the country? Ideas matter. Wu Yujin's view on world history shared the theoretical framework for this series. Rooted in a tradition of Marxist historical materialism, Wu strived to reconcile the tension between temporal and spatial dimensions in the world-historical narrative. Marxist scholars in the past had developed a teleological, temporal schema to narrate the development of historical time from primitive society, slave society, feudal society, and capitalist society, to communism, which Wu called the "vertical dimension" of world history. Yet as the contemporary globalization process only unfolded after the nineteenth century, Marxist historians around the world after Marx and Engels were to discover a narrative on how to document the spatial process, which he called "the horizontal dimension." Trained as an early modernist, Wu adopted the interaction between the sedentary and the nomadic worlds as a dominant theme.[42] His view influenced Chinese historians' conceptions of world history for the years to come.

Qi by and large followed Wu's idea. However, as their research fields differ, he further developed it with an emphasis on the modern and contemporary world in contrast to Wu's specialty in ancient and early world history. In the 2000s, Qi organized another team of scholars and edited a four-volume textbook on world history.[43] In it, he further underscored the significant role of contemporary globalization within a

---

[41] Xu Lan, "Qi Shirong xiansheng daiwo zoushang xueshu zhi lu" [How Mr. Qi Shirong Took Me to the Path to Academe], in *QSXZ*, 160.

[42] This summary is based on Wu Yujin, "Zonglun" [Introduction], in *shijie shi*, Part 3, vol. 1, i–ixxx. The original text was first published as an entry in the *Encyclopedia of China*, volume on foreign history.

[43] Qi Shirong, ed., *Shijie shi* [World History] (Beijing: Gaodeng jiaoyu chubanshe, 2006–2007).

world-historical context.[44] In reviewing his works, one will find that Qi's most valuable contribution to the rise of global views of history in China, that is, he promoted a new narrative of world history where globalization is being placed at the very center.

Peter Novick in his modern classics discusses failed attempts by American historians to repress their subjectivity in historical research. To have sheer objectivity is a "noble dream," yet impossible to achieve. To a certain degree, historical works always have to reflect historians' certain subjective views.[45] World history is not an exception. Scholars in the West often apply their own experiences to writing about the world overlooking the significant contributions of non-Western civilizations.[46] In terms of periodization, for example, they insist on a divide between ancient, medieval, and modern. This view has a great impact on the modern transformation of Chinese historiography. Generations of Chinese scholars have embraced such a view but are confused about how to correlate Chinese history to each stage in this tripartite schema of world history. Ample research has been devoted to the questions of locating ancient or medieval periods in Chinese history.[47] In this chapter, let us focus on the modern question.

What does being "modern" entail? Scholars have been debating the question over a century.[48] However, to the public in the West, the contemporaneity of their own society defines the outlook of being modern for non-Western societies. As Senator Kenneth Wherry of Nebraska in 1940 famously put, "With God's help, we will lift Shanghai up and up, ever up, until it is just like Kansas City."[49] This hubris further

[44] Yang Gongle, "Sixiangzhe de shengming shi buxiu de—chentong daonian Qi Shirong xiansheng" [Thinkers Will Never Die: Commemorating Mr. Qi Shirong with a Broken Heart], in *QSXZ*, 92.

[45] Novick, *That Noble Dream*.

[46] Many scholars have written on this topic. See, for example, Dipesh Chakrabarty, *Provincializing Europe: Postcolonial Thought and Historical Difference* (Princeton: Princeton University Press, 2008).

[47] The most comprehensive survey on this topic, see Feng Tianyu, *"Fengjian" kaolun* [Re-examining "Feudalism"] (Beijing: Zhongguo shehui kexue chubanshe, 2010).

[48] For Chinese historians' efforts to define the "modern" period in Chinese historiography, see Li, *Reinventing Modern China*.

[49] Martin Goldstein, *American Foreign Policy: Drift or Decision* (Wilmington, Delaware: Scholarly Resources Inc., 1984), 28.

climaxed by the end of the Cold War, when Francis Fukuyama proudly announced that the triumph of Western liberal democracy had ended thousands-of-years debate on the question of political ideology. The West provides all the answers![50] Indeed, when historians are developing standards by which to define the characteristics of a "modern" society, they often seek their roots in Western historical phenomena such as the French Revolution, the Industrial Revolution, Judeo-Christian tradition, and even Greco-Roman Classical Antiquity.[51]

Marxist historians in the Soviet Union criticized this framework of world history for its Eurocentric slant and added a "contemporary" period after the "modern." They argued that the bourgeois was the leading class in the revolutions that induced the triumph of global capitalism. Yet the October Revolution of 1919 world history opened the next chapter of development, a period when the working class was about to lead the transition to an international communist movement. Such a view was introduced to China along with the world history textbook edited by the Soviet Academy of Science. It once dominated the scene of world-historical studies giving rising to the field of contemporary world history, *shijie xiandai shi* (世界现代史).[52]

Qi Shirong played a leadership role in developing the field of contemporary world history in China. He served as chair of the Association of Contemporary World-Historical Studies for several terms. He also educated several generations of leading scholars in this research area. But most importantly he proposed a theoretical framework for contemporary world history in China. As a historian who grew up under Soviet influence, he was familiar with the Soviet periodization of contemporary history. According to Soviet scholars, the modern period of world history was divided into two parts, the rise of capitalism before the Paris Commune of 1871 and the fall of capitalism after it.[53] He disagreed

---

[50] Francis Fukuyama, *The End of History and the Last Man* (New York: Free Press, 1992). This book is based on an article that Fukuyama published in 1989, "The End of History?" *The National Interest,* no. 16, (Summer 1989): 3–18.

[51] A conservative view on the rise of Europe, see David Landes, *Revolution in Time: Clocks and the Making of the Modern World* (Cambridge, MA: Harvard University Press, 2000 [1983]), and a most poignant critique, see Jacky Goody, *The Theft of History* (Cambridge: Cambridge University Press, 2007).

[52] Zhang, "Xiong zhong ziyou yibu shijie shi," 205.

[53] Martin, *The Making of a Sino-Marxist Worldview*, especially ch.4.

with such a view, for he argued that the German and American capitalist economies certainly continued to grow in the late nineteenth century.[54] In collaboration with Wu Yujin, Qi revised the Soviet periodization of contemporary history and replaced the October Revolution with the opening of the twentieth century. In citing Lenin's view, he contended that the world entered an age of global imperialism in the late nineteenth and early twentieth century, which was the beginning of the contemporary period. This was especially the case if one takes a global view other than the Eurocentric one into consideration. For, as Qi observed, the nineteenth century was indeed a European century; but as the United States in America and Japan in Asia joined the global powers at the beginning of the twentieth century along with the awakening of the peoples in Asia, world history thus became truly global.[55] This global thinking is Qi's significant contribution to world-historical studies.

Yet the spatial dimension of the global cannot be separated from the temporal dimension of the contemporary, as Qi further explained. He pointed out that one could only grasp the special nature of contemporary history through the lens of globalization. According to him, contemporary history was world history, one that China and the world could not be separated anymore. In arguing so, Qi engaged a profound issue in world-historical studies in China since the Republican, even late Qing, period.

Educated elites in traditional China had long believed that China was the center of the world and that the Chinese civilization achieved the most sophisticated development in a historical scope. This view was only shattered by the late Qing when world history knowledge, imported from Japan and the West, was written into national history textbooks, as argued by historian Ge Zhaoguang.[56] While giving up on the Sinocentric view of world history, world historians in China over the course of the entire twentieth century faced a lost sense of temporality, and they were trying to figure out China's place within a world-historical context. What time

---

[54] Zhang "Xiong zhong ziyou yibu shijie shi," 205.

[55] Zhang, "Xiong zhong ziyou yibu shijie shi," 205–206; *Shijie shi*, part 3, vol. 1: 1; Qi Shirong, "Guanyu kaizhan shijie xiandaishi yanjiu de jige wenti" [Several Questions Concerning the Unfolding of World-Historical Studies], *Lishi jiaoxue wenti* [Issues of Historical Pedagogy], no. 2 (March 1988): 2.

[56] Ge, "The Evolution of a World Consciousness in Traditional Chinese Historiography."

was China's present vis-à-vis global capitalism? How to compare China's past to European antiquity? These seemingly easy questions now required new answers. In terms of understanding China's contemporary position in the world, for example, the 1929 guidelines to national history textbooks in the Republican period told Chinese students that the contemporaneous world was dominated by the struggles between "powerful nations" and "weak peoples," and that, being a weak country, China could only survive the world struggles by uniting with peoples in the colonial and semi-colonial world.[57] World historians in China in the early People's Republic also celebrated the solidarity of Chinese people with the global anti-colonial movements and promoted a world-historical mission for China's communist revolution.[58]

In contrast to the earlier views, Qi transcended the struggles of global imperialism in revolutionary historiography and pointed out global entanglement as the dominant feature of the history of the twentieth century. Writing in the post-Cold War context, he stated,

> The bipolar world history dominated by the competition between two superpowers the United States and the Soviet Union has ended, and the world is moving towards a multipolar order. Nowadays, any big country [*daguo*], no matter how powerful it is, cannot dominate the world; it is impossible for it to give orders to other countries anymore.

This was driven by economic development. He continued,

> In the sphere of economy, the trend of the internationalization, integration, and corporatization of production and capital continued on a daily basis. Nowadays, there exist various conflicts as well as connections among developed countries, among developed and developing countries, and, to a certain degree, among developing countries. Any country must rely on the international market. Isolationism is a dead end.

The globalization of the world economy predetermined cultural relations, a belief that he held within the tradition of historical materialism.

---

[57] Culp, "'Weak and Small Peoples' in a 'Europeanizing World'," 216–217.

[58] Huaiyu Chen, "The Rise of 'Asian History' in Mainland China in the 1950s: A Global Perspective," *Global Intellectual History* 7, no. 2 (2022): 282–302.

Yet he recognized the significant role of culture and ideology in forming contemporary consciousness. He further elaborated on this point,

> In the sphere of culture, thanks to the invention of the modern facilities of transportation, communication, and print, the scale and velocity of cultural exchange has reached an astonishing level, which has widened people's views and increased their mutual understandings. On the other hand, various systems of ideologies influenced each another and combated each another. Yet the general trend is that people are increasingly aware that the ideological differences should not bother the harmonious coexistence among nations.

For all these reasons, Qi believed that the twentieth century demanded its own historical narrative, one that was centered on globalization, and he called it "contemporary world history."[59]

Qi's promotion of contemporary world history in China has met with some criticism among historians, to be sure. For quite a long period, many historians believed that "contemporary" and "history" were concepts that contradicted each other. To them, the contemporaneity belonged to the studies on politics and current affairs.[60] He countered these challenges with two propositions. First, the current state of globalization was rooted in a historical process, and both the Western and Soviet experiences contributed to it. For Chinese scholars, Qi argued, it was important not only to break the self-isolated view of the world but also to rethink the failed Soviet experimentation of modernization and to digest its historical lessons. Second, reversely, studying the contemporary world would help historians to better understand the past. Coming from the Tsinghua tradition of macroscopic view in historical studies, Qi underscored the integrated nature of world-historical time. He argued that nowadays some historians in the West lost confidence in projecting the future. But he insisted, "if we develop a holistic understanding of the human past through its contemporaneity, we will discover that, at any rate, human history is a progressive movement; from the primitive, isolated, the dispersed human settlements [we] had developed into an integrated, connected community." He further predicted, "Although the

---

[59] Zhang, "Xiong zhong ziyou yibu shijie shi," 207.
[60] Zhang, "Xiong zhong ziyou yibu shijie shi," 207.

road is torturous, the future is bright." History could help people to gain confidence in future developments.[61]

How to study contemporary history? Qi developed a set of guidelines on this. In a conversation with another leading historian in the field, he pointed out that to study contemporary world history, first, one had to utilize declassified archives from various sources. Thanks to the Freedom Information Act, the archives in the West had become largely available for scholars to study world history. The problem was that the sources were not too limited, but overwhelming in number. Thus, world historians needed to further develop theoretical mindsets to grasp the Zeitgeist of the period of their studies. They had to critically examine the nature of the sources, as many were written for contemporary interests. Equally important, he reminded us of the contingent nature of contemporary history. As history was still unfolding, historians needed to be aware that their conclusions were not conclusive[62] (Fig. 3.1).

As a historian, Qi contributed to the theoretical framework of studying the contemporary world. As a pioneer, he also applied his belief in utilizing multinational archival sources to his own works of historical studies. In 1985, Qi represented China to attend the XVI International Congress of Historical Sciences in Stuttgart, Germany, and delivered a presentation on China's role in the Second World War.[63]

In this article, he challenged the Eurocentric mindset of WWII studies, which often overlook non-European countries' contributions. Based on various sources, ranging from Japanese government archives and Chinese memoirs to secondary scholarship from the West, he re-evaluated the role of China's War of Resistance in this global effort of the anti-Fascist movement. He pointed out that after the outbreak of the war in Asia in 1937 all the way to the Japanese attack on Pearl Harbor, China was the only country fighting global fascism in Asia. Thus, China was the main battlefield of the war in the Asian continent.[64] As an article written nearly four decades ago when China's contact with the foreign world was by and large

---

[61] Zhang, "Xiong zhong ziyou yibu shijie shi," 208.

[62] Zhang, "Xiong zhong ziyou yibu shijie shi," 208–210.

[63] Qi Shirong, "Zhongguo kangri zhanzheng zai di'erci shijie dazhan zhong de diwei he zuoyong" [The Role and Contribution of China's Anti-Japanese War of Resistance in the Second World War], *Lishi yanjiu* [Historical Research], no. 4 (1985): 118–133.

[64] Qi, "Zhongguo kangri zhanzheng zai di'erci shijie dazhan zhong de diwei he zuoyong," 133.

1985年9月摄于西德·杜案报大学

Fig. 3.1 Qi Shirong in Tübingen, Germany with international scholars, September 1985 (Courtesy of Capital Normal University)

limited, we may find that some of Qi's arguments need further clarification. However, his effort to engage global conversations and to rethink world history beyond a Eurocentric framework remains laudable (we will discuss this issue in Chapter 6). His pursuit of multinational archives influenced his students and world historians in China as well.[65]

We can only include a preliminary reflection on historian Qi Shirong's contribution to world-historical studies in this chapter, for its primary focus is to understand the rise of global history in China. Qi remains one of many scholars who contributed to the development of world-historical studies during this period. Yet, one of his lasting legacies is his effort to place globalization at the center of a world-historical narrative. From his work, the next generation of scholars, many of whom are his students,

---

[65] Xu, "Qi Shirong xiansheng daiwo zoushang xueshu zhi lu," 157.

started to treat globalization more seriously, resulting in the rise of global views of history as defined by Liu Xincheng introduced at the opening of this chapter. Qi and Liu both teach at the same institution, Capital Normal University, which was the first one in China to establish the Center for Global History. This connection is by no means accidental. Therefore, from both the institutional perspective and the intellectual genealogy, one may argue that this effort of placing globalization at the center of a world-historical narrative is the prime mover of the rise of global history in China. It started as an intellectual trend at the early age of Opening-up and Reform, and gradually crystalized into a field of scholarly studies today.

Part II

Practice

In North America and Western Europe, global history has firmly established itself as field of scholarly research, yielding remarkable works that enable scholars to transcend Eurocentric biases, reframe global connections, and contextualize changes through comparison. Take Columbia University Press's "Columbia Studies in International and Global History" as an example. Since 2007, it has published more than twenty volumes spanning topics ranging from non-Western intellectual history and comparative political thought to global migration and international development.[1] The pursuit of global historians has evolved into increasingly diverse endeavors.

A similar trend is emerging in China, where scholars from various backgrounds have contributed to works on "quanqiu shi," the Chinese equivalent of global history. In the following chapters, I discuss three promising approaches through which Chinese scholars engage with the global dialogue on global history. These approaches include global intellectual history, contextual comparison (with a focus on world-historical analogy), and studies on "global moments" within Chinese history. While not exhaustive, this discussion offers researchers a first-hand glimpse into the evolving landscape of global history practices in China.

---

[1] https://cup.columbia.edu/series/columbia-studies-in-international-and-global-history?page_number=2

CHAPTER 4

Global Intellectual History

Abstract Global history challenges Eurocentric biases, emphasizes global connections, and utilizes contextual comparisons. However, its relationship with world history remains contentious. The second part of the book delves deeper into this issue by examining the practice of global history in China, with a particular focus on conceptual history. While some scholars in East Asia conflate global history with world history, this chapter demonstrates that global conceptual history has become a prominent subject among Chinese historians today. Rather than focusing solely on comparison, it emphasizes the interplay between local knowledge and transnational concepts. Through a case study on the translation of the term "republic" from English into Chinese via Japan, this chapter illustrates the dynamic relationship between the local, the regional, and the global in historical studies.

Keywords Global intellectual history · Conceptual history · Translation · Republicanism in China · Intellectual history · Global history and world history

Global history challenges Eurocentric biases, underscores global connections, and employs contextual comparisons. Yet its relationship with world history remains contentious. For some scholars, it is synonymous with

X. Fan, *Global History in China*,
https://doi.org/10.1007/978-981-97-3381-1_4

world history. Patrick Manning, a prominent world historian, asserts that "world history is the story of connections within the global human community."[1] According to this perspective, world history aligns closely with global history, both aiming to highlight the interconnectedness evident in historical research, suggesting minimal differences between these two approaches. While Georg Iggers (1926–2017), Q. Edward Wang, and Supriya Mukherjee acknowledge subtle distinctions, noting that "global history" often delves into more recent periods in history coinciding with the twentieth-century "globalization," they believe that term "global history" and "world history" practically overlap and are ultimately interchangeable.[2] In general, world historians in recent decades, especially those from the "California School" such as Kenneth Pomeranz, Roy Bin Wong, Andrew Gunder Frank, and Jack Goldstone, have shared global historians' objective of challenging embedded Eurocentrism in historiography. They compare economic development trajectories between East Asia and Western European in the early modern world, challenging the conventional narrative attributing the rise of the Industrial Revolution to the "unique Western cultural tradition."[3] Their work has significantly influenced global historians.

In East Asia, many scholars often equate "global history" with "world history," too. In Japan, historians invented a unique way of categorizing history after the Meiji Restoration. They divided history into three parts, including national history, history of the West, and the history of the East. If the history of the West refers to European and North American history, the history of the East, known as "toyoshi" (東洋史), separates Japan from its neighboring countries, especially China.[4] Until today such disciplinary structure persists in Japan's higher education system. Although an increasing number of Japanese historians are becoming fascinated with

[1] Manning, *Navigating World History*, 3.

[2] Iggers et al., *A Global History of Modern Historiography*, 329–330.

[3] For a critical review of the "California School," see Peer Vries, "The California School and Beyond: How to Study the Great Divergence?" *History Compass* 8, issue 7 (July 2010): 730–751; for a Eurocentric view on the uniqueness of "Western civilizational tradition" embodied in the clock ware, see Landes, *Revolution in Time*.

[4] Stefan Tanaka, *Japan's Orient: Rendering Pasts into History* (Berkeley: University of California Press, 1993).

global history, criticism remains.[5] Historian Kishimoto Mio's recent essay is a good example. In it, she defines "global history" by outlining its five characteristics, which include interrogating subjects over extended time periods, addressing expansive themes, provincializing Europe in narration, tracing transregional interlinkages, and exploring novel themes such as epidemics, environment, and population.[6] She then criticizes "global history" for still being Eurocentric citing works by scholars from the "California School" as examples. She argues that these scholars have foregrounded "Europe" as the "active shaper" in their comparative studies of world history. It is not our plan to further engage with such a critique. However it appears to be that there is a conviction among some Japanese scholars that the California School's comparative approach presents the major thrust of global history.

In contrast, the other camp of scholars underscores the differences between global history and world history. Some scholars in Europe are concerned with the troubled legacy of *Weltgeschichte* starting in the post-Enlightenment era. They criticize historians such as Ranke and his followers for placing the nation-state at the center of historical narratives and philosophers such as Hegel, Marx, and Max Weber for their Eurocentric *Weltanschauung* (worldview).[7] Sebastian Conrad, for example, rejects the notion that global history is "direct heirs of older traditions of world history writing."[8] Cautioning against unfettered comparisons "without connections and broader context," he contends that global history surpasses mere connectedness.[9] According to him, global historians must grapple with "large-scale structured integration" and delve into the "problem of causation up to the global level." This nuanced perspective challenges scholars to delve deeper into the complexities inherent in the global historical narrative.[10] Therefore, scholars in this

[5] Haneda Masashi, "Japanese Perspectives on 'Global History'," *Asian Review of World Histories* 3, no. 2 (July 2015): 219–234; Beckert and Sachsenmaier, *Global History, Globally*.

[6] Kishimoto Mio 岸本美緒, "Gurōbaru hisutorī ron to 'Kariforunia gakuha'" [Global History Theory and the "California School"], *Shisō* [Thought], no. 1127 (2018): 80.

[7] Sachsenmaier, *Global Perspectives on Global History*, 22–25.

[8] Conrad, *What Is Global History*, 37.

[9] Conrad, *What Is Global History*, 42.

[10] Conrad, *What Is Global History*, 67.

camp feel uncomfortable endorsing the comparative approach adopted by the California School to global history.

In China, historians have also produced some significant works on comparative studies within the framework of "world history." Influenced by Marxist historical materialism, Chinese historians during the Maoist era passionately debated the economic nature of pre-modern Chinese society. Some of them essentialized China's past as "feudal" in contrast to Western Europe's "modern development," while others attempted to identify the "seeds of development" of traditional Chinese social and economic structures. The latter's study is known as the debate on the "sprouts of capitalism."[11] Regardless of their strong ideological rhetoric, some of these works such as the ones by Fu Yiling 傅衣凌 (1911–1988) remain instrumental for studies of economic history in post-Mao China.[12] Rooted in this tradition, for example, Fu's student Li Bozhong 李伯重 places industrialization within a global context and traces the economic development of the Yangzi Delta region in comparison with the industrialization process in Western Europe. Li's work echoes the studies by scholars such as Roy Bin Wong and Kenneth Pomeranz from the "California School."[13] Zhong Weimin 仲偉民 also studies the opium and tea trade and places Qing China within an integrated global economic system of the nineteenth century.[14] Despite this significant legacy, as the next chapter will show, some historians in China are, theoretically speaking, not fully comfortable with the comparative approach to historical studies. Instead, they attempt to highlight the global entanglement in the making of modern China through concepts and ideas. The rise of global intellectual history is a good example.[15]

[11] Arif Dirlik, "Chinese Historians and Marxist Concept of Capitalism," *Modern China* 8, no. 1 (1982): 105–131.

[12] On Fu Yiling's work, see Dirlik, "Chinese Historians and Marxist Concept of Capitalism," 112.

[13] For example, Li Bozhong, *Jiangnan de zaoqi gongyehua, 1550–1850* [Early Industrialization in the Yangzi Delta] (Beijing: Shehui kexue wenxian chubanshe, 2000).

[14] Zhong Weimin, *Chaye yu yapian: shijiu shiji jingji quanqiuhua zhong de Zhongguo* [Tea and Opium: China in the Nineteenth Century Economic Globalization] (Beijing: Zhonghua shuju, 2010).

[15] By no means, I am dismissing works done by scholars who are working on global trade, migration, and environmental changes. Yet a focus for this chapter is on intellectual history and history of concepts.

Intellectual history has become a prominent topic in contemporary Chinese historiography, a point underscored by historian Ge Zhaoguang. In a talk delivered at Princeton University, Ge delves into the significance of intellectual history, referencing Taiwanese scholar Chin-Shing Huang's perspective on the "decline" of intellectual history in the West.[16] Ge stated that, in contrast, scholars in China maintain a profound interest in intellectual history, to the extent that some believe that it has led to the "imbalance of academic structure" (學術格局的失衡).[17] Ge identifies three crucial roles for intellectual history in China. First, it serves to uncover the root causes of change in modern society, politics, and culture by delving into the past. Secondly, it engages in a dialogue with emerging theories and methodologies from the West and Japan. Lastly, it responds to the impact of new historical sources discovered since the 1970s. While not all scholars may fully endorse Ge's agenda of using intellectual history to trace the historical roots of contemporary China, his observation on the necessity for intellectual history to embrace diversity in research methodology remains a valid and pertinent point.[18]

Yet one needs to face the troubled legacy of intellectual history in modern China. In earlier generations, Chinese intellectual historians often fell into the trap of cultural essentialism. Well-known scholars including Liang Shuming 梁漱溟 (1893–1988), Qian Mu 錢穆 (1895–1990), and Lei Haizong were proponents of overarching historical narratives that provided "macroscopic views" of the past. They engaged in a comparative examination of ideas spanning East and West, ancient to modern, employing philosophical and deductive analyses to explore cultural traits

---

[16] The talk took place in summer 2010, as reported in *Wenhui bao* (May 22, 2010), https://www.gmw.cn/01wzb/2010-06/01/content_1139054.htm.

[17] Ge Zhaoguang, "Sixiangshi weihe zai dangdai Zhongguo ruci zhongyao" [Why Is Intellectual So Important in Contemporary China?], *Aisixiang* [The Love for Intellectual Thought] (December 2021), cited from *Wenhuibao*, https://www.aisixiang.com/data/130011.html.

[18] For a critique review of Ge's view on continuity of Chinese culture, see Peter Perdue, "A Single Entity," *London Review of Books* 43, no. 10 (May 20, 2021); equally problematic, some mainstream intellectual historians in the West still mainly focus their research on Europe without including sufficient input from non-European intellectual traditions. A recent example can be found in Richard Whatmore, *What Is Intellectual History?* (Cambridge: Polity Press, 2015).

from a world-historical perspective.[19] Scholars working within this tradition often found themselves at odds with counterparts trained in modern higher education systems, who emphasize evidence-based and positivist approaches to historical studies.[20]

In the face of such challenges, a new generation of scholars in China is embracing more diverse approaches to the study of intellectual history, including the perspective of global intellectual history. For some Chinese scholars, the rise of global intellectual history (*quanqiu sixiangshi,* 全球思想史) necessitates a re-evaluation of the European intellectual tradition, contextualizing it within the broader framework of global cultural exchanges and knowledge transfers.[21] On the other hand, others seek to reintegrate China into a world-historical context. Advocates of this approach contend that the shaping of modern Chinese identities is intricately woven into global networks of knowledge exchange, linguistic transfers, and the circulation of ideas. Among these scholars, a particularly outspoken group demonstrates a keen interest in the conceptual processes that contributed to the development of modern knowledge systems, echoing a European continental tradition known as *Begriffsgeschichte* (conceptual history). As a result, the history of concepts has emerged as a promising approach for intellectual historians in China to engage with global history. To provide an overview of this shift, this chapter explores both the theory and practice of global conceptual history.

The rise of global conceptual history is predicated on the belief that the evolution of modern China transcends mere social, economic, and political transformations, encompassing a profound shift in language perception and practice.[22] Recent scholarship underscores this shift in the

[19] For Liang Shuming's work, see Guy Alitto, *The Last Confucian: Liang Shu-ming and the Chinese Dilemma of Modernity* (Berkeley: University of California Press, 1986); on Lei Haizong's cultural comparison, see Fan, *World History and National Identity in China,* 70–73.

[20] An example is the debate between Evelyn Rawski and Ping-ti Ho. The latter embraced a view of "macroscopic history" passed down from his teacher Lei Haizong. Fan, "The Anger of Ping-ti Ho," especially 150 and 153.

[21] Li Hongtu, "Quanqiu sixiangshi: chongsi xiandai quanqiu zhixu de sixiang qiyuan" [Global Intellectual History: Reexamining the Intellectual Origins of the Modern World Order], *Huadong shifan daxue xuebao* [Journal of East China Normal University] 52, no. 5 (2020): 8.

[22] Jing Tsu, *Kingdom of Characters: A Tale of Language, Obsession, and Genius in Modern China* (London: Penguin, 2022); Yurou Zhong, *Chinese Grammatology: Script*

state's endeavor to "standardize the language," leading to the establishment of "Guoyu 國語" and "Putonghua 普通話." This protracted process unfolded amid decades-long political negotiations, often marked by arbitrary interventions from modernizing political regimes. As a result, the "modern" iteration of this language is significantly more centralized and standardized than its ancient roots.[23]

People are increasingly aware that this transformative process unfolded during a period when China experienced heightened interactions with the outside world. Undoubtedly, there were instances of resistance, misunderstandings, and imperial clashes, but these cross-cultural exchanges ultimately played a pivotal role in shaping modern Chinese languages and the worldviews of the Chinese people.[24]

Scholars in China, Japan, and Europe have directed their focus toward concepts and vocabularies to trace these changes. In China, early-generation linguists such as Wang Li 王力 (1900–1986) and Lü Shuxiang 呂叔湘 (1904–1998) were attuned to the historical shifts in the Chinese language. In the 1980s, debates arose regarding the emergence of "modern Chinese." Influenced by the periodization in the history of Chinese literature, Wang argued that the modern Chinese language came into being only after the May Fourth movement in the early twentieth century when writers embraced vernacular Chinese in literary works. In contrast, Lü Shuxiang extended the "modern" (近代) period in the history of the Chinese language back to the late Tang period. Both scholars downplayed the significant period in the late Qing and early Republic when intense linguistic exchanges occurred between China and the rest of the world. Wang Li referred to the time from 1840 to 1919

Revolution and Literary Modernity, 1916–1958 (New York: Columbia University Press, 2019).

[23] Gina Anne Tam, *Dialect and Nationalism in China, 1860–1960* (Cambridge: Cambridge University Press, 2020); Shen Guowei, *Xiyu wanghuan: Zhong-Ri jindai yuyan jiaosheshi* [New Language Boomerang: The History of Linguistic Exchanges between China and Japan in Modern Times] (Beijing: Shehui kexue wenxian chubanshe, 2020).

[24] For recent work on how culture misunderstandings could lead to conflicts between China and foreign countries, see Henrietta Harrison, *The Perils of Interpreting: The Extraordinary Lives of Two Translators between Qing China and the British Empire* (Princeton: Princeton University Press, 2021); for how imperial politics shaped linguistic practice, see Liu, *The Clash of Empires*.

as a "transitory stage" (*guodu jieduan*, 過渡階段) in the history of the Chinese language.[25]

Influenced by the German tradition of *Begriffsgeschichte*, contemporary scholars in China have increasingly turned their attention to this "transitory stage." In the late 1970s, Wolfgang Lippert published a groundbreaking work in German on the reception of Marxist terminologies in the East Asian context.[26] While extensively delving into political discourse and vocabularies, this work illuminates the substantial interweaving of the Chinese and Japanese languages in translating Western terminologies during the late Qing and early Republic periods. Subsequently, German sinologists collaborated with their Chinese and Japanese counterparts, producing foundational works on the translation of Western concepts in China in the ensuing decades.[27]

In recent years, similar projects have emerged in China. Political scientist Li Lifeng 李里峰 highlights that the "transitory stage" in Chinese history aligns with what Reinhart Koselleck describes as "Sattelzeit" (the Saddle period). Via the translation, Sattelzeit is introduced to Chinese scholars as a transitional stage before and after the French Revolution, roughly spanning the century from 1750 to 1850.[28] Defined as a period marked by intensive yet unstable changes in concept formations, it mirrors the moment in history when new concepts like democracy, republic, revolution, and class erupted in public discourse in the German linguistic context. During this time, these new concepts shaped the consciousness of the civic sphere, while old concepts such as aristocracy and hierarchy lost their original meanings and influence on the Zeitgeist.[29] Scholars like Li Lifeng draw parallels between the early modern period in Europe and the late Qing and early Republic in China, launching research initiatives

---

[25] Shen, *Xinyu wanghuan*, 14–15.

[26] Wolfgang Lippert, *Entstehung und Funktion einiger chinesischer marxistischer Termini: Der lexikalisch-begriffliche Aspekt der Rezeption des Marxismus in Japan und China* (Wiesbaden: F. Steiner, 1979).

[27] For example, Michael Lackner, Iwo Amelung, and Joachim Kurz, *New Terms for New Ideas: Western Knowledge and Lexical Change in Late Imperial China* (Leiden: Brill, 2001).

[28] Fang Weigui, "'Anxingqi' yu gainianshi: jianlun Dong-Ya zhuanxingqi gainian yanjiu" [The "Saddle Period" and the History of Concepts], *Dong-Ya guannianshi jikan* [East Asian Journal of History of Concepts], no. 1 (December 2011): 90.

[29] Fang, "'Anxingqi' yu gainianshi," 92.

to trace linguistic changes. Over the past decade, they have published numerous monographs, collectively advocating for the pursuit of "a global history of localized concepts" (全球本土化的概念史), exemplified by the *Xueheng Erya* (學衡爾雅) book series. Edited by scholars like Sun Jiang 孫江 and Li Lifeng based at Nanjing University, the series released seven titles by June 2023, covering the Chinese receptions of concepts such as Feudalism [封建, *fengjian*], Race [人種, *renzhong*], National character [國民性, *guominxing*], Science [科學, *kexue*], National Language [國語, *guoyu*], Rule of Law [法治, *fazhi*], and Utilitarianism [功利主義, *gongli zhuyi*].[30]

By concentrating on conceptual changes, scholars have developed a more nuanced understanding of the intricacies involved in the modern transformation of East Asia, particularly the dynamic linguistic exchanges between China and Japan. Examining this process, Japan-based scholar Shen Guowei 沈國威 outlines three directions of linguistic flows in translating Western concepts between the two countries: loan words from Chinese to Japanese, loan words from Japanese to Chinese, and words with Sino-Japanese origins.

For the flow from Chinese to Japanese, Shen further distinguishes the transfer of loan words from China to Japan into two stages. The first period, beginning in the late sixteenth century, saw the introduction of new concepts such as 基督 (Jesus), 幾何 (geometry), and 熱帶 (tropical areas), translated by Jesuit missionaries from China to Japan. The second period, from 1807 to the 1880s, involved words such as 銀行 (bank), 陪審 (jury), and 化學 (chemistry), translated by Protestant missionaries. After the Meiji Restoration, Japan supplanted China as the center of East Asian knowledge exchange with the West. From the late nineteenth century to the May Fourth period, an increasing number of Japanese loanwords (often known as "和語") that first appeared in Japanese were introduced to Chinese, including terms like 哲學 (philosophy), 科學 (science), and 個人 (individual). Another group of words underwent a dynamic process of Sino-Japanese exchange. they initially appeared in Chinese, underwent transformations in meaning in Japanese,

---

[30] Sun Jiang, "Quanqiu bentuhua de gainianshi" [A Global History of Localized Concepts] (book series launch speech at Nanjing University), *Pengpai xinwen* [The Paper News] (13 June 2023), https://m.thepaper.cn/newsDetail_forward_23461626 (accessed 17 June 2023).

and were eventually reintroduced into the Chinese language. A notable example is the word *gonghe* (共和).[31]

Today, China is officially referred to as "Zhongguo renmin gonghe guo" 中華人民共和國 (the People's Republic of China). While all the characters in this name originated in classical Chinese, the entire combination acquired its current meaning only in the twentieth century. The translation of "republic" into Chinese serves as a case study, capturing the dynamic exchange between China, Japan, and the West. Moving from theory to practice, the following section in this chapter provides a brief conceptual history of the term "republic" in China.

The concept of "republic" is steeped in historical transformations, with its origins often traced back to the Western Classical tradition, if not the earlier Mesopotamian city-states. In 510/509 B.C., the Romans expelled their tyrannical king, marking the founding of a "res publica" by virtue of political practice rather than a pre-existing idea.[32] By the middle of the second century B.C., Polybius, the Greek historian, offered a conceptualization of the Roman constitution through a Greek political philosophical perspective. His work contributed to the classical canons on republicanism. In the ensuing centuries, the notion of "republic," encapsulated by the term "republicanism," proliferated in modern Europe and North America through the Renaissance in Italian city-states, the Enlightenment in Europe, and the revolutions in the Americas. As a result, it became an integral part of the Western political tradition and continues to be practiced in contemporary politics.

Republicanism was relatively unfamiliar in China before the Opium War. However, the late nineteenth century witnessed a surge in cultural exchanges between China and the rest of the world. The introduction of republicanism to China followed a two-step process: the dissemination of the idea and the translation of the concept. The latter proved to be a contentious process, in line with Koselleck's perspective on the Sattelzeit. It took over half a century of negotiation for this translational stage to reach completion. The Sino-Japanese term "gonghe" (共和) eventually emerged as the standardized and stabilized translation for "republic," acquiring a sense of equivalence in meaning. Simultaneously with the

[31] Shen, *Xinyu wanghuan*, 26–29.

[32] It means people's affairs or people's property. "*res pulica, res populi.*" Cicero, *De Re Publica*, I. 25. 39.

translation, republicanism solidified as a core idea for the Chinese revolution. As a result, a new Chinese nation was established based on the foreign idea and concept of republicanism. To this day, China remains a People's Republic. In this section of the chapter, I will retrace the conceptual history of the term "republic" from the 1840s to the 1910s, which can be considered China's "Sattelzeit."

Despite the pioneering efforts of missionaries in facilitating knowledge exchange between China, Europe, and North America, information on the Western political system in Chinese publications before the Opium War was sporadic. One early missionary publication, the *Eastern Western Monthly Magazine* 東西洋考每月統計傳 (1833–1838), provided some insights.[33] In this periodical, the term "Zi'zhu'zhi'li" (自主之理) was adopted to denote Western republicanism.[34] According to the author, "Zi'zhu'zhi'li" conveyed the idea that individuals could pursue their actions freely under legal regulations, with each person, including the emperor, being equally subject to this legal system.[35] A similar case is found in *Xia'er guanzhen* 遐邇貫珍 (1853–1856). In this journal, missionaries asserted that the constitutions of England and America were "basically the same in their political system, with all power emanating from the people."[36] In both instances, the early introduction of Western republicanism underscored constraints on monarchical power and the exercise of individual rights. Notably, during this period, there was no standardized translation for the term "republic" in Chinese.[37] The absence of specific vocabulary in Chinese presented a barrier for those seeking to describe Western politics to Chinese readers.[38]

[33] According to the editors, the aim of the newspaper is to show to the Chinese that the west also has the same civilized culture as China. Huang Shijian, "Preface," in *Eastern Western Monthly Magazine*, ed. Aihanzhe, collected by Huang Shijian (Beijing: Zhonghua Shuju, 1997), 13.

[34] For example, *Eastern Western Monthly Magazine*, 296, 330, 361.

[35] *Eastern Western Monthly Magazine*, 339.

[36] "Huaqiguo Zhengzhi" [American Politics], *Xia'er guanzhen* [Chinese Serial] (Hong Kong: Xianggang Zhonghuan Yinghua Shuyuan, 1854), Vol. 2, 4–5.

[37] In 1844, the American missionary S. W. Williams translated "republic" as "Heshengguo" 合省國. William, *An English and Chinese Vocabulary in the Court Dialect* [Ying-Hua yufu lijie] (Macao, 1844).

[38] *Eastern Western Monthly Magazine*, 339.

The English word "republic" was likely first translated into Chinese as "minzhu" 民主, a term that, confusingly, now means "democracy" in the contemporary Chinese language. Unfortunately, based on existing sources, it is challenging to determine precisely when this translation first appeared in China and who was the initial proponent. However, W. A. P. Martin, known as "Ding Weiliang" 丁韙良 (1827–1916), is among the earliest known individuals to have adopted such a translation. In 1864, at the request of the Qing court, he translated Wheaton's *Elements of International Law* into Chinese as 萬國公法 (*Wanguo gongfa*) and used "Minzhu" to replace "republic" in this influential book.[39] Chinese diplomat Guo Songtao 郭嵩燾 (1818–1891), during his visit to Europe, consistently referred to "republic" as "minzhu" in his diaries, which indicates the wide influence of this republic-as-minzhu translation among late Qing scholar-officials.[40]

The compound term "minzhu" emerged as a neologism in the last decades of the nineteenth century. Breaking down the components, "min" refers to "the people" (demos) in Chinese, and "zhu" means "to have the power to decide."[41] Translated, "minzhu" signifies "the people deciding," carrying an equivalent meaning to "democratic." In contemporary Chinese, "minzhu" has indeed become the standard translation for "democracy." As highlighted in Fang Weigui's research, without contextual information, it becomes challenging to discern the precise meaning of "minzhu Guo" (民主國) in Chinese. Does it refer to a democratic state or a republic?[42] However, due to linguistic ambiguity, the blending of republicanism with democracy is a distinctive feature in this phrase

[39] Henry Wheaton, *Wanguo gongfa* [Elements of International Law], trans. W. A. P. Martin, in *Han'guk kŭndae pŏpche saryo ch'ongsŏ* (Sŏul: Asea Munhwasa, 1981), 97, 254–255, 277; *Wanguo gongfa* was introduced by Korea and Japan soon after its publication in China. See Wang Xiaoqiu, *Jindai Zhong-Ri wenhua jiaoliushi* [The History of Modern Cultural Exchanges between China and Japan] (Beijing: Zhonghua shuju, 2000), 52–53.

[40] Guo Songtao, *Lundun yu Bali riji* [London and Paris Diaries], ed. Zhong Shuhe (Changsha: Yuelu chubanshe, 1984), 156, 562, 563.

[41] Yuezhi Xiong, "'Liberty', 'Democracy', 'President': The Translation and Usage of Some Political Terms in Late Qing China," in *New Terms for New Ideas*, 74.

[42] Fang Weigui, "'Yihui,' 'minzhu,' 'gonghe' gainian zai Xifang yu Zhongguo de chuanbian" [The Transformation of Concepts "Parliament," "Democracy," and "Republic" in China and the West], *Ershiyi shiji* [The Twenty-First Century] 58, no. 2 (April, 2000): 54.

of translation, as seen in the rendering of the "Republic of China" as "Zhonghua Minguo" (中華民國).

In the last two decades of the nineteenth century, this translation appears to have become standardized. For instance, in 1880, a missionary newspaper called *Huatu xinbao* 華圖新報 [The Chinese Illustrated News] translated the American term "republican party" as "minzhu dang."[43] Furthermore, in 1890, another diplomat, Xue Fucheng 薛福成 (1838–1894), noted in his diaries the existence of a political system called *er'li'bo'li'ke*,[44] which he translated as "Minzhu Guo."[45] These instances indicate a growing trend toward the standardization of the term "minzhu" to convey the concept of republicanism in Chinese.

The translation of "republic" as "minzhu" also encapsulates a spatial aspect in the understanding of world politics, deeply rooted in a political taxonomy. According to this classification, there are three categories of political forms (in Greek, *politeia*) in the world: "*junzhu* 君主 (monarchy), *minzhu* 民主 (republicanism), and *junmin gongzhu* 君民共主 (a combination of monarchy and republicanism)." This taxonomy appeared frequently in the works of Chinese scholars in the late nineteenth century. For example, Zheng Guanying 鄭觀應 (1842–1922) wrote in 1880, "there are *Junzhu guo, minzhu guo,* and *junmin gongzhu guo* in the West."[46] In the same year, Huang Zunxian 黃遵憲 (1848–1905) also noted, "There are hundreds of countries all around the world. There are people since there are countries, and there are kings since there are people. Among the hundreds of countries, there is a political form where one person rules, which we call it *zhuanzhi*; there is a political form where the people rule, which we call it *minzhu*; there is a political form where the king and people rule together, which we call it *junmin gongzhu*."[47] Other scholars like Wang Tao 王韜 (1828–1897), He Qi 何

---

[43] *Huatu xinbao* [The Chinese Illustrated News], vol. 8 (Taipei: Taiwan xuesheng shuju, 1966), 162. "Minzhu dang" refers to "Democratic Party" in contemporary Chinese.

[44] It is the Chinese pronunciation of "republic".

[45] Xue Fucheng, *Chushi Ying-Fa-Bi-Yi siguo riji* [Diaries of Mission to Britain, France, Belgium, and Italy] (Changsha: Yuelu chubanshe, 1984), 104.

[46] Xia Dongyun, ed. *Zheng Guanying wenji* [Collected Essays by Zheng Guanying] (Shanghai: Shanghai renmin chubanshe, 1982), 175.

[47] Huang Zunxian, *Riben guozhi* [Treatise on Japan] (Guangzhou, 1898).

啓, and Hu Liyuan 胡禮垣 also followed this political taxonomy in their works.

These Chinese leading intellectuals played a pivotal role in advocating Western knowledge during the early years, and their acceptance of the political taxonomy had a profound impact on the development of Chinese political thought.

The underlying ideas behind this taxonomy included:

1. The assertion that the Chinese political system was not a "junmin gongzhu" like the West but a "junzhu" (monarchy).
2. The recognition that both "minzhu" and "junmin gongzhu" were viable alternatives for the political system in China.
3. The understanding that a "minzhu guo" rejects monarchical power.

However, inherent logical flaws exist within this taxonomy, most notably the use of "minzhu" to represent the equivalence of "republic." This poses a challenge when attempting to translate the term "democracy." As a result, in the history before 1900, Chinese scholars rarely discussed the meaning of democracy as extensively as they did republicanism. This linguistic complexity can be seen as a potential barrier to the further spread of liberal ideas in China during that era.

The subsequent stage in this transitional period was dominated by Japanese influence. Despite the word "gonghe" 共和 having a long tradition in the Chinese linguistic context, it was in Japanese that the term "republic" was initially translated as "gonghe."[48] In 1876, Okamoto Kansuke published *Wanguo shiji* in Chinese, frequently using "gonghe" instead of "republic."[49] His book was introduced into China before 1879, and with the increasing influence of Japan, this new translation gained followers in China. In 1894/1895, a journal in Hunan *Xiangxue xinbao* 湘學新報 quoted Okamoto's works and reiterated his translation

[48] Ogura kin'ichi argues that it was Mitsukuri Shōgo 箕作省吾 (1821–1847) who first coined the term 共和 as a translation of "republic" in 1844. This was then apparently popularized by Fukuzawa Yukichi's 福沢諭吉 in *Seiyō jijō* 西洋事情. Ogura Kin'ichi, ed. 小倉欣一 *Kinsei Yōroppa no higashi to nishi* 近世ヨーロッパの東と西 [Eastern and Western Europe in Early Modernity] (Tokyo: Yamakawa shuppansha, 2004), 12.

[49] Okamoto Kansuke, *Wanguo shiji* (Shanghai: Shenbao guan, 1879), Vol. 6: 14, 16; Vol. 8: 17, 18.

of "gonghe" as republic.[50] Notably, intellectuals like Huang Zunxian and Wang Tao, who had close connections with scholars in Japan, also adopted "gonghe" to translate "republic" in their works during this stage. However, given that the old taxonomy model was still dominant at this point, the "gonghe-as-republic" translation was not fully justified. Authors in *Xiangxue Xinbao* used this translation but did not display significant interest in it. They still at times reverted to the old taxonomy within the same journal.[51]

After the failure of the 1898 Reform, numerous Chinese reformists sought refuge in Japan. They were soon joined by a substantial number of Chinese students who went to Japan for educational purposes. With the increased influence of Japanese political writings on these students and political exiles, the new translation of "republic" gained popularity among them. In 1898 the famous journalist and public intellectual Liang Qichao translated a Japanese political novel *Jiaren Qiyu* 佳人奇遇 into Chinese. In it, he occasionally adopted "gonghe-as-republic" translation.[52] Soon after (in 1899) he published an essay in which he replaced the taxonomy "*junzhu, minzhu,* and *junmin gongzhu*" with "*zhuanzhi* 專制, *gonghe* and *lixian* 立憲.[53] Liang reiterated this new taxonomy in 1901, marking a significant shift in the conceptual framework used to discuss political systems.[54]

In 1903, a young Chinese student named Zou Rong 鄒容 (1885–1905) published a pamphlet titled "Revolutionary army" (*geming jun,* 革命軍) in Shanghai. Having just returned from Japan, he was heavily influenced by republican ideas. In this publication, Zou fiercely attacked the Qing dynasty, calling on the Chinese people to fight against Manchu tyranny in order to establish a "Republic of China" (中華共和國).[55]

---

[50] *Xiangxue xinbao* [New Journal for Studies in Hunan] (Taipei: Taiwan huawen shuju, 1966), 2008, 2034, and 2055.

[51] *Xiangxue xinbao*, 2080–2090.

[52] Liang Qichao, "Jiaren qiyu" [Curious Encounters of a Beauty], *Qingyi Bao* [The China Discussion] (Beijing: Zhonghua shuju, 1991), vol. 2: 123, 127.

[53] Liang Qichao, "Geguo xianfa yitonglun" [On Constitutions of Various Countries], *Qingyi Bao*, Vol. 12: 747.

[54] Liang Qichao, "Li xianfa yi" [On Drafting the Constitution], *Qingyi Bao*, Vol. 81: 5164.

[55] Zou Rong, *Geming Jun* [Revolutionary Army], in *Xinhai geming qian shinianjian shilun xuanji* [The Selected Works on the Debates During the Decade Before the 1911

Table 4.1 Translating political taxonomy in late Qing

"Republic"		
Junzhu 君主	Minzhu 民主	Junmin Gongzhu 君民共主
Zhuanzhi 專制	Gonghe 共和	Lixian 立憲

While Zou did not provide detailed reasons for his preference for a republic over other political forms, his influence played a significant role in spreading republicanism throughout the country. Another political activist, Hu Hanmin 胡漢民 (1879–1936), commented in his memoir that "Zou Rong wrote *Geming jun*, which was even more straightforward, with which nothing could be on its same level. Immediately his book came into fashion throughout the Yangtze River area. Because of its easy style, it was welcomed by all the middle and lower classes."[56] In 1904, a Shanghai magazine repeated the new taxonomy, confirming the rising popularity of the "gonghe-as-republic" translation[57] (Table 4.1).

As discussed, according to the old taxonomy, there were primarily two outlets for change in Chinese politics in the late Qing period: "*minzhu* and *junmin gongzhu*." The new translation replaced *minzhu* with *gonghe*, and now the new alternatives became "*gonghe* or *lixian*." Following this subtle change in translation, a significant debate unfolded between Chinese revolutionaries and constitutionalists in Japan. Eventually, this debate stabilized the "gonghe-as-republic" translation in the first decade of the twentieth century, marking a crucial shift in the conceptual landscape of political discussions among Chinese intellectuals.

In 1905, anti-Manchu revolutionaries launched a newspaper called *Minbao* 民報 to promote republicanism among Chinese students and

Revolution], eds. Zhang Zhan and Wang Renzhi (Beijing: Salian shudian, 1960), 676–677.

[56] Hu Hanmin, "Hu Hanmin zizhuan" [Autobiography by Hu Hanmin], in *Geming wenxian* [Documents on the Chinese Revolution], ed. Zhongguo guomindang zhongyang dangshi shiliao bianzhuan weiyuanhui (Taipei: Zhongyang wenwu gongyingshe, 1965), Series 3: 384–385.

[57] Xinhua, "Lun Zhongguo wu guoquan" [On China Not Having National Sovereignty], *Dongfang zazhi* [The Eastern Miscellany] 1, no. 5 (July 1904): 1042.

political exiles in Japan.[58] According to Hu Hanmin, this initiative represented the next step in revolutionary mobilization following the efforts of figures like Zou Rong. He argued that revolutionaries like Zou and Zhang Taiyan 章太炎 (1869–1936) focused too much on destruction without proposing concrete solutions. The mere expulsion of the Manchu rulers, according to Hu, could not be the sole solution to China's problems. He believed these revolutionaries were lacking in political ideas, relying primarily on support from the lower classes.[59]

Between 1905 and 1906, there were approximately 8,000 Chinese students in Japan, viewed as a valuable resource for potential future revolutionaries. During this period, both the revolutionaries, advocating for radical change, and the constitutionalists, aiming to preserve the monarchy while calling for reform, mobilized various resources to build revolutionary propaganda and garner support. In 1906, Liang Qichao, one of the leading voices among the Constitutionalists, published an essay in *Xinmin congbao* 新民叢報 denouncing revolution as a means of progress. Liang presented a two-fold argument. Theoretically, he cited the German scholar Konrad Bornhak (1861–1944) to caution that revolution might not necessarily bring about a true "gonghe" (republic) but instead lead to "zhuanzhi" (tyranny) in China. In terms of practical considerations, Liang maintained that the Chinese people were not yet sufficiently enlightened to be ready for a republican political form.[60]

Liang Qichao's criticisms of republicanism sparked a fierce response from *Minbao*. Both sides engaged in a series of articles discussing how to shape the future of China. Wang Jingwei 汪精衛 (1883–1944), a Chinese student in Japan, and Liang Qichao were the respective leading figures in the two camps. This exchange, known as the "Wang-Liang debate," garnered significant attention among the Chinese educated

[58] See "Benshe Jianzhang" [Regulations for Our Society] on the cover page of first volume. Also, Hu Hanmin, "Minbao Zhi Liuda Yuanze" [The Six Principles of *Minbao*], *Minbao* Vol. 3.

[59] Hu, "Hu Hanmin zizhuan," 385.

[60] Liang Qichao, "Kaiming zhuanzhi lun" [On Enlightened Absolutism], in *Xinmin congba* [New People's Newspaper], issues 73, 74, 75, 77 (1906); Wang Jingwei, "Bo 'Xinmin congbao' zuijin zhi feigeming shuo" [A rebuttal against the recent anti-revolutionary rhetoric in *Xinmin congbao*], *Minbao*, no. 4 (April 28, 1906).

elite.[61] Despite the debates, republicanism emerged as the dominant political theory for the anti-Qing movement. In alignment with this intellectual trend, a new Republic of China was eventually founded in 1911, marking a transformative moment in Chinese history and politics.

The conceptual history of translating republicanism in late Qing China represents a brief chapter on the extensive exchange of ideas, concepts, and vocabularies between China, Japan, and the West during the nineteenth and twentieth centuries. This case study illuminates the "Sattelzeit" of linguistic changes in China's modernizing centuries. Following the Opium War, the Chinese translation of republicanism underwent a period of dramatic change marked by competing modes of translation.

The translation "minzhu as republic" appears to have been initially adopted by Protestant missionaries, who rearranged the Chinese characters 民 and 主 to create a new compound. On the other hand, the translation "gonghe as republic" was a product of Japanese scholars recycling classical Chinese vocabulary and infusing them with new meanings derived from Western republicanism. This study underscores that the translation of republicanism in China was not a simple, one-dimensional process of reception. Instead, it reflects a dynamic cross-cultural exchange, illustrating a boomerang effect in the transfer of concepts and ideas within East Asia and between China, Japan, and the West.

From the beginning of the twenty-first century, Chinese scholars have undertaken a thematic re-examination of the formation of modern Chinese thought through the lens of the history of concepts. Notably, alongside the *Xueheng* series, scholars like Fang Weigui, Shen Guowei, and Zhang Ke 章可 have made significant contributions to enhancing Chinese scholars' understanding of global concepts. This endeavor has propelled global conceptual history into one of the most dynamic movements within the realm of global intellectual history in China.

[61] On the theoretical bases of the two parties, see Michael Gasster, "Reform and Revolution in China's Political Modernization," in *China in Revolution: The First Phase 1900–1913*, ed. Mary Wright (New Haven: Yale University Press, 1968), 77–78.

CHAPTER 5

The World as Historical Analogy

Abstract Global historians in China critique the Eurocentric biases prevalent in existing world history scholarship. This chapter, part of the broader discussion on the practice of global history in China in Part II, exemplifies how global history can effectively challenge Eurocentric biases within the framework of international law. It begins by examining scholars' critique of the theoretical limitations of comparison as a method in world-historical studies. It then explores the utilization and misrepresentation of historical analogies through Eurocentric lenses, particularly within international relations theories. Using the assertion of ancient China's engagement with international law as a case study, this chapter argues that the wealth of Chinese historical records offers valuable insights to debunk the narrow perspectives inherent in modernity discourse.

Keywords Historical comparison · Historical analogy · Historiography · International relations · World history · Global history · Use and abuse of history

In China today, global history attracts scholars not just from the field of professional studies of history but also a board range of disciplines including politics, law, international studies, and area studies. As I will address the impact of area studies on global history in this book's conclusion, this current chapter focuses on the intersection between global history, law, and international relations theories in China. It appears to me that Chinese scholars of international relations and international law are particularly frustrated with the existing international law system's exclusion of Chinese experience. Not only do they challenge its Eurocentric nature, but they also go one step further to suggest that international law might even have originated in ancient China.

To some Chinese scholars, the critique of the Eurocentric international law is first and foremost a critique of world/global history.[1] In a long review essay of Carl Schmitt's *The* Nomos *of the Earth*, for example, political philosopher Liu Xiaofeng 劉小楓 questions the genealogy of global historiography. He challenges the view of historians Georg Iggers, Q. Edward Wang, and Supriya Mukherjee who trace the origin of global history to William McNeill' *The Rise of The West*.[2] Liu thinks that McNeill's work remains Eurocentric as the latter specifically writes about the rise of the West. Liu instead argues that the German conservative scholar Carl Schmitt had already established a "global history" by publishing *The* Nomos *of the Earth* in 1950 thirteen years before McNeill.[3] Liu is not a professional historian, and people might not be convinced by his assertion that Schmitt is a "global historian." But what Liu proposes is stimulating. He invites us to rethink the logical behind the international legal system through Schmitt's concept "globales Lienendenken" (global linear thinking).

As a renowned conservative thinker in contemporary China, Liu Xiaofeng is against the liberal views of cosmopolitanism and globalization. To him, the recent discourse of "global history" in the West has shifted the focus from nation-states to social life too prematurely. This

---

[1] Non-professional historians pay less attention to the subtle divide between global history and world history in China.

[2] Georg Iggers, Q. Edward Wang, and Supriya Mukherjee, *A Global History of Modern Historiography* (London: Routledge, 2013). Liu cited from this book's Chinese translation by Yang Yu, *Quanqiu shixueshi: cong 18 shiji dao dangdai* [Global Historiography: From the 18th Century to the Present] (Beijing: Peking University Press, 2011), 411.

[3] Carl Schmitt, *The* Nomos *of the Earth in the International Law of the* Jus Publicum Europaeum, trans. G. L. Ulmen (New York: Telos Press, 2006); Liu Xiaofeng, "Ouzhou wenming de 'ziyou kongjian' yu xiandai Zhongguo: du Shimite *dadi de fa* zhaji" [The "Free Space" for European Civilization and Modern China: Notes on Reading Schmitt' *Der Nomos der Erde*], *Sixiang pinglun* [RUC Perspectives], no. 4 (2018): 67.

change is hinged upon a false assumption of a total triumph of European values in the name of world citizens (*shijie gongmin*, 世界公民). Through Schmitt, he contends that nation-states remain at the center of global conflicts and world politics because the logical of *Lienendenken* persists. According to him, this idea of "line-making" is the fundamental logic through which European and American powers dominated the world. It means to draw boundaries between enemies and friends and civilizational self and others through international law. The rise of America and its challenge of the European-centered international law are the signs of epoch-making world-historical changes. Yet he argues that such global linear thinking persisted after the shift of the power from Europe to the United States. He hints at the possibility that China's rise would introduce a new possibility to challenge the linear politics through this country's revolutionary legacy of guerilla warfare. Although Liu does not further explain how the legacy of guerilla warfare serves as an anti-thesis to *Lienendenken*, one would assume that the thrust of his critique is to remind us that the artificial boundaries between the West and others are at the center of Eurocentric power politics.

Historians in the non-West have noticed this tilted balance between the West and the rest. Postcolonial critic Dipesh Chakrabarty famously calls to "provincialize" Europe to shift away from Europe and to reconstruct a locally focused historiography.[4] So is historian Paul Cohen. His critique of American scholarship on China studies and his call for a China-centered approach remains inspirational to present-day scholars after his book's first publication in the 1980s.[5] Writing an indigenous history from a local perspective is a great contribution to our knowledge of history, to be sure; but the focus on the local seems contradictory to global historians' agendas to write about global connectedness.

Not endorsing his ideological position in this essay, I think that Liu's call to deconstruct the power-invested "lines" between the West and the rest is highly useful. As this chapter shows through a case study on international laws in China, the assertions on the exception of international law to China involve imperial agendas to separate the West from the rest. At the same time, the line-drawing practice is at the core of old world-historical comparisons. Separating China from the West or vice

---

[4] Chakrabarty, *Provincializing Europe*.
[5] Cohen, *Discovering History in China*.

versa almost always involves drawing a clear line between the two, forcing them to become separate entities. As Japanese historian Kishimoto Mio argues, a major theoretical flaw of world historians from the "California School" is their effort to sustain the linear paradigm between the center and periphery.[6] Therefore, I encourage scholars to think about alternatives, especially to delve into investigating the role of specific conceptual infrastructures that bridge the gap between local, national, and global experiences—what I term "world-historical analogies."

From comparison to analogy, this chapter focuses on Chinese scholars' critique of Eurocentrism, especially those who focused on the history of international law and international relations. They have achieved this by employing alternative world-historical analogies, often drowning creative interpretations and reinterpretations of ancient Chinese history, with applications extending beyond the border of today's Chinese nation. Rather than advocating for a wholesale replacement of the old (arguably Eurocentric) with the alternative (arguably Sinocentric), I argue that these efforts represent a significant legacy for today's global historians today. They contribute to the construction of a more egalitarian narrative of the globalized human past. In this context, global history in China is not just a reinvention of world-historical works by professional historians; it also involves a synthesis of various intellectual traditions in the country, including fields such as law, international relations, and classical studies.

But first, let us rethink the theoretical pros and cons for global historians to engage with comparison.

Comparison stands as a frequently employed methodology in historical research, and, as a result, there exists a wealth of studies on historical comparison within modern historiography. In a speech delivered at the Fourth European Social Science History Congress in The Hague in 2002, for example, German historian Jürgen Kocka proposes a categorization of historical comparisons based on their purposes. He delineates four categories, namely heuristic, descriptive, analytical, and paradigmatic, explaining that historical comparisons serve diverse functions in historiography. These functions range from identifying questions and problems, clarifying profiles of individual cases, and asking and answering causal

---

[6] Kishimoto, "Gurōbaru hisutorī ron to 'Kariforunia gakuha'," 88.

questions, to providing a means for historians to distance themselves from their known cultural positions.[7]

Historians in North America have devoted attention to historical comparison, too. Patrick Manning, a prominent world historian, classifies comparisons into three categories based on their meanings. He articulates, "[to] compare is to bring two or more things together (physically or in contemplation) and to examine them systematically, identifying similarities and differences among them."[8] In the first and most limited sense, comparisons involve juxtaposing two isolated units, such as colonized societies impacted by metropolitan rule. Secondly, some form of influence may induce changes in both units, prompting scholars to decide whether to emphasize the similarities or differences between the cases. Historians can also place these units with a larger system of comparison. In this scenario, these objects being compared are generally independent of each other, as seen in civilizations and cultures examined by Oswald Spengler and Arnold Toynbee. Thirdly, Manning highlights units in comparison are both in contact with one other and mutually influence each other, as exemplified by thee intertwined relationship between China, Japan, and Korea in East Asia.[9]

Despite the various ways of categorization, historians generally concur that comparison constitutes a fundamental approach in historical studies. At the same time, they express concerns about some of its potential pitfalls. Kocka identifies three "serious methodological reasons that make comparison difficult." Firstly, as historians aim to incorporate more cases in their studies, they increasingly rely on secondary literature, having less time and ability to delve into primary sources. Secondly, for comparison to occur, historians must extract these cases from their contexts, leading to the observation that, "the comparison breaks continuities, cuts entanglements, and interrupts the flow of narration."[10] Thirdly, comparison faces the inherent challenge of dealing with totality. Each individual case encompasses various perspectives, and one can only elect a few of them for comparison. Thus, Kocka argues that comparison involves "selection,

---

[7] Jürgen Kocka, "Comparison and Beyond," *History and Theory* 42, no. 1 (Feb. 2003): 39–41.

[8] Manning, *Navigating World History*, 279.

[9] Manning, *Navigating World History*, 280.

[10] Kocka, "Comparison and Beyond," 41.

abstraction, and de-contextualization." In other words, it is not feasible to compare totalities.[11]

As scholars grapple with the methodological challenges of comparative history, some also delve into the ontological aspect of historical comparison, particularly questioning the extent to which two cases are comparable. Chinese historians Liu Jiahe and Chen Xin contribute to this discourse by introducing the concept "incommensurability" into Chinese historiography. Originating from Thomas Kuhn's 1962 classic *The Structure of Scientific Revolutions*, this term originally meant "to have no common measure" and later took on a new meaning to "characterize the holistic nature of the changes that take place in a scientific revolution."[12] If paradigmatic shifts occur at the holistic level, then incremental and local changes become incomparable. Liu and Chen apply this idea to historiography, asserting that historical comparison must adhere to the logic of the unity of incommensurability and commensurability. To put it simply, they argue that the coexistence of similarities and differences is a prerequisite for comparison.[13] Without similarities, they are deemed incommensurable, and without differences, there is no need for compare. Building upon this logical understanding, they contend that comparison forms the fundamental condition for making sense of the world.[14]

Liu explains the criteria for comparison in the earlier article. In it, he asserts that the very existence of differences is a precondition for meaningful historical comparison. Within the same historical period, comparisons among different countries, nations, and social groups hold significance. However, within the same country, nation, and social group, comparisons become meaningless. What about cases from different times and different places? Liu contends that they are comparable if they are placed within the same theoretical or conceptual frameworks. For example, although the ancient Western Zhou dynasty and medieval

[11] Kocka, "Comparison and Beyond," 41.

[12] Eric Oberheim and Paul Hoyningen-Huene, "The Incommensurability of Scientific Theories," *The Stanford Encyclopedia of Philosophy* (Fall 2018 Edition), ed. Edward Zalta, https://plato.stanford.edu/entries/incommensurability/.

[13] Liu Jiahe and Chen Xin, "Lishi bijiao chulun: bijiao yanjiu de yiban luoji" [A Preliminary Analysis of Historical Comparison: General Logic in Comparative Studies], *Beijing shifan daxue xuebao* [Journal of Beijing Normal University (Social Science Edition)], no. 5 (2005): 70.

[14] Liu and Chen, "Lishi bijiao chulun," 71.

Europe may not seem comparable on the surface, they become comparable if both were characterized by the existence of feudalism.[15] He argues that world history, by its nature, is always a unity of differences, involving a process of holistic abstraction while acknowledging local particularities. In this context, perspectives matter, and identifying the correct theoretical and conceptual frameworks is crucial for effective comparison.[16] Thus, Liu emphasizes that the key to meaningful historical comparison lies in recognizing and navigating the intricate interplay between differences and commonalities within the chosen frameworks.

The crucial role of establishing a shared perspective serves as a common thread unifying historiographies on comparison in both the East and the West. Historian Stefan Berger, in his essay on comparative history, similarly raises questions about the importance of theoretical and conceptual frameworks in the comparative endeavor. Berger expresses a more optimistic view, stating that "anything can be compared with something else." However, he also emphasizes the need for careful consideration when selecting the theoretical and conceptual framework for the comparison. According to Berger, it is essential to choose cases that align with the specific questions one aims to address. He urges scholars to be mindful of the theoretical foundations they employ, emphasizing that the effectiveness of a comparison hinges on the thoughtful selection of cases that align with the intended research inquiries.[17]

Determining the right question for a meaningful comparison requires a return to theoretical consciousness.[18] For example, in the context of examining whether both cases are influenced by nationalism, it is ineffective and potentially misleading to solely compare aspects such as "enmity towards foreigners and willingness to defend one's country against foreign

[15] Liu Jiahe, "Lishi de bijiao yanjiu yu shijie lishi" [Comparative Studies in History and World History], *Beijing shifan daxue xuebao*, no. 5 (1995): 47.

[16] Liu, "Lishi de bijiao yanjiu yu shijie lishi," 51.

[17] Stefan Berger, "Comparative History and Transnational History," in *Writing History: Theory and Practice*, eds. Stefan Berger, Heiko Feldner, and Kevin Passmore (London: Bloomsbury, 2010), 193.

[18] As global historians have reminded us, lives and ideas do not often fit into the neatly labelled boxes of "geographies and time periods." Shellen Wu, *Birth of the Geopolitical Age: Global Frontiers and the Making of Modern China* (Stanford: Stanford University Press, 2023), 9.

invasions." These elements are not the necessary conditions for the existence of nationalism. Instead, a more pertinent question might delve into the broader conceptual foundations and manifestations of nationalism within each case, allowing for a more nuanced and insightful comparative analysis. In essence, the key lies in formulating questions that align with the theoretical underpinnings and complexities of the phenomena being compared.[19]

The process of establishing theoretical conditions for historical comparison poses its own set of challenges. Berger delves into the postcolonial critique of concept transfers and knowledge formation, acknowledging the complexities inherent in this endeavor. While he ultimately succeeds in establishing the logical conditions for historical comparison, it becomes evident that historians can no longer sidestep the theoretical discussion of the concepts central to their comparative efforts. Historical comparison, according to Berger, has evolved into a primary arena for theoretical deliberation, encompassing discussions on concepts, ideas, frameworks, and structures. In other words, the theoretical underpinnings have become integral to the very fabric of historical comparison, shaping the way in which historians approach and interpret the past through comparative lenses.

Due to the demanding theoretical preconditions for comparison, world historians in China have generally exhibited less enthusiasm toward this methodology. In the Maoist era, when historical materialism emerged as a state ideology, historians were compelled to embrace "forced analogies" derived from Marx's writings, such as the Asiatic Mode of Production and feudalism. They engaged in debates regarding the implications of these analogies within the context of Chinese history.[20] Since the 1980s, Chinese scholars have only achieved "limited-scoped achievements" in comparative studies. Considering this phenomenon, Li Jianming 李劍鳴, a prominent global historian in China today, cautions researchers about the formidable nature of comparison. He emphasizes the critical importance of establishing an analytical framework before engaging in comparison, stressing that this process demands a thorough and accurate command of knowledge about both entities being compared. Often, due

---

[19] Berger, "Comparative History," 193.

[20] As for the "forced analogy" on the Asiatic Mode of Production debate, see Fan, *World History and National Identity in China*, Chapter 4.

to a lack of knowledge about the counterpart in the comparison, Chinese historians tend to juxtapose one party against a "flawed" or "imagined" image of the other. Li underscores the necessity of overcoming this limitation to ensure more accurate and meaningful comparative analyses.[21]

In this chapter, I acknowledge the intricate discussions surrounding the establishment of effective historical comparisons through theoretical and conceptual frameworks. However, I propose that, rather than exclusively focusing on comparison, historians should seriously consider historical analogy as a distinctive form of comparison. Unlike comparisons, which involve negotiation between similarities and differences, as Liu adeptly demonstrates in his dialectical analysis of comparison. In contrast, analogies serve as the "building blocks" through which the precondition of similarity is established. In global history, this inherent similarity between cases situated in different temporal and spatial contexts warrants historians' attention. As historicism dominates the current mode of historical thinking, the conceptualization of this similarity becomes a more intriguing question than merely identifying differences. By emphasizing historical analogy, historians can delve into the nuanced connections and shared characteristics between disparate cases, offering a valuable perspective that goes beyond the conventional focus on divergences.

According to the *Oxford English Dictionary*, an analogy is a comparison primarily serving a heuristic function. It is defined as "a comparison made between one thing and another for the purpose of explanation or clarification." The process of analogy can be described as follows: if object A resembles object B in having characteristic X, then it is expected that B might have a characteristic Y that is similar to X ($AX:BX::AY:BY$). As such, analogy involves drawing connections between two entities based on shared characteristics, allowing for a deeper understanding or clarification of one through the comparison with the other.[22]

---

[21] Li Jianming, *Lishi xuejia de xiuyang he jiyi* [Historians' Education and Their Craft] (Shanghai: Shanghai Sanlian Shudian, 2007), 329, 334.

[22] David Hackett Fischer, *Historians' Fallacies: Toward a Logic of Historical Thought* (New York: Harper and Row, 1970), 243; Yuen Foong Khong, *Analogies at War: Korea, Munich, Dien Bien Phu, and the Vietnam Decisions of 1965* (Princeton: Princeton University Press, 1992), 7.

Historians widely employ analogies as "heuristic instruments for empirical inquiry," "explanatory devices in their teaching," and "embellishments in their writing."[23] In a previous essay for Bloomsbury, I discussed some theoretical falls in the use and disabuse of analogies in history.[24] On this issue, David Hackett Fischer's overview in the early 1970s remains relevant today as he highlighted some common fallacies in historians' application of analogical thinking.[25] Similarly, Chinese scholars engaged in discussions about the nature of historical analogy in the early 1980s. Wu Yinhua 吳寅華, for example, took a logical approach to construct three categories of analogous analysis: analogy based on the nature of things, analogy based on relations of things, and analogy based on historical models.[26]

Wu Yinhua outlined four preconditions framing analogous relations between historical events. The first and foremost is the commensurability of historical events. He emphasized that productive historical analogization involves comparing the nature of things rather than their appearances. In other words, two things in comparison must share a similar nature. Thirdly, he underscored the significance of counterarguments in analogy. While encouraging the identification of commensurability, he urged the recognition of dissimilarities exposed through analogy. Finally, he advocated for a quantitative method to carefully measure historical entities in comparison.[27] Despite these efforts, decades later, historians still find themselves falling into similar traps when utilizing historical analogies.

In China, there is a saying, "前事不忘后事之师" (learn from the past to guide the future) underscores the significant role of historical knowledge in political decision-making. Analogies are deeply ingrained in a

---

[23] Fisher, *Historian's Fallacies*, 244.

[24] Xin Fan, "Historical Analogies, Historia Magistra Vitae." In *Bloomsbury History: Theory and Method Articles* (London: Bloomsbury Publishing, 2021). http://dx.doi.org/10.5040/9781350970885.074.

[25] Fisher, *Historian's Fallacies*, 243–9.

[26] Wu Yinhua, "Lishi leibi de leixing he yaoqiu" [The Categorization of and Prerequisites for Historical Analogy], *Jianghan luntan* [Jianghan Tribune], no. 9 (June 1982): 32–34.

[27] Wu, "Lishi leibi de leixing he yaoqiu," 34–35.

world-historical narrative that sustains Western dominance in global politics. The Munich analogy, for instance, is frequently cited in the history of American foreign relations.

On July 21, 1965, during a National Security Council (NSC) meeting, American President Lyndon B. Johnson deliberated with his advisors on whether to send one hundred thousand troops to South Vietnam. While Under Secretary of State George Ball opposed the decision, colleagues McGeorge Bundy, Dean Rusk, and Robert McNamara argued in favor. The U.S. ambassador to South Vietnam, Henry Cabot, summarized their position, stating, "I feel there is a greater threat to start World War III if we don't go in. Can't we see the similarity to our own indolence at Munich?"[28] The decision to escalate U.S. military involvement in Vietnam had complex reasons, but this Munich analogy serves as an example of how politicians adopted historical lessons to justify their actions. However, the subsequent colossal failure of U.S. involvement also highlights the potential abuse of historical analogies.

A similar case reveals a more structured flaw in the use of historical analogy, namely, the Eurocentric bias. During the Cuban Missile Crisis, a heated debate unfolded among officials in the Kennedy administration upon discovering that the Soviet Union had secretly transported missiles to Cuba. Hawks, like Secretary of State Dean Acheson, advocated military intervention, proposing a surgical strike to eliminate the threat. Opponents drew an analogy between this proposed action and Japan's sneak attack on Pearl Harbor. In the midst of this intense debate, a statement by Robert Kennedy played a pivotal role in steering toward a peaceful resolution. He argued,

For 175 years we had not been that kind of country. A sneak attack was not in our tradition.[29]

Two noteworthy points about Robert Kennedy's use of analogy emerge: first, analogies often draw from well-known historical events, and second, in the use of analogies, Western politicians frequently exhibit biases

---

[28] Khong, *Analogies at War*, 3.

[29] FRUS, 1961–1963, Vol. 11, Cuban Missile Crisis and Aftermath, Recording of Meeting, 31. Record of Meeting. https://history.state.gov/historicaldocuments/frus1961-63v11/d31#:~:text=For%20175%20years%20we%20had,a%20lot%20of%20Russians%20too.

against other nations, reflecting a deeply ingrained Western-centric world-view. This Eurocentric bias can influence decision-making processes and contribute to a skewed interpretation of historical analogies.

Indeed, policy advisors and scholars in international relations often utilize world-historical analogies, such as the "Thucydides' Trap," to anticipate the potential impact of China's rise on the international order. For example, in his notable 2015 article in *The Atlantic*, Graham Allison discusses the rise of China and foresees a perilous future marked by a likelihood of military conflicts between the United States and China. He draws on an insight from the Athenian historian Thucydides, who, in his well-known history of the Peloponnesian War, argued that conflicts arise when a rising power encounters a ruling power.[30] Despite Chinese leaders rejecting this metaphor, Allison insists on its applicability to the future relations between America and China. To support his claim, Allison and his research team conducted a survey of cases over the last five hundred years where rising powers encountered existing ones. They concluded that the majority of these cases (twelve out of sixteen) eventually resulted in war. By referencing China's rise to world-historical precedents, Allison emphasizes the grave danger of potential conflicts.[31] In essence, scholars of international relations often employ a metaphor invented thousands of years ago in the Greek peninsula and draw from a world history extending back to the last five hundred years of European global dominance to predict the future trajectory of China.

At the same time, historical analogy can play a pivotal role in deconstructing Eurocentric world-historical narratives, particularly within global anti-colonial movements. The twentieth century witnessed the rise and fall of colonialism as a global world order, and its history is often narrated as a tale of conquest and resistance. On one hand, it chronicles how industrialized Western powers expanded their influence beyond cultural zones and political boundaries, establishing unequal relationships with people worldwide. On the other hand, it recounts how communities on the receiving end strove to combat Western imperial

---

[30] Graham Allison, "The Thucydides Trap: Are the U.S. and China Headed for War?" *The Atlantic* (September 24, 2015). https://www.theatlantic.com/international/archive/2015/09/unitedstates-china-war-thucydides-trap/406756/.

[31] Graham Allison, *Destined for War: Can America and China Escape Thucydides' Trap?* (New York: Houghton Mifflin Harcourt, 2017).

aggressions, aiming for political self-determination and economic independence. While earlier works tended to concentrate on the dominance of
the West, such as the rise of the West, recent scholarship has increasingly
focused on anti-colonial struggles by people in the non-Western world.
Historical analogy, in this context, serves as a powerful tool to illumi-
nate parallels between different anti-colonial movements, challenging and
dismantling Eurocentric perspectives that have traditionally dominated
historical narratives. By emphasizing shared experiences of resistance and
independence across diverse regions, historical analogy contributes to a
more inclusive and nuanced understanding of the complex dynamics in
the global anti-colonial movements.

The so-called anti-colonial struggles go beyond mere resistance to
the Eurocentric world order of Western imperial aggressions and colonial dominance; they are also tangible projects of "world-making." Over
the course of century-long struggles, people in the colonial world have
recognized that their fate as an independent nation is intricately tied
to the global state of affairs. They have come to realize that true self-
determination is unattainable without a comprehensive transformation
of the existing world order. However, the concept of "world-making"
remains somewhat abstract in the current scholarship on anti-colonial
studies.

The concept of world-making, to me, encapsulates an idea, an argument, and a possibility. It starts as an idea, one intended to be realized
through concrete actions. This idea is often presented as a persuasive
argument, offering the possibility of liberation and self-determination,
frequently associated with a radical and, at times, violent struggle.
However, it goes beyond mere physical resistance; it encompasses the
envisioning and construction of a new world order. Leaders in the
colonial world, grappling with the question of what comes after the
empire, face the challenge of providing answers. In navigating the experiences of the past and the horizons of expectation for their nations,
they frequently employ world-historical analogies in their world-making
projects. Through contrast and comparison, they connect the promise of
their individual nations' destinies to cross-cultural references in their anti-
colonial struggles on the world stage. In this way, world-making becomes

a complex and multifaceted process, intertwining historical analogies, cultural references, and the pursuit of a liberated future.[32]

In the next chapter of this book, I will argue that Chinese political elites, both in the Nationalist Party and the Communist Party, were fully aware that China's national struggle was interconnected with the global anti-colonial and anti-imperial movements during the Sino-Japanese War of Resistance. This global consciousness has been an undercurrent in modern Chinese intellectual thought, forming a significant legacy that frames the rise of global history in China today. However, in this chapter, I will center my discussion on a more profound critique of the international legal system, which originates from a world-historical analogy drawn from ancient Chinese history—the origins of international law in ancient China.

To European imperialists of the nineteenth century, international law served as both a body of knowledge and a tool for controlling colonial subjects. The maxim "knowledge is power" underscored the imperative to closely guard access to such knowledge. A case in point is the aftermath of the Second Opium War (1856–1860), where the Chinese government granted permission to American missionary William A. P. Martin (1826–1916) to translate Henry Wheaton's *Elements of International Law* into Chinese. Upon learning of this, M. Klecskowsky, the French chargé d'affaires in China, responded with a harsh remark: "Who is this man who is going to give the Chinese an insight into our European international law? Kill him—choke him off; he'll make us endless trouble."[33]

In the nineteenth century, Europeans harbored complex sentiments regarding human sympathy. While extending such sympathy to a Chinese subject might have been beyond their contemplation, the idea of killing an American for such an arbitrary reason would have been deemed unimaginable in that historical context. Klecskowsky's casual comment may appear to be a bad, and even harmless, joke. However, one aspect of this seemingly random remark holds some truth: during the nineteenth century, international law was fundamentally "European." In a way, this

[32] Adom Getachew, *Worldmaking After Empire: The Rise and Fall of Self-Determination* (Princeton University Press, 2019).

[33] W. A. P. Martin, *A Cycle of Cathay: or China, South and North with Personal Reminiscences* (New York: Fleming H. Revell Company, 1896), 234; Rune Svarverud, *International Law as World Order in Late Imperial China: Translation, Reception and Discourse, 1847–1911* (Leiden: Brill, 2007), 91.

incident also exemplifies the apprehension among European imperialists about sharing knowledge of international law with colonial subjects, viewing it as a potential source of trouble and resistance.

The Eurocentric roots of the international law system are evident, with the Treaty of Westphalia laying its foundation and figures like Hugo Grotius and Niccolò Machiavelli shaping its principles. Concepts rooted in European history, such as nation-states and popular sovereignty, occupy a central place in its vocabulary. Despite awareness of this bias, escaping such Eurocentrism in international law studies remains challenging. In a recent project, for example, the *Oxford Handbook of the History of International Law* aimed to engage in a "global historical" endeavor, transcending the "incomplete" and "Eurocentric story" of international law history. However, a critical reviewer noted that nineteen out of the twenty-one contributors were "white European men." The encounters discussed in the volume all involved Europe, neglecting relations between non-European countries, like those between China and Japan.[34] The neglect is obvious.

Language serves as a significant challenge. As Europeans expanded their dominance through imperial aggression and colonial control, they imposed their interpretation of international law as the global standard. The establishment of international treaty systems involved negotiations where legal terms were translated from one linguistic context to another. This knowledge transfer process was asymmetrical, with non-European knowledge being selected, appropriated, and sometimes reinvented through the European lens. For example, in *The Clash of Empires*, Lydia Liu examines how, in the negotiation of the Treaty of Tianjin (1885), European translators forcefully paired the Chinese term *yi* with the English "barbarian," and the term acquired a much more discriminative overtone thereafter in its original linguist context.[35] This translingual

---

[34] Anne-Charlotte Martineau, "Overcoming Eurocentrism? Global History and the *Oxford Handbook of the History of International Law*," *The European Journal of International Law* 25, no. 1 (Feb. 2014): 330.

[35] Liu, *The Clash of Empires*; Li Chen also discusses the crucial role of language to international relations among empires in the eighteenth and nineteenth centuries. Li Chen, *Chinese Law in Imperial Eyes: Sovereignty, Justice, and Transcultural Practice* (New York: Columbia University Press, 2015), especially Chapter 2, 69–111.

process has had a transformative impact on the Chinese understanding of statehood and its place in the world order.[36]

The law creates reality. International law provides rules and regulations that both constrain states (the laws of war) and empower them (the law of sovereignty).[37] It frames relations among states as it is translated from European to non-European languages, and a Eurocentric system of knowledge takes root. This system not only influences but also reflects the "infrastructure" of political imagination used by scholars in international relations to predict the globalized future. However, if the study of international law and international relations continues to *"speak a thoroughly Eurocentric language,"* transcending this narrow view of Eurocentrism remains a complex challenge.[38]

In the remainder of this chapter, I will delve into a school of thought positing the existence of international law in ancient China, specifically during the Spring and Autumn Period (771–476 BCE). Despite the dismissal of this perspective by many scholars due to its perceived nationalist and assertive stance in China's foreign policy, I will highlight an alternative genealogy of this thought. In the late nineteenth century, W. A. P. Martin, a Western missionary, systematically presented this perspective in both its original English publication and its subsequent Chinese translation. Since this school of thought has resurfaced at various junctures in Chinese history, it prompts us to consider how non-European legacies of this nature could contribute to contemporary theories of international relations. Recognizing such a legacy, as I will argue later in this chapter, marks the initial stride toward establishing a more egalitarian vision of the globalized future. This is particularly significant in emphasizing the role of political idealism in a world increasingly dominated by power politics.

William Alexander Parsons Martin, known as "Ding Weiliang" in Chinese, was an American missionary, translator, and educator who dedicated sixty-six years of his life to China. Hailing from Indiana, he received his college education from Indiana University and the Presbyterian Seminary in New Albany. In 1850, Martin arrived in China with his newlywed wife and engaged in Christian work in Zhejiang province for about a decade before serving as an interpreter for American diplomats during the

---

[36] To borrow Lydia Liu's term, see Liu, *Translingual Practices.*

[37] Simmons, "International Law and International Relations," 188.

[38] Martineau, "Overcoming Eurocentrism?," 331.

negotiation of the Treaty of Tianjin. In the 1860s, he began working for the American Minister to China, Anson Burlingame (1820–1870; known as "Pu Anchen" in Chinese). By 1869, Martin had assumed the presidency of the School of Combined Learning (Tongwen guan) in Beijing, one of the earliest state institutions offering Western-style education in China. In 1895, he was appointed as the inaugural president of the Imperial University of Peking, the precursor to the renowned Peking University.

In addition to his missionary endeavors, Martin gained renown for introducing the principles of international law to China. During the 1860s, he stood among the pioneers in translating Western works on international law into Chinese.[39] His translation of Henry Wheaton's *Elements of International Law* achieved wide circulation not only in China but also across the entire East Asian region.[40] Beyond his role as a translator, Martin displayed a keen intellectual interest in China. Serving as a professor of international law, he introduced a diverse array of subjects covering Chinese history and culture to Western audiences. His autobiography detailing life in China also became a bestseller in the United States.[41]

From 1880 to 1882, Martin served as an advisor to the Chinese delegation in Europe. During this period, he presented a paper at the Congress of Orientalists in Berlin on September 13, 1881. This research notes that, for the first time, he argued for the existence of international law in ancient China—a notion he had contemplated as early as 1864.[42] He actively promoted this thesis both within China and internationally. Subsequently, a revised version of the Berlin paper, titled "Traces of International Law in Ancient China," was published in the *International Review* in January 1883 and later in several other sources.[43] In 1894,

[39] Svarverud, *International Order as World Order*, 88.

[40] Svarverud, *International Order as World Order*, 93.

[41] Martin, *A Cycle of Cathay*.

[42] Martin briefly mentioned this idea in the English preface to his translation of Wheaton. Svarverud, *International Law as World Order*, 98–100.

[43] W. A. P. Martin, "Traces of International Law in Ancient China," *International Review* 14 (January 1883): 663–677; The *International Review* (1871–1883) was a trade magazine published by A. S. Barnes & Co. Based in New York, the journal held a progressive view and expected to speak to audiences both in Europe and America.

Martin included the article, now renamed "International Law in Ancient China," in his scholarly collection, the *Hanlin Papers*.[44]

Meanwhile, Martin's assistant Wang Fengzao 王鳳藻 (1851–1918) translated the article into Chinese and published it as *Zhongguo guoshi gongfa luelun* in 1884. Two years later, the Chinese translation surfaced in Japan under the title *Sina kodai bankoku kôhô*.[45] In the lead-up to the 1898 Reform, influential opinion leader and open-minded journalist Liang Qichao incorporated the translation into the *Xizheng congshu* [Book series on Western politics], a collection that he edited to disseminate Western knowledge in China. The text thus gained wide circulation in late Qing China.

Penned over a century ago, Martin's article remains captivating for contemporary readers due to its straightforward arguments. Initially, he aligned with the prevailing notion that China, throughout its extensive history, was isolated from the rest of the world, despite its interactions with neighboring Asian countries within its tribute system. However, the intriguing twist lies in Martin's creative interpretation of Classical sources, where he discerned a parallel world in ancient China comparable to his contemporary era. Through this comparison, he posited that an international order not only could but did exist in ancient China, potentially constituting the Chinese origin of international law. As such, Martin rejected the Eurocentric assumption that Chinese civilization stood in opposition to the modern world order. On the contrary, he argued that this order, deeply rooted in international law, might align harmoniously with China.

To fully grasp Martin's thesis, it is essential to delve into his understanding of historical time, particularly the periodization of "ancient" and "modern" in this article. Both concepts are highly contested in Chinese historiography, as demonstrated by various debates introduced by Huaiyin Li in *Reinventing Modern China*.[46] Dominant perspectives often trace the beginning of modern times in Chinese history to the mid-nineteenth century, specifically the First Opium War. Martin's definition of "modern" Chinese history appears expansive, spanning two thousand

---

[44] W. A. P. Martin, *Hanlin Papers: Essays on the History, Philosophy, and Religion on the Chinese* (Shanghai: Kelly & Walsh/The Tientsin Press, 1894).

[45] Svarverud, *International Law as World Order*, 100.

[46] Li, *Reinventing Modern China*, 19, 31, 103 and ff.

years from Qin's consolidation of the Chinese empire in 221 BCE to his own time.

Martin characterized the modern period in Chinese history based on China's interactions with the rest of the world, outlining three stages paralleling Western historical events.[47] The first stage, from the Punic Wars to Europe's discovery of the Cape of Good Hope in 1488, marked a period of complete isolation from the West. The second stage saw limited commercial contact with Western countries over the next three and a half centuries, during which China acquired some knowledge about major European states without fully grasping their strength. The third stage commenced after China's defeats in the Opium Wars, as the Chinese recognized the imminent threat of Western expansion following the opening of the Suez Canal.

While Martin echoed the prevalent belief in Chinese isolationism during the "modern" period of Chinese history, his perspective on China's antiquity was both creative and intriguing. He proposed that Qin's unification of China served as the dividing line between the "ancient" and "modern" periods. In the former, China was not a consolidated state but a fragmented world where independent "states" or "principalities" shared a common root of civilization and equal status. Essentially, China constituted a territorial scope of the "world" in this earlier period, where various regional states interacted and formed dynamic relationships.

The enduring continuity of Chinese civilization has been a widely accepted belief in Sinological studies. However, recent scholarship has begun to challenge this notion, particularly during non-Chinese dynasties' conquests like the Yuan and Qing. Scholars, utilizing Manchu-language sources in the study of Qing history, argue that the success of the Manchu dynasty is less a continuation of the "Chinese" civilization and more influenced by the Inner Eurasian political tradition.[48] At the same time, scholars have shifted away from perceiving China as a homogeneous nation and focused on its rich local diversity. To some extent, Martin's

---

[47] Martin, "Traces of International Law in Ancient China," 64.

[48] Concerning the rise of "New Qing History," an approach to studying Qing history by utilizing Manchu language archives, scholars have offered some excellent surveys, e.g., see Evelyn Rawski, "Reenvisioning the Qing: The Significance of the Qing Period in Chinese History," *Journal of Asian Studies* 55, no. 4 (1996): 829–850.

view of ancient China foreshadows these nuanced understandings of time and space in historical studies.

Addressing the spatial dimension, Martin dismissed the fundamental differences between ancient China, ancient Greece, and Rome. In ancient times, he noted, the "vast domain of China" was divided among several independent principalities. These principalities, sharing a common blood-line, possessing an advanced civilization, and bound by a common language,[49] mirrored conditions not dissimilar to those in ancient Greece and Rome—widely regarded as the origins of international law. While the scope of Chinese civilization was undoubtedly more extensive than its Greek counterpart, the distinction lay in the organizational structure. Unlike the Greek states, described as a "cluster of detached tribes," the Chinese states formed a fragmented empire inheriting laws and civilization, akin to how modern European states inherited those of Rome.[50]

Concerning the temporal dimension, Martin avoided a binary understanding of the relationship between the past and present. Unlike later historians embroiled in debates over periodization in Chinese history, he did not explicitly define when the "ancient" period commenced or concluded in this article. He vaguely alluded to it as the latter part of the Zhou dynasty (Eastern Zhou). Although aware that this period could be further divided into two ages—what he termed the "coordinated States" (lie-kuo) and the "warring States" (chan-kuo)—he chose not to pinpoint specific dates. The transition from one age to the other marked the gradual decline of the central power of Zhou emperors, succeeded by the ascendancy of regional powers of feudal states. He labeled the first age as characterized by an "orderly and pacific" order, while the second represented a time of intense politics.

Martin's overarching understanding of this transition aligned with common views in Chinese historiography. Similar to Classical Antiquity in the West, the latter part of the Zhou dynasty represented a foundational stage in Chinese history, witnessing the formation of major philosophical traditions such as Confucianism, Daoism, and Mohism.[51] However, his

---

[49] Martin, "Traces of International Law in Ancient China," 64.

[50] Martin, "Traces of International Law in Ancient China," 65.

[51] Benjamin Schwartz, *The World of Thought in Ancient China* (Cambridge, MA: Harvard University Press, 1989), 2, and ff.

choice of terminology was not flawless. While the term "Warring States period" accurately described the second age—from the partition of the powerful regional state Jin in 475 BCE to Qin's unification of China in 221 BCE—the term "lieguo" for the first age was less conventional. In China, few learned individuals would typically refer to it as "lieguo." Instead, the more widely accepted term is the Spring and Autumn period (771 to 476 BCE; known as "chunqiu"). Recognizing this anomaly, Martin's translator, Wang Fengzao, replaced "lieguo" with "chunqiu" in Martin's preface to the Chinese translation of his original text.[52]

Nevertheless, in his somewhat superficial and intuitive grasp of ancient Chinese historiography, Martin honed in on a pivotal point—the existence of a "family of States" resembling "the great States of Western Europe." According to Martin, these entities were "united by the ties of race, literature, and religion, engaged in active intercourse, both commercial and political." For such a system to function, Martin speculated that there must have been *jus gentium* (law of nations).[53]

To substantiate this claim, Martin embarked on a creative examination of Confucian classics, notably the *Book of Rites*. He asserted that he had identified traces of "a law, written or unwritten, and more or less developed, which they recognized in peace and war."[54] This included a set of rules and institutions in early China, such as "the interchange of embassies," treaty agreements with sacred dispositions in *mengfu* (Palaces of Treaties), the pursuit of a balance of power, neutrality maintenance in war, and the professional practice of diplomacy.[55] His sources included Confucius, Mencius, the *Book of Rites*, and *Kuo-yu* ("Guoyu" in Pinyin; *Discourses of States*).[56] Martin provided an example of a treaty between the Prince of Zheng and a coalition of invading princes in 544 BCE, legitimized by solemn religious powers.[57]

[52] E.g., Ding Weiliang [W. A. P. Martin], *Zhongguo gushi gongfan* [International Law in Ancient China], trans. Wang Fengzao (Beijing: Tongwen Guan, 1884), juan 1, pages 1b, 4b.

[53] Martin, "Traces of International Law in Ancient China," 65–66.

[54] Martin, "Traces of International Law in Ancient China," 77.

[55] Martin, "Traces of International Law in Ancient China," 66.

[56] His translator Wang Fengzao adds *Zhanguo ce* 戰國策 (Stratagems of the Warring States) to the list in the Chinese translation.

[57] Martin, "Traces of International Law in Ancient China," 72–73.

Transitioning from peace to war, Martin elucidated the "practice of international law" in ancient China, drawing parallels to modern Europe. This included protecting the persons and property of non-combatants, proper attack procedures, justifications for war, the pursuit of a balance of power, the sacred right of existence for fiefdoms originating from "the imperial throne," and the rights of neutrality. He even speculated, "Textbooks on the subject of international relations may have existed in ancient China."[58]

Martin's thesis on international law in ancient China held particular significance, especially in the sensitive late nineteenth century. He presented and published the article in the 1880s, a time when a group of open-minded Chinese mandarins, led by the Prince of Gong, had initiated the Self-Strengthening Movement. This movement aimed to introduce Western sciences and technologies, reform the education system, and bolster the military. While the Qing government established official diplomatic relations with other countries and invited Westerners for various roles, conservative forces within the government resisted, viewing Chinese and Western cultures as fundamentally incompatible. For them, the introduction of Western modernity was only a detrimental blow to the preservation of the Chinese identity.

As a translator and educator employed by the Chinese government, Martin was acutely aware of the perilous potential of the discourse of cultural difference, a challenge he faced in both China and the West. In the preface to the Chinese translation, he noted that when he asserted the existence of international law in ancient China, Westerners often refused to believe it. He wrote this paper to persuade them.[59] More significantly, he argued that if international law was not alien to China, then the Chinese were "by that fact more disposed to accept the international code of Christendom, which it is no utopian vision to believe will one day become a bond of peace and justice between all the nations of the earth."[60] In the nineteenth century, well before the present, Martin had already recognized the embedded Eurocentrism in international law and the crucial role of non-Western history in shaping a globalized future society.

---

[58] Martin, "Traces of International Law in Ancient China," 77.

[59] Ding, "Preface," 1a.

[60] Martin, "Traces of International Law in Ancient China," 77.

The originality of Martin's thesis may be subject to challenge. He appears to be of among the first in the West to embrace such a viewpoint. However, it is evident that his interactions with Chinese scholars and translators left a discernible impact on his perspectives. Unlike the predominant teleological framework that characterized much of the twentieth-century narratives of modern Chinese history, late Qing scholarly officials held more contested views regarding time and space in world-historical thinking.[61]

In contrast to later Marxist historians who sought to fit Chinese historical events into a Eurocentric framework, identifying stages such as slavery, feudal society, and modernity, late Qing scholars experimented with adopting a China-centered historical framework to narrate world-historical events. Martin's contemporaries, including Guo Songtao and Xue Fucheng, for example, explored comparisons between European countries and the United States with ancient Chinese dynasties.[62] Martin acknowledged this influence, stating in the conclusion of his paper, "Chinese statesmen have pointed out the analogy of their own country at that epoch with the political divisions of modern Europe."[63] While influenced by his Chinese counterparts, Martin's views, in turn, had an impact on subsequent generations of Chinese scholars, and one of such scholars influenced by Martin was He Bingsong.

He Bingsong is recognized as a leading figure of the Chinese "New Historiography School," which aimed to incorporate social scientific methods into historical studies.[64] Educated in the United States during

---

[61] Prasenjit Duara, *Rescuing History from the Nation: Questioning Narratives of Modern China* (Chicago: The University of Chicago Press, 1995).

[62] On this point, see Jenny Day, *Qing Travelers to the Far West: Diplomacy and the Information Order in Late Imperial China* (Cambridge: Cambridge University Press, 2018), 73, 80.

[63] Martin, "Traces of International Law in Ancient China," 77. It is hard to find the exact names of the "Chinese statesmen" that Martin referred to. But Zhang Sigui was certainly one of them who expressed similar opinions that international law existed in ancient China in his preface to Martin's translation of Wheaton. Svarverud, *International Law as World Order*, 99.

[64] Peng Minghui, *Taiwan shixue de Zhongguo chanjie* [The Chinese Complex in Taiwanese Historiography] (Taipei: Maitian Chubanshe, 2001), 36–40; 55–59.

the 1910s, he belongs to the early wave of Chinese returnees who significantly influenced the landscape of historical research.[65] As a student, he pursued studies at the University of California, the University of Wisconsin, and Princeton University. He collaborated with the eminent Chinese scholar Hu Shi, co-editing the *Chinese Students' Monthly*, an influential English-language journal among overseas Chinese students in the United States.[66] Upon returning to China, He held positions in various educational institutions, serving both as an educator and administrator, enjoying a highly successful career. His notable roles included being a professor at Peking University and the principal of Zhejiang No. One Middle School in the 1920s—two renowned institutions during China's New Cultural Movement. The former, located in the north, and the latter, a cultural hub in the south, emerged as centers of intellectual dynamism during this transformative period in Chinese history.[67] Subsequently, He held positions in publishing houses and higher education sectors, ultimately becoming the president of Jinan 暨南 University in the 1930s and 1940s, a well-known institution among Chinese diasporas in Southeast Asia.

During his time at Princeton, He Bingsong published an English-language article in the *Chinese Students' Monthly* in February 1916, reiterating Martin's thesis.[68] In the 1920s, he published its Chinese translation in at least two different venues.[69] Evaluated by today's professional standards, this article, both in its original English version and its subsequent Chinese translations, exhibits significant overlaps and is characterized by plagiarism. To underscore the similarities between He and

[65] As for the role of Chinese student returnees in transforming Chinese historiography, see Q Edward Wang, *Inventing China Through History: The May Fourth Approach to Historiography* (Albany: State University of New York Press, 2001).

[66] On Hu Shu's biography, see Jerome Grieder, *Hu Shih and the Chinese Renaissance: Liberalism in the Chinese Revolution* (Cambridge, MA: Harvard University Press, 1970).

[67] For instance, in his memoirs, the journalist Cao Juren 曹聚仁 (1900–1972) offers a vivid portrayal of vibrant cultural dynamics of the school during the time of the New Cultural Movement. See Cao Juren, *Wo yu wo de shijie* [My World and Me] (Beijing: Renmin chubanshe, 1983).

[68] P. S. Ho, "International Law and Customs of Ancient China in Time of Peace," *The Chinese Students' Monthly* 11, no. 4 (1916): 238–250.

[69] He Bingsong, "Zhongguo gudai guoji fa" [International Law in Ancient China], *Fazheng xuebao* [Journal of Law and Politics] (1920): 5–13; "Chuqiu shidai guoji fa", 3–7.

Martin and to avoid any potential confusion stemming from translation, let us focus on the original text, the English-language version in 1916. Examining the initial sentences on its first page, He wrote:

> The Period during which these ancient Chinese states rose and fell was the latter half of the Chou [i.e., Zhou] Dynasty [Martin, 65], which was an age of intense political activity. The states, twelve in number [Martin, 66], were created by the voluntary subdivision of the national domain by the founder of the Chou Dynasty [Martin, 65]. The throne of each state being hereditary, decentralization and a feeling of independence naturally sprang up [Martin, 65].[70] (Underlined segments appear in Martin's text)

We can recognize a substantial portion of this paragraph in Martin's work, particularly in the subsequent two sentences.

> The period during which [the Chinese States] rose and fell was the latter half of the dynasty of Cheo [i.e., Zhou] ... The several States were created by the voluntary subdivision of the national domain by the founder of the dynasty...[71]

In addition to these two sentences, various segments of He's text also manifest in different sections of Martin's work, spanning from page 65 to 66. The extent of sentence borrowing renders He's article nearly a revised iteration of Martin's essay.

In this article, He Bingsong not only replicated sentences from Martin but also "borrowed" essential evidence without direct citation. To substantiate the existence of treaties in ancient China, Martin presented two critical pieces of evidence in the midst of his article: the term "mengfu" (Palace of Treaties) and a sample treaty between "the Prince of Cheng and a coalition of princes who invaded his territories B.C. 544."[72] The former signifies the very presence of treaties, and the latter serves as direct evidence. He Bingsong quietly "borrowed" the term and included

---

[70] Ho, "International Law and Customs of Ancient China in Time of Peace," 238. He, "Chuqiu shidai guoji fa," 3.

[71] Martin, "Traces of International Law in Ancient China," 65.

[72] Martin, "Traces of International Law in Ancient China," 72.

it alongside a sample treaty that closely resembled Martin's example.[73] Toward the end of his article, He appeared to lose patience and simply quoted Martin's conclusion without altering a single word. While he did cite Martin as a source, the act of copying sentences, borrowing evidence, and echoing conclusions does not constitute original research.

At the same time, He Bingsong augmented Martin's article in several aspects. For instance, he expanded on Martin's discussion of the practice of envoy exchanges and introduced more direct evidence from Classical sources.

In his version, Martin briefly touched upon the matter of envoy exchanges, contending that the negotiation of a treaty was the "highest function of an envoy" and underscored the religious sacredness of the exchange.[74] On this subject, He Bingsong deviated from Martin. In his article, with less emphasis on treaty negotiations, he instead further categorized envoy exchanges into four types, including regular visits, coronations, attendance at funerals, and expressions of sympathy.[75] This divergence between the two texts highlights different interests in studying the topic. As a missionary, Martin was more concerned with the religiosity and sacred ceremonies of ancient Chinese diplomacy, while He Bingsong was focused on understanding the practical details of its implementation.

Moreover, He Bingsong displayed a greater awareness of historical periodization. He replaced the term "lieguo" in Martin's text with the Spring and Autumn period. As discussed earlier, Martin, not formally trained as a historian, employed vague and at times confusing periodization for the "ancient" period in Chinese history. The term "lieguo" and its designation for a specific period in early Chinese history, for instance, was rarely used. Wang Fengzao, Martin's Chinese translator, found no appropriate Chinese words to translate it. Similarly, He Bingsong struggled with the translation while writing in English, borrowing the term "coordinated states" from Martin but using "ancient China in time of Peace" in the title. However, in his Chinese article, he took a step further by connecting the dots between "lieguo" and "chunqiu," the latter being a well-defined period in early Chinese history. In doing so, he pinpointed

---

[73] Ho, "International Law and Customs of Ancient China in Time of Peace," 244, 246.

[74] Martin, "Traces of International Law in Ancient China," 72.

[75] Ho, "International Law and Customs of Ancient China in Time of Peace," 240–241.

Table 5.1 Publications on international law in ancient China

Year	Author	Title
1899	Hu Weiyuan 胡薇元	公法導源
1911	Lan Guangce 藍光策	春秋公法比義發微
Early 1910s	Liu Renxi 劉人熙	春秋公法內傳
1924	Zhang Xinzheng 張心徵	春秋國際公法
1926	Xu Chuanbao 徐傳保	國際法與古代中國,第一部分:思想
1931	Xu Chuanbao 徐傳保	古代中國國際法遺跡
1931	Chen Guyuan 陳顧遠	中國國際法溯源
1933	Ning Xiewan 寧協萬	現行國際法
1937	Hong Junpei 洪鈞培	春秋國際公法
1941	Lei Haizong 雷海宗	中國古代外交
1962	Liu Boji 劉伯驥	春秋會盟政治
1990	Wang Tieya 王鐵崖	中國與國際法——歷史與當代
1991	Li Hengmei 李衡眉	春秋戰國國際法略述
1994	Chen Shicai 陳世材	中國國際法之源流
1998	Wang Tieya 王鐵崖	國際法引論
1999	Sun Yurong 孫玉榮	古代中國國際法研究
2004	Zhao Yanchang 趙彥昌	春秋時期國際法研究

Source Cited from Zeng Tao[76]

the origins of international law in China to a more specific time frame between 770 and 476 BCE.

Martin and He Bingsong represent just two among numerous scholars in the twentieth century who subscribed to the belief in the existence of international law in ancient China. Scholars specializing in Chinese legal history have observed this recurrent pattern and conducted various surveys to analyze its implications. One source indicates that at least fifteen scholars have put forth similar assertions across seventeen distinct sources throughout the extended duration of China's twentieth century, as outlined in the following list (Table 5.1).

This list is not exhaustive; a recent update includes two additional entries (Tan Zhuohong and Qian Mu).[77] Judging from this, one could

[76] Zeng Tao, "Jindai Zhongguo de guojifa fuhui lun" [The Hermeneutical Theory of International Law in Modern China], *Fashi xuekan* [Journal of the History of Law] 11, no. 2 (2007): 217–239.

[77] Jin Yao, "Dongfang guojifa puxi de chongxin faxian" [The Eastern International Law Pedigree], *Shehui kexue qianyan* [Advances in Social Sciences] 7, no. 8 (2018): 1169.

argue for the deep-seated nature of this idea within Chinese scholarship on international law. It is within this spectrum of thought that contemporary scholars like Yan Xuetong 閻學通 are making renewed efforts to replace the current international legal system with one rooted in Chinese origins.

In 2011, Princeton University Press published Yan's collection titled *Ancient Chinese Thought, Modern Chinese Power*, which features several of his essays exploring various aspects of applying ancient Chinese philosophy to predict China's rise as a global power in the contemporary world.[78] The book situates Yan's thesis within the context of debates in international relations theories and includes English translations of critiques originally published in Chinese-language sources.

In contrast to Martin and He Bingsong, Yan treats interstate politics in pre-Qin China as a premise of analysis and spends little time justifying its existence. Instead, he focuses on revitalizing ancient Chinese political thought in contemporary international politics. He delves into the works of a wide range of Chinese thinkers, including Guanzi, Laozi, Confucius, Mencius, Mozi, Hanfeizi, and Xunzi, actively involved in discussions of "pre-Qin interstate" politics. Despite his well-known hawkish position, he argues for the recognition and promotion of moral justification in international politics, suggesting that leaders of a rising China should pursue a world vision based on humane authority within a global hierarchy rather than a power-hungry hegemony. His position wavers between realism and idealism. Daniel Bell, Yan's then colleague and the introducer of this volume, observes Yan's position akin to that of neoconservatives in the United States. He believes that Yan's worldview is profoundly shaped by his experiences with recent political events in China, stating, "if American neoconservatives are liberals mugged by reality, Chinese realists are idealists mugged by the surreal events of the Cultural Revolution."[79] Individual experience plays a significant role in shaping people's worldviews.

At the same time, this is more than just about individual experience. Yan does not mention any influence from previous thinkers like Martin or He Bingsong in his works. However, placing his work within context

[78] Xuetong Yan, *Ancient Chinese Thought, Modern Chinese Power* (Princeton: Princeton University Press, 2013) especially the chapter: "A Comparative Study of Pre-Qin Interstate Political Philosophy", 21–69.

[79] Daniel Bell, "Introduction," in *Ancient Chinese Thought, Modern Chinese Power*, 1.

reveals that it is just one of various attempts to find international law in ancient China over the course of the entire twentieth century. To some extent, his work is a recent manifestation of a genealogy of knowledge often overlooked by mainstream scholars. It lingers in the marginalized position of the knowledge system of international law and never becomes the mainstream view. However, when the moment is right, it will once again resurface from the forgotten place and challenge dominant views. The purpose of this chapter is to recognize this repeated pattern and reconstruct a genealogy of knowledge about the thesis "international law in ancient China." But what does this genealogy really tell us?

In this chapter, I delve into the significance of comparison and analogy as crucial approaches to global historical studies. While acknowledging the value and widespread use of the former, I contend that Chinese historians demonstrate a heightened awareness of the intricacies and challenges associated with comparison as a historical method. Consequently, comparison tends to be less favored among global historians in China. In the course of outlining the field's landscape, I present my own intervention as a scholar aiming to position global history within the context of the ascent of modern Chinese thought and contemporary world historiographies. I argue that, beyond the realm of professional historical studies, scholars of international law have strategically employed a world-historical analogy—the Chinese origins of international law—as a means to confront the deeply ingrained Eurocentrism in Western international relations theories.

Through an examination of three cases involving scholars, both Chinese and foreign, who adopted the thesis of "international law in ancient China," spanning from the late nineteenth century to the early twenty-first century—from American missionary W. A. P. Martin to Republican historian He Bingsong, and PRC foreign policy specialist Yan Xuetong—I illustrate how these scholars, at distinct moments in China's extensive twentieth century, shared a belief in the existence of international law in ancient China under three common premises:

First and foremost, proponents of the thesis argue that ancient China and the contemporary world share structural comparability. Similar to the geopolitical landscape of today, as well as that of the early twentieth or late nineteenth century, China before the unification of the Qin dynasty was characterized by political fragmentation. Various independent states, largely united by commonalities in culture, language, and ethnicity, engaged in constant competition and negotiation. Importantly, this competition was conducted in an orderly fashion. Much like the

"Western" states in the late nineteenth century, the intra-war period, and
the post-Cold War era, the regional states in ancient China adhered to
certain rules in diplomatic relations during times of peace. They also
placed value on specific principles during times of war, actively seeking
a balance of power and respecting wartime neutrality. According to these
scholars, these observed rules and principles bear a striking resemblance
to what we commonly understand as "international law," constituting the
second shared premise. Lastly, all these scholars believe that delving into
the study of ancient Chinese thought on international law has the potential to offer valuable guidance for understanding contemporary global
dynamics.

Due to the evident similarities in their ideas, one might be tempted to
explore potential influences from one scholar to another. This is particularly evident in the case of He Bingsong, where it is clear that Martin had a
substantial impact on his thinking. Similarly, there is a curiosity about the
extent to which their fellow "Chinese statesmen" influenced Martin, as he
acknowledged in his own writing. Identifying the exact sources of influence on Yan Xuetong's views may pose some challenges. However, Daniel
Bell emphasizes the impact of the Cultural Revolution on Yan's generation in the introduction to Yan's book, pointing out that national debates
on Confucianism and Legalism during the later stages of the radical movement have left an imprint on Yan. This influence is especially noticeable
in Yan's efforts to emphasize the significance of ancient philosophies in
modern politics.[80] But how original are their ideas? More importantly,
we need to ask: Must an idea have only one origin, and if not, how many
times can the same idea be conceived in different times and spaces?

For historians of thought, there is still insufficient evidence to establish
a clear intellectual lineage through which the same idea was transmitted
from one generation to another in an identifiable pattern of influence.
The three case studies presented in this chapter reveal not only conver-
gences but also divergences in their thinking. For example, He Bingsong,
in contrast to Martin, placed more emphasis on diplomacy in times of
peace than in times of war. Among the three scholars discussed, Yan
engaged in the most thorough examination of various schools of ancient
Chinese thought, highlighting their respective contemporary values. The

---

[80] Known as, "Criticize Lin (biao), Criticize Confucius Campaign"; as for scholarship
on this topic, see Qiu Jin, *The Culture of Power: The Lin Biao Incident in the Cultural
Revolution* (Stanford: Stanford University Press, 1999).

extensive list of scholars who have endorsed such a view, dispersed across various scholarly disciplines and historical periods, only contributes to the complexity of the issue. It may prove challenging to construct a coherent narrative detailing the transmission of this thesis throughout history.

Hence, we must seek a more effective approach to analyze these case studies, aiming not to place them within the lineage of thought but within the genealogy of knowledge. For genealogy, I refer to the Foucauldian tactics, which is to "look for the anonymous rules governing discursive practices along with the network of power relations of which these rules are a part."[81] In this study, I do not presume the existence of an "empty sameness" persisting throughout history, nor do I inquire about the origi- nator of this idea and the influence one scholar had on another.[82] Instead, I contemplate what the repetitive occurrences of this thesis in Chinese intellectual culture throughout the entire twentieth century can reveal about the power dynamics of global cultural encounters.

In conclusion, I posit that, on one hand, international law, rooted in the European knowledge system, symbolizes the expanding Western influence on the global stage. On the other hand, ancient historiography, grounded in Chinese culture, upholds the resilient identification of the locals. The notion of "international law in ancient China" is not merely a discourse of knowledge but also a "zone of contact," where individuals negotiate the relationship between the local and global in the formation of self-identification within the transnational system of law and order.[83]

The repeated occurrences do not necessarily imply the existence of an international order in ancient China. Instead, they suggest that the belief that international law is alien to Chinese culture is a highly contested idea. The most contested aspect of such an assertion is not about the

---

[81] Michel Foucault offers some preliminary remakes on genealogy as his "tactics" in his opposition and struggle against "the coercion of a theoretical, unitary, formal and scientific discourse." Michel Foucault, "Two Lectures," in *Power/Knowledge: Selected Interviews & Other Writings, 1972–1977* (New York: Pantheon Books, 1980), 85; To further under- stand Foucault's usage of genealogy, see Larry Shiner, "Reading Foucaul: Anti-Method and the Genealogy of Power-Knowledge," *History and Theory* 21, no. 3 (1982): 388.

[82] Foucault, "Truth and Power," in *Power/Knowledge*, 117.

[83] Here I cite Li Chen's concept on "contact zones," by which he refers to "not just the physical and social spaces in which Chinese and Western persons and things meet but also the cultural and discursive spaces in which Chinese and Westerns, languages, perceptions, and sentiments come to influence or constitute each other." Chen, *Chinese Law in Imperial Eyes*, 10.

definition of law or the periodization of ancient history. It revolves around the underlying assumption that Chinese civilization is fundamentally different from the Western one, whether in its roots in classical antiquity or its representation in contemporary European politics. In this context, attempting to replace Eurocentric international law with a China-centered perspective seems a futile effort to counter-cultural chauvinisms. It merely represents one perspective over another. However, returning to the common legacy of the human world becomes a necessary step toward constructing a more egalitarian form of global history. As I will demonstrate in Chapter 7 of this book, this new form of global history is inherently political, and its continual interpretations and reinterpretations offer diverse visions of a globalized future.

CHAPTER 6

The Global Moment

Abstract This chapter places the question of global moments in global history within the context of the ongoing discourse among historical theorists and world historians in China regarding the role of the national in shaping global history. Some scholars advocate for the composition of global history with distinctive Chinese characteristics, emphasizing the inherent national character essential to historical practice. This chapter diverges from this perspective to scrutinize a pivotal moment that significantly influenced modern Chinese identities—the War of Resistance. It argues that even during the initial stage of the conflict, before the outbreak of the Pacific War, when the Nationalist government in China purportedly confronted Japanese aggressions without substantial foreign aid, a global conceptual framework remains crucial for comprehending the motives behind the resistance. Despite the Nationalist leaders' profound concerns for the nation's survival, diverse political forces within China proposed various interpretations of China's struggle with Japan within a global context. These ranged from anti-colonial rhetoric and anti-imperial aspirations to anti-fascist alliances and anti-Western racial discourse. By uncovering the global dimensions within the national narrative, this chapter encourages a departure from the simplistic binary distinctions prevailing in current historiography in China.

Keywords WWII · Global moment · Sino-Japanese war of resistance · Anti-fascist movements · Anti-colonialism · Chiang Kai-shek

© The Author(s), under exclusive license to Springer Nature
Singapore Pte Ltd. 2024
X. Fan, *Global History in China*,
https://doi.org/10.1007/978-981-97-3381-1_6

In the spring of 2014, historian Klaus Mühlhahn delivered a talk in Shanghai addressing the re-conceptualization of the May Fourth Movement, traditionally viewed as a pivotal moment in modern Chinese intellectual history, within a global context. Drawing upon the insights of Jürgen Osterhammel, Mühlhahn argued that a series of radical social and political changes from the nineteenth century onward—spanning the American Revolution, the French Revolution, the Haitian Revolution, Ottoman Tanzimat Reforms, the Meiji Restoration, the Mexican Revolution, and the 1911 Revolution in China—were not solely driven by national and regional factors but were also influenced by global discourse and international events. Consequently, these events could be understood as part of a "global moment" (全球時刻), and a history of mutual influence within an integrated world system is yet to be fully explored and documented.

Mühlhahn advocated for "global history" (全球史) as a novel approach to studying histories that transcends national perspectives. He outlined four key features of this approach:

1. Investigating significant events within the broader global context: This involves placing historical events in a wider international framework to better understand their interconnectedness and global implications.
2. Rejecting philosophical speculations: Mühlhahn emphasized the importance of moving away from speculative philosophies embedded in earlier works by universal historians like Oswald Spengler and Arnold Toynbee. Instead, he underscored the need for evidence-based historical research.
3. Moving beyond the national framework: Departing from the national-centric approach introduced by Rankean historians, Mühlhahn advocated for a perspective that transcends national boundaries to capture the global dynamics at play.
4. Emphasizing cross-cultural comparisons and transcending Eurocentrism: Mühlhahn highlighted the significance of cross-cultural comparisons, aiming to overcome Eurocentric biases and integrate

relational knowledge and area studies into the study of global history.[1]

Mühlhahn then moved from abstract conceptualization to a concrete application, using the May Fourth Movement as a case study to demonstrate how global history can prompt Chinese historians to reconsider the relationship between the national and the global. He drew upon the work of global historian Erez Manela, highlighting a cluster of significant events worldwide in 1919. These events ranged from the Paris conference in Europe to the 1919 Revolution in Egypt, the Amritsar Massacre in India, the March First Movement in Korea, and the May Fourth Movement in China. Mühlhahn, aligning with Manela's perspective, argued that 1919 represented a turning point in global history, marking the beginning of a series of anti-imperial and anti-colonial movements that gained unstoppable momentum throughout the twentieth century.

Written ten years ago, Mühlhahn's talk made a significant contribution by anchoring the global circulation of ideas, particularly in the context of anti-colonialism and anti-imperialism, within the physical network of connections facilitated by communication revolutions. These revolutions were spearheaded by technologies like the telegram, cable, and steamboat shipment, complemented by the movement of people through foreign study journeys, labor migration, and cultural exchanges organized by non-governmental organizations.[2] He illustrated how Chinese intellectuals were acutely aware of global events in the early twentieth century, and these events directly influenced their decision to participate in the May Fourth Movement. During student protests, for example, Shanghai students took to the streets to share stories about anti-colonial struggles in Korea, Vietnam, and India. Mao, through his edited newspaper, consistently reported on events in India, Egypt, Turkey, Afghanistan, Poland, and Hungary. As such, he made a convincing case that, to a certain

[1] He Yan, "Yu Kaisi jiangyan: cong quanqiushi de jiaodu kan Wusi Yundong" [Talk by Klaus Mühlhan: Rethink the May Fourth Movement Through Global History], *Wenhui bao* (May 5, 2014). https://www.whb.cn/zhuzhan/guandian/20140505/6316.html.

[2] He, "Yu Kaisi jiangyan." On propaganda's role in promoting international communication during the movement, see Rudolf Wagner, "Reconstructing the May Fourth Movement: The Role of Communication, Propaganda, and International Actors," *Journal of Transcultural Studies* 12, no. 2 Supplement (October 2021): 6–44. (posthumous publication based on his keynote speech at Harvard University and Heidelberg University in 2019).

degree, China's May Fourth Movement was intricately connected to the global anti-colonial movement.[3]

A decade later, substantial progress has been made in global history within China. A growing number of scholars now acknowledge the profound impact of global history on the broader historical landscape. Not only do they engage in their own research endeavors but they have also been instrumental in the establishment of new journals and book series dedicated to global history. As a result centers specifically focused on global historical studies are being founded. It is not an overstatement to assert that contemporary Chinese historiography is undergoing a significant global historical turn. However, within the community of those intrigued by global history and closely monitoring its evolution in China, a debate has emerged regarding the extent to which global history in China should exhibit a distinctly Chinese character.

While acknowledging the continued validity and utility of the national framework for studying Chinese history, this chapter seeks to assert the indispensability of global perspectives in comprehending the modern transformation of China. Global historians have successfully redefined the May Fourth movement as a global historical event, prompting a reconsideration of numerous pivotal moments in "Chinese history" within a broader context of comparison and interconnection. In this chapter, I adopt the Sino-Japanese War of Resistance as another case study, and argue that even during the initial phase of the war, prior to the outbreak of the Pacific War, when the Nationalist government in China purportedly confronted Japanese aggressions without substantial foreign aid, a global framework of conceptual references remains highly relevant for scholars to grasp the motivations behind the resistance.

This discussion unfolds in four parts. The first part elucidates the relevance of the national framework in studying the war in China. Subsequently, the next three sections invite the reader to contemplate on the global dimensions of the war. These sections explore how Chinese leaders perceived it as integral to the global anti-imperialist movement, how media and political elites conceptualized it through global comparisons

---

[3] He, "Yu Kaisi jiangyan." Recent scholarship has further confirmed the international dimension of the movement. See, for example, Shakhar Rahav, "Beyond Beijing: May Fourth as a National and International Movement," *Journal of Modern Chinese History* 13, no. 2 (January 2019): 325–331.

and references, and how the war is remembered and studied as a global historical event.

Let us start with the first.

The war with Japan in the 1930s and 1940s is commonly referred to as the "War of Resistance against Japan" (*Kang-Ri zhanzheng*, 抗日戰爭) in China. While wars inherently involve opposing parties, this particular conflict stands out as a pivotal episode encapsulating both the suffering and rejuvenation of the Chinese people in the twentieth century. Scholars widely concur that this war influenced the shaping of modern Chinese identities. Its national significance becomes allegedly even more pronounced when contrasted with the limited acknowledgment it receives in contemporary public discourse in Japan.[4] To a considerable extent, this war has been perceived as a distinctly "Chinese" event.

First of all, from a historical perspective, one could argue that the War of Resistance marked a significant and transformative shift. That is, since the Opium Wars, the Chinese state consistently found itself on the losing end of major conflicts with foreign powers. Historians note a recurring pattern during this period—each time conflict arose, Chinese armies suffered swift defeats, and governments readily surrendered. Even in the midst of the Nationalist revolution's momentum during the Northern Expedition, the intervention of Japanese armies in Jinan forced Chinese troops into a reluctant withdrawal. This incident became a source of deep shame in Chiang Kai-shek's personal recollections. In May 1927, he commenced his diary entry on that day with a fervent call to cleanse the stain of shame, a ritual he continued daily for the next two decades.[5] However, in the intricate tapestry of Chinese history, the year 1937 marked a departure from this disheartening trend. Despite the conflicting narratives of the war, the Nationalist government, led by Chiang Kai-shek, did not retreat but instead chose to confront the Japanese aggression. This decision, while resulting in significant sacrifices and the loss of its

---

[4] It is contested on the scholarly level about how relevant the war memories in today's Japan are. But in terms of popular memories, many refer it "ignorance," "amnesia," and "denial" of ordinary Japanese people's view on the war. Philip Seaton, *Japan's Contested War Memories: The "Memory Rifts" in Historical Consciousness of World War II* (Routledge, 2007), 2.

[5] Grace Huang, *Chiang Kai-shek's Politics of Shame: Leadership, Legacy, and National Identity in China* (Cambridge, MA: Harvard University Press, 2021), 29, 50.

finest troops, set the stage for a remarkable resilience that saw the country resisting for a formidable eight years.

This achievement becomes even more impressive when considering the consensus among scholars that, during the initial years of the war, China stood in isolation, confronting Japan without significant external support. Not only did the Chinese government receive limited foreign aid, but scholars also highlight the fact that, during this period, certain Western governments, including the United Kingdom, regarded China as a potentially hostile state. This led to the implementation of discriminatory policies against Chinese subjects in territories under their control, both within the homeland and in colonies such as India, as documented in a recent study by Yin Cao.[6] While working with China as an ally, the U.S. servicemen in China also exhibited hostile racial feelings against their Chinese partners.[7] Against all odds, the Chinese resistance, however, persisted. This starkly contrasts with all the Chinese surrenders and defeats prior to this war.

Secondly, contemporary records to some extent support this assertion. For example, in a notable speech delivered to the nation after the Marco Polo Bridge Incident on July 7, 1937—often considered the war's starting point—the Chinese national leader, Chiang Kai-shek, extolled the "national" significance of the conflict with Japan. In his address, he emphasized that the war with Japan was an act of resistance (抗戰). Chiang articulated that the peace-loving Chinese people were acutely aware of their country's status as a "weak nation" (弱國) and had no intention of provoking conflicts with Japan.[8] However, the relentless Japanese aggressions left the Chinese nation with no option for further retreats and compromises. Chiang asserted that, as war became inevitable, China's only choice was sacrifice—to fight back. He characterized it as a war of resistance because the Chinese people were not actively provoking the conflict but were compelled to cope with one forced upon them. It represented the last resort. Chiang went on to proclaim that engaging in this war was a moral responsibility to the Chinese nation, stating, "Even though we are a weak country, we have no choice but to preserve

[6] Cao, *Chinese Sojourners in Wartime Raj.*

[7] Zach Fredman, *The Tormented Alliance: American Servicemen and the Occupation of China, 1941–1949* (Chapel Hill: University of North Carolina Press, 2022).

[8] This concept echoes the Nationalist perception of China's position in the world as one of the "ruoxiao minzu." See Smith, *Chinese Asianism*, 209–211.

our nation's bloodline and cannot disregard the responsibility that our ancestors entrusted to us."[9]

Similarly, Chinese historians of the time celebrated the "national" significance of China's war with Japan, viewing it not merely as a destructive force but as a catalyst for the formation, transformation, and rejuvenation of the Chinese nation. Lei Haizong, for example, characterized the War of Resistance as a nation-building endeavor. In a 1938 political opinion piece during the height of the resistance, he advocated for enduring the current suffering and cautioned against seeking a swift and decisive victory. Lei argued that China, akin to a sick patient, had deep-rooted "sickness," and only "through the baptism of swords, fire, and warfare" could the nation thoroughly "cleanse all the past dirt and impurity" to forge a new life.[10] Likewise, Qian Mu, a prominent figure in the modern Chinese cultural conservative movement, labeled the war as "a struggle for survival," not only for the Chinese nation but also for Chinese culture (文化爭存 and 民族爭存).[11] In this context, one could posit that the war marked a pivotal moment in the rise of cultural conservatism in modern Chinese intellectual history.[12]

Thirdly, this national framework remains compelling for contemporary scholars studying the war. One of its convincing aspects is the stark reality that, during the initial years from 1937 to 1941, China received minimal foreign aid and support from other countries—it was effectively fighting Japan alone. The eight years of conflict were not only characterized by attrition but also profound suffering. The toll was devastating, with at least 14 million people in China losing their lives due to the war, and over

[9] Chiang Kai-shek, "Guanyu Lugouqiao shijian zhi yanzheng biaoshi" [A Solemn Statement on the Marco Polo Incident] (known as "Lushan Speech"), in *Zongtong Jiang gong sixiang yanlun zongji* [The Complete Collection of President Mr. Jiang's Thought and Speeches] (Taipei: Zhongguo guomindang zhongyang weiyuanhui dangshi weiyuanhui, 1984), vol. 14: 582–585.

[10] Lei Haizong, "Jianguo—zai wang de disanzhou wenhua" [Nation-building: The Third-Cycle Culture in Sight], in *Zhongguo wenhua yu Zhongguo de bing* [Chinese Cultural and Chinese Military] (Beijing: Shangwu yinshuguan, 2014), 162.

[11] Qian Mu, "Lishi jiaoyu jidian liuxing de wujie" [Several Popular Misunderstandings in History Education], in *Zhongguo lishi yanjiu fa* [Methods to Study Chinese History] (Beijing: Jiuzhou chubanshe, 2019), 159–165.

[12] Fan, *World History and National Identity*, Chapter 2.

80 million being displaced, becoming refugees. This agonizing experience has left an indelible imprint on China's national memory.[13]

At the same time, a contemporary trend in studying China's past involves placing the War of Resistance and its symbolic significance within the broader context of the country's twentieth-century nation-building process. Scholars such as Hans van de Ven, for example, present a compelling argument that the Chinese were not only fighting against Japan but also among themselves. As such, the War of Resistance was not the conclusion of conflicts with imperial powers but a continuation of the struggles between the Nationalists and the Communists. This perspective integrates the Civil War and even the Korean War into the study of the extended conflict in China from 1937 to 1952.[14] Indeed, the Chinese state has recently expanded the duration of the war from eight years to fourteen, beginning with the resistance against the Japanese invasion of Manchuria in 1931. Chinese President Xi Jinping has expressed support for this extended periodization of the war on various occasions, although he also emphasizes the initiation of the full-scale war in 1937.

However, the national framework alone falls short in fully explaining the conviction of Chinese leaders regarding the eventual survival of the nation during the war. Chiang Kai-shek consistently emphasized the importance of Chinese culture and the necessity to foster nationalism and patriotism in wartime China. Yet, he also recognized the significant impact of international politics on the war's outcome.

In a lucid analysis presented to army leaders in 1934, before the full-scale military conflict, Chiang underscored the global aspect of the impending war with Japan and foresaw China's ultimate success despite Japan's overwhelming advantage. He candidly admitted that, in contrast to Japan's preparations, China was entirely unprepared for future conflicts. From a purely military standpoint, he argued, China might not even survive, given its lack of modernization and the inferiority of its army compared to Japan's. However, by transcending the national framework and adopting an East Asian or Pacific perspective, Chiang asserted that there was hope. He thus provided an analysis grounded in the Nationalists' anti-imperialist agendas.

[13] Rana Mitter, *Forgotten Ally: China's World War II, 1937–1945* (Boston: Houghton Mifflin Harcourt, 2013), 5.

[14] Hans van de Ven, *China at War: Triumph and Tragedy in the Emergence of the New China, 1937–1952* (Profile Books, 2017), 4.

Citing Sun Yat-sen's perspective, Chiang argued that China was a semi-colonial country (次殖民地).[15] The term "semi-colonial" referred to China not being a colony of a single country but rather under the joint control of various world powers. China's position was even worse than a normal colony. But exactly because of this dreadful situation, it was hard for Japan to change the status quo. For if Japan wanted to do so, it had to fight world powers in the first place. In other words, before becoming the hegemon of East Asia annexing China, Japan had to defeat the "world." Chiang did not believe that Japan could achieve such a goal, and, thus, through a manipulation of its position as a semi-colony for world powers China remained hopeful.[16] Therefore, Chiang's confidence in China's eventual victory against Japan was, in part, grounded in his observations and judgment of global politics.

One might contend that Chiang's view on global geopolitics could be perceived as mere rhetoric. This perspective is reflected in the current official stance of the CCP, which links Chiang's discourse to his non-resistance policy during wartime and heavily criticizes it.[17] However, it is noteworthy that the Japanese government consistently viewed Chiang's attempt to internationalize Sino-Japanese conflicts as a significant threat. For example, during negotiations in October 1935, Japanese Foreign Minister Kōki Hirota 廣田弘毅 (1878–1948) urged the Chinese government to abandon its "using barbarians to control barbarians" (以夷制

---

[15] For contemporary scholarly discussion on the concept "Semi-colonialism," see Rebecca Karl, *The Magic of Concepts: History and the Economic in Twentieth-Century China* (Durham: Duke University Press, 2017), especially Chapter 4. "The Economic as Lived Experience: Semicolonialism and China." Also, Anne Reinhardt, *Navigating Semi-Colonialism: Shipping, Sovereignty, and Nation Building in China, 1860–1937* (Cambridge, MA: Harvard Asia Center, 2018).

[16] Chiang Kai-shek, "Jiang weiyuanzhang jiang: Diyu wairu yu fuxing minzu" [Secretary Chiang Speaks: Resisting Foreign Aggressions and Reviving the Nation], *Zhonghua minguo zhongyao shiliao chubian–Dui Ri kangzhan shiqi* [The Preliminary Collection of Important Historical Materials from the Republic of China: The War of Resistance Era. First Edition; shortened as "ZMZSC"], vol. III (Zhongguo guomindang zhongyang weiyuanhui dangshi weiyuanhui: 1981), 107–108.

[17] For example, Zhou Lisheng and Zhou Yanpei, "Zhongguo gongchandang guanyu minzu fuxing de huayu biaoda" [The Chinese Community Party's Discourse on the Rejuvenation of the Chinese Nation], *Renmin wang* [People's Net] (March 16, 2022), http://theory.people.com.cn/n1/2022/0316/c40531-32376508.html.

夷) policy. He explicitly discouraged China from seeking support from European and American powers to constrain Japan.[18]

In contrast to the GMD's emphasis on nationalism and global strategic considerations, the Communists' perspective on the war was deeply rooted in the global politics of anti-fascism and anti-imperialism. The Chinese Communist Party(CCP) articulated its stance during the Seventh Plenum of the Communist International in Moscow, where party spokesman Wang Ming 王明 (1904–1974), assisted by Hu Qiuyuan 胡秋原 (1910–2004), delivered the CCP's announcement against Japanese aggression in August 1935. In this declaration, they echoed the strong nationalist rhetoric seen in Chiang's speeches, characterizing the impending conflict with Japan as a "live-or-die moment" for the Chinese nation. However, the statement also provided a world-historical reference, citing the example of Ethiopia—a small country in Africa with eight million people—that successfully resisted Italian fascist aggression, emphasizing that China, with its 400 million population, could certainly defend itself. Toward the conclusion of the statement, the CCP called for a broad coalition, urging all peoples engaged in anti-imperial struggles, including working masses within Japan, as well as those in Korea and Taiwan, to collaborate with those sympathetic to the Chinese national liberation movement.[19] As a protege of Stalin, Wang Ming continued to promote the anti-fascist coalition after his return to China in 1937.[20]

Despite Wang Ming's sidelining by Mao during the power struggles in Yan'an, the CCP did not abandon the connection between China's war against Japan and the global anti-fascist movement. In 1939, Pan Zi'nian 潘梓年 (1893–1972), the director of the CCP's news agency Xinhua in Chongqing, published an essay that further emphasized the link between the national and the global aspects of the conflict. Pan began

---

[18] "Zhu Ri dashi Jiang Zuobin zhi Dongjing baogao yu Guangtian waixiang tanhua dian" [Telegram on Chinese Ambassador in Tokyo Jiang Zuobin's Report on His Conversation with Japanese Foreign Minister Kōki], in *ZMZSC*, vol. III, 641.

[19] "Wei kangri jiuguo gao quanti tongbao shu" [Letter to All the Compatriots to Resist Japan and Save the Nation].

[20] Hans van de Ven, *War and Nationalism in China, 1925–1945* (London: Routledge, 2002), 173.

with a resounding statement about the global nature of China's war of resistance.[21]

Three themes underpinned Pan's assertion—democracy, national liberation, and international anti-fascist movements. According to Pan, the concept of democracy served as a bridge between the national and the global. He argued that democracy was crucial not only for the national agenda, mobilizing various social elements for national liberation, but also for the global agenda of anti-fascist movements. He believed that "our war of resistance, in essence, was to pursue peace among nations through democratic movements, which cannot be separated from international anti-fascist struggles, and, in fact, it also burst out riding the high tides of international anti-fascist struggles."[22]

Pan predicted that, due to its democratic nature, China's national liberation movement would receive global support. At the same time, he argued that the world also needed China. The "United Front" established in China, he believed, would become a model for all struggling "weak and small nations." To these nations, aiding China was akin to helping themselves. Pan even suggested that within oppressor nations like Japan, there were peace-loving masses. He argued that Japanese fascist "robbers" not only exploited the Chinese but also their own people.[23] While the logic of such an analysis may not fully convince a modern reader today, it is clear that both the Nationalists and the Communists understood that placing China's war against Japan within a global context was essential for anticipating final victory.

Similarly, for the Nationalist government, the war with Japan transcended military tactics and extended into the realm of propaganda and ideas. The government utilized various tools to instill confidence in China's eventual victory through state propaganda apparatuses. Shuge Wei's study highlights the Nationalist state's efforts to promote China's war with the Allies through English-language newspapers.[24] Notably, influential China experts like Theodore White were involved in the Chinese state's propaganda machinery. Chiang Kai-shek, leveraging his

---

[21] Zinian [Pan Zinian], "Zhongguo kangzhan yu guoji fan-Faxisi douzheng" [China's War of Resistance and International Anti-fascist Struggles], in *ZXZSZLHB* 3, no. 3: 47.

[22] Zinian, "Zhongguo kangzhan yu guoji fan-Faxisi douzheng," 49–50.

[23] Zinian, "Zhongguo kangzhan yu guoji fan-Faxisi douzheng," 50–51.

[24] Shuge Wei, *News under Fire: China's Propaganda Against Japan in the English-Language Press, 1928–1941* (Hong Kong: Hong Kong University Press, 2017).

American-educated wife Madame Chiang, fostered positive relations with foreign leaders and the Western public. They frequently invited China experts such as Pearl Buck (1892–1973), Sven Hedin (1865–1962), and Lin Yutang 林語堂 (1895–1976) to meet with them. The Communists, even though isolated in remote areas during the war, actively cultivated relationships with foreign journalists like Edgar Snow (1905–1972). They worked to present a positive image of the CCP's efforts in the war and insisted on rhetoric emphasizing the formation of a broader anti-fascist coalition in China's resistance against Japanese aggression. The propaganda efforts of both the Nationalists and the Communists played a crucial role in shaping international perceptions of China's role in the war.

Indeed, at the early stages of the war, a notable example of global attention was the reference to Madrid during the Battle of Wuhan. In *Competing Visions of World Order*, Sebastian Conrad and Dominic Sachsenmaier argue that a global moment may not only have political and economic significance but must also carry symbolic meaning. With the mobilization of global movements, the rise of information technology, and enhanced communication infrastructures, various communities focused their attention on specific moments in global history.[25] While WWII was undoubtedly such a global moment, the Battle of Wuhan stood out, attracting attention from around the world even as China was fighting Japan alone. The symbolic significance of events like the Battle of Wuhan extended beyond their immediate geopolitical context, resonating as key markers in the broader narrative of global history during WWII (Fig. 6.1).

Stephen MacKinnon's survey highlights that during the Battle of Wuhan, a substantial number of foreign observers visited the city, showcasing the international attention garnered during this critical period. Among the notable visitors were Evans Carlson (U.S. Marines), Joseph Stilwell, and his assistant David Barrett (U.S. Army), Frank Dorn (also U.S. Army), Claire Chennault (U.S. Air Force), Jacques Guillermaz (French attaché), Henri de Fremery (Dutch; close to He Yingqin), and A. I. Cherepanov (Soviet foreign mission). Reports about the war emanated from the Chinese city, disseminated to foreign governments and

---

[25] Sebastian Conrad and Dominic Sachsenmaier, "Introduction," in *Competing Visions of World Order: Global Moments and Movements, 1880s–1930s*, eds. Sebastian Conrad and Dominic Sachsenmaier (Palgrave, 2007), 13–15.

Fig. 6.1 Chinese Solider in Wuhan by Robert Capa, sourced from public domain, https://en.wikipedia. org/wiki/Robert_ Capa#/media/File:Chi nese_Soldier.jpg

news agencies. Renowned war photographer Robert Capa (1913–1954), known for his left-leaning views and having recently left Madrid, also visited Hankou. For many leftists, China's struggle against Japan was seen as a continuation of the global left movement against fascist aggression, extending from Madrid to Wuhan. Capa's photographs of Wuhan were featured in *Life* magazine, serving to highlight the bravery of the Chinese resistance. Wuhan, following in the footsteps of Madrid, gained special symbolic meaning within the global anti-fascist movement.[26] The city became a focal point, connecting various narratives of resistance against fascist aggression across different geopolitical contexts.

Understanding the historiography is crucial for gaining insight into the global dimensions of China's war with Japan. Historically, Western studies of World War II were heavily dominated by a Eurocentric framework, largely overlooking China's significant role in the conflict. As noted by Rana Mitter, many failed to recognize China's contribution to the Second World War, with a profound bias leading them to believe that

[26] Stephen MacKinnon, *Wuhan, 1938: War, Refugees, and the Making of Modern China* (Berkeley: University of California Press, 2008), 100–101.

"China's role in the war is a historical byway, not worthy of the full examination that is the due of the major powers involved."[27] Furthermore, this Eurocentric perspective extended to historians in the Soviet Union who also downplayed China's role. They asserted that "the conflicts and struggles allowed Japan to place relatively insignificant amount of its military manpower in China to conduct the flight," relegating China to a minor role in preventing Japan from invading Russia's Far East.[28]

In recent years, there has been a significant shift in the historiography of China's war with Japan, largely attributed to the growing influence of global perspectives within the study of World War II. Increasingly, the global significance of this conflict is being recognized and underscored. The examination of the Sino-Japanese War of Resistance appears to be experiencing a "global turn" as well, which signifies a broader and more inclusive approach to the analysis and understanding of historical events.

In English-speaking academia, scholars like Hans van de Ven and Rana Mitter have spearheaded the introduction of new global perspectives to comprehend the intricacies of China's war with Japan. They assert that at various historical junctures, this conflict held global significance. Rana Mitter, for example, contends that the war not only stands as a pivotal moment in shaping modern Chinese identities but also serves as a catalyst for restoring China as a major global power.[29] In a parallel vein, Hans van de Ven argues for conceiving China's war with Japan as part of a broader anti-colonial and anti-imperial movement, which profoundly impacted Western powers' colonial control in regions such as China, India, and Southeast Asia. To delve into more specific instances, both Rana Mitter and Barak Kushner advocate for viewing the conclusion of the East Asian conflict as a global narrative encompassing post-war reconstruction, anti-colonial decolonization, and the international reconfiguration of legal orders in East Asia, Asia, and beyond.[30]

---

[27] Mitter, *Forgotten Ally*, 9.

[28] Cited from Han Yongli, "Zhongguo xuezhe guanyu Zhongguo kangzhan zai dierci shijie dazhan zhong diwei yanjiu shuping" [A Review of Chinese Scholars' Study the Role of China's War of Resistance in the Second World War], *Wuhan daxue xuebao* [Wuhan University Journal (Humanity Sciences)] 59, no. 4 (July 2006): 481–482.

[29] Mitter, *Forgotten Ally*, 13–14.

[30] Barak Kushner, *Men to Devils, Devils to Men: Japanese War Crimes and Chinese Justice* (Cambridge, MA: Harvard University Press, 2015); Rana Mitter, "State-building

Chinese historians, by contrast, have already actively advocated for acknowledging the global significance of China's War of Resistance against Japan. In this context, the global framework shaping studies of this conflict does not simply involve the transfer of historical knowledge but rather represents a global convergence in reevaluating the national narrative through a broader historical analysis. An early instance of this perspective emerged in 1980 when the Chinese delegation, attending the XV International Congress of Historical Sciences in Bucharest after the Cultural Revolution, emphasized China's contribution to the global war effort. Historian Liu Simu 劉思慕 (1904–1985), speaking on behalf of the team, asserted, "The Chinese people's War of Resistance is not just one to defend the survival of the nation and to pursue national liberation, but also an indispensable part of the anti-fascist war of the peoples of the entire world."[31] They highlighted two significant aspects, the first of which, reiterated in subsequent works, was acknowledged in the statement issued by the Third Communist International. This aspect emphasized that China's resistance forced Japan into a protracted war of attrition, hindering the latter from pursuing its global agendas, including invasion plans against the Soviet Union and collaboration with the Axis powers.[32]

The Chinese delegation raised a second point, which remains relevant today; scholars in the West have often failed to comprehend the nature of China's War of Resistance—employing the strategy of fighting the strong with weakness (以弱戰強). They elaborated that since these Western scholars could not identify decisive battles akin to those in Stalingrad, El Alamein, Midway, and Normandy, they struggled to acknowledge China's significant contribution. Contemporary Western historians, such as Hans van de Ven and Stephen MacKinnon, endorse Chinese historians' view, challenging the Eurocentric nature of the traditional analytical framework rooted in Clausewitz's perspective on conventional warfare.[33]

After Disaster: Jiang Tingfu and the Reconstruction of Post-World War II China, 1943–1949," *Comparative Studies in Society and History* 61, no. 1 (2019): 176–206.

[31] Liu Simu, Wang Zhende, Hou Chengde, and Ma Xinmin, "Zhongguo kangri zhanzheng jiqi zai di'erci shijie dazhan zhong de diwei he zuoyong" [China's War of Resistance and Its Role and Contribution in the Second World War], *Shijie lishi* [World history], no. 4 (1980): 7.

[32] Liu et al., "Zhongguo kangri zhanzheng," 9–12.

[33] Van de Ven, *China at War*, 6.

Hans van de Ven goes a step further, contending that the Communists in China developed a novel strategy for conducting a "national liberation war" by combining mobilization in the countryside with the creation of a tightly disciplined party to provide cohesion. This approach included the assertion of a powerful ideology to unite and motivate followers, avoiding confrontation on the battlefield until victory was nearly assured, and politicizing all aspects of life, including education, villages, courtrooms, media, and even the family.[34] This model, he argues, had a lasting impact, serving as inspiration for anti-colonial movements in Asia, Africa, and Latin America during the era of decolonization and continues to influence such movements today.[35]

Five years later, Chinese historians once again attended the International Congress. This time, historian Qi Shirong reaffirmed China's significant contribution to the global stage through more robust research, drawing from various primary sources in Chinese, Japanese, and English. He began by presenting "facts" that from July 7, 1937, to September 3, 1939, China was the sole country fighting fascism. He highlighted how China inflicted substantial causalities on Japan, pulling it into a protracted war of attrition. He understood China's participation alongside the allies in the Pacific theatre, actively engaging in the conflict in Burma. He then argued that China's war effort not only thwarted Japan's plans to invade the Soviet Union but also played a role in delaying the onset of the Pacific War, facilitating American involvement. Furthermore, he emphasized China's noteworthy contributions to Burma.[36] As we have seen in the discussions in the first chapter regarding Qi's role in advancing global history in China, Qi's paper is another example of his contribution to the rise of global history in China. It serves as a valuable resource for future scholars seeking to more comprehensively integrate China's war into the global history of World War II.

Thanks to these earlier efforts, the global nature of China's War of Resistance has increasingly become a consensus among historians today. At the same time, a new generation of scholars is broadening the scope of studies on this war beyond China's interactions with Western allies

[34] Van de Ven, *China at War*, 7.

[35] Van de Ven, *China at War*, 7.

[36] Qi, "Zhongguo kangri zhanzheng zai di'erci shijie dazhan zhong de diwei he zuoyong," 118–133.

and the Soviet Union to include Southeast Asia, South Asia, and Inner Eurasia.[37] Recent Chinese scholarship aligns with the global interest in exploring anti-colonial and anti-imperial movements during the war and their continued impact in post-war Asia and beyond.

From the global perspectives to Chinese historiography, one could also notice that the study of China's War against Japan has undergone paradigmatic shifts in recent decades. Thanks to the tireless efforts of some PRC historians, grounded in solid archival work, an increasing number of scholars now acknowledge the major contribution of the GMD to the War of Resistance. The once-tainted image of Chiang Kai-shek has become more balanced.[38]

In addition to this changing perspective within the national framework, another significant transformation has occurred by placing China's war with Japan within a global context. In this chapter, three aspects briefly discussed highlight the utility of such a global framework for studying the war: First, leaders from both the Nationalists and the Communists in China predicted victory based on their views regarding the global nature of China's struggle against Japan; second, as the war unfolded, both the Chinese public and elites, along with foreign observers, consistently referred to a global framework of world-historical context to comprehend China's survival and destiny; third, in contemporary Chinese historiography, there is an increasing acknowledgment of the global significance of China's anti-fascist struggle when reflecting on how the war is remembered. In light of these considerations, it is safe to argue that China's War of Resistance is not merely a significant event in Chinese history but also holds global significance.

The War of Resistance, undoubtedly, represents only one episode in modern Chinese history. However, scholars, both within China and internationally, have been endeavoring to establish connections between these

[37] Just to list two examples, Cao, *Chinese Sojourners in Wartime Raj*; Kankan Xie, "Ambivalent Fatherland: The Chinese National Salvation Movement in Malaya and Java, 1937–41," *Journal of Southeast Asian Studies* 52, no. 4 (2021): 677–700. Both Cao Yin and Xie Kankan are teaching in China.

[38] For example, PRC historians such as Yang Tianshi 楊天石 have called for a more balanced view in evaluating Chiang Kai-shek's role in modern history. This has been echoed by their counterparts in the West such as the work by Alexander Pantsov, *Victorious in Defeat: The Life and Times of Chiang Kai-shek, 1887–1975* (New Heaven: Yale University Press, 2023).

moments in "Chinese history" and broader global changes. In English-language scholarship, an illustrative example is Erez Manela, who situates China's May Fourth movement within the context of international anti-colonial nationalist movements that emerged after the Paris Conference following the Great War. This occurred concurrently with the initiation of Gandhi's nonviolent resistance movement in India, the 1919 Revolution in Egypt, and the March First Movement in Korea.[39] Similarly, in her influential work on Chinese nationalism, Rebecca Karl argues for the "simultaneous growth of nationalism and a global historical logic in China" during the late Qing period, marking a global moment when "China entered the world."[40] While international scholars seek "global moments" in modern Chinese history, this chapter contends that scholars in China have historically recognized the global and international dimensions of events, such as those related to China's War of Resistance. The ongoing efforts to reassess the relationship between the national and the global represent a crucial step for the future development of global history in China.

[39] Erez Manela, *The Wilsonian Moment: Self-Determination and the International Origins of Anticolonial Nationalism* (Oxford: Oxford University Press, 2007), 9.

[40] Karl, *Staging the World*, 8.

Part III

Conclusion

CHAPTER 7

The Rise of Area Studies and Global History

Abstract This concluding chapter of the book scrutinizes the emergence of area studies and their potential repercussions on global history. It revisits the political fervor characterizing the rise of international studies and foreign studies during the 1960s and 1970s, marked by a pronounced anti-imperialist stance. Early world historians and international studies scholars leveraged history to propel the ideological aspirations of the global revolution, leaving a legacy that contemporary scholars in area studies in China are now embracing. In recent years, the burgeoning funding opportunities accompanying the ascent of area studies have greatly facilitated fresh research endeavors for historians in China dedicated to global history. Nonetheless, global historians are currently navigating a complex landscape, encountering both opportunities and challenges as they endeavor to navigate the intricate nexus between history and politics in the early years of the twenty-first century.

Keywords Area Studies · Global History · Anti-imperialism · Marxist Ideology · Cultural Revolution · Theory on Disorder · Politics and History

If American neoconservatives are liberals mugged by reality, Chinese realists are idealists mugged by the surreal events of the Cultural Revolution.

© The Author(s), under exclusive license to Springer Nature   135
Singapore Pte Ltd. 2024
X. Fan, *Global History in China*,
https://doi.org/10.1007/978-981-97-3381-1_7

—Daniel Bell (2011)[1]

In 1972, amid the fervor of the Cultural Revolution, *Red Flag* (Hongqi, 紅旗), a prominent propaganda journal representing Maoist radical political perspectives, unveiled a series of four essays advocating for the study of world history. The following year, these essays were compiled into a pamphlet titled "On Studying Some World History."[2] Infused with passionate anti-imperialist rhetoric, these essays explore the pivotal role of world history in advancing the revolutionary cause.

Penned under the pseudonym "Shi Jun" 史軍, the anonymous authors open the first essay with a resolute assertion, defining "change" as the Zeitgeist of the contemporary era.[3] Its salient nature is "tianxia daluan" (天下大亂), or "global upheaval" as rendered in the English translation.[4] The authors posit that "luan" (亂) is a positive force, contextualizing upheaval within class theories. They celebrate these changes by which "the imperialist-ruled old world is headed for collapse and a socialist new world is advancing to victory."[5] The authors contend that this juncture signifies a moment when "a weak nation can defeat a strong, a small nation can defeat a big."[6]

The importance of studying world history during this period is under-scored. Internationally, it fosters solidarity between the Chinese people and those of Asia, Africa, and Latin America in their shared struggles against imperialism and colonialism.[7] On the domestic front, a grasp of world history aids in comprehending Marxism and Mao Zedong's contributions to the Chinese revolution. The authors emphasize the interconnectedness of the international and national realms, stating that "Chairman Mao always proceeds from the overall situation in class struggle both at home and abroad, and examines these questions in the

---

[1] Daniel Bell, "Introduction," in *Ancient Chinese Thought, Modern Chinese Power* (Princeton: Princeton University Press, 2011), 1.

[2] Shi Jun, *Du yidian shijieshi* (Beijing: Renmin chubanshe, 1973); Shih Chun, *On Studying Some World History* (Peking: Foreign Languages Press, 1973).

[3] Shi Jun, *Du yidian shijieshi*, 1; Shih Chun, *On Studying Some World History*, 2.

[4] Shi Jun, *Du yidian shijieshi*, 2; Shih Chun, *On Studying Some World History*, 3.

[5] Shih Chun, *On Studying Some World History*, 4.

[6] Shih Chun, *On Studying Some World History*, 5.

[7] Shih Chun, *On Studying Some World History*, 8.

context of the entire international situation." To illustrate, they point to the failure of some party members to recognize the world-historical nature of China as a "semi-colonial" country, resulting in the defeat of the great revolution in 1927.[8] With world history wielding significance on both global and national scales, the authors encourage readers to "study some world history" and implore researchers to publish accessible world history books for the working-class populace.

The subsequent essays in this pamphlet delve into specific facets of world history, addressing inquiries related to modern and contemporary history, the history of imperialism, and the history of national liberation movements. Due to space constraints, we will not be able to venture into further details in this chapter. Nevertheless, the overarching objective of all four essays remains consistent: to wield world history as a tool for fostering revolutionary radicalism among the masses. While undoubtedly a piece of propaganda, the publication of these essays, in hindsight, signifies a symbolic moment for the emergence of area studies in China.

During this period, the establishment of research centers with a focus on the study of foreign regions laid the institutional groundwork for contemporary area studies. Meanwhile, many scholars in this field today came of age during the Maoist era, and the discourse of anti-colonialism and anti-imperialism has indelibly shaped their worldview. A noteworthy example of this enduring influence is evident in the contemporary critiques of globalization by Chinese political scientists, who often perceive it as an extension of American imperialism—a theme that will be explored further in this chapter.

Tracing the roots of area studies to the political radicalism of the 1960s and 1970s enables a nuanced understanding of the intricate interplay between international studies (foreign studies), world history, area studies, and global history in China. The rise of area studies presents both opportunities and challenges for present-day global historians in the country.

As previously discussed in earlier chapters, contemporary historians often downplay the historiographical significance of world history during the radical era of the Cultural Revolution. The tumultuous decade of the Cultural Revolution saw the suspension of world history education at numerous universities and research institutions. However, the essays

---

[8] Shih Chun, *On Studying Some World History*, 10–11.

featured in *Red Flag* serve as a reminder of an intrinsic theme in the evolution of global history in China: the intricate interplay between history and politics. While present-day historians in China are typically driven less by political considerations in their research, there persists a historical tendency for the state to shape the narrative of history in alignment with its ideological agendas. Exactly during the radical years of political upheaval in the 1960s and 1970s, the communist government embarked on establishing new research centers in international studies to serve its foreign policy objectives.[9]

In its formative years, the People's Republic of China adopted a "leaning on one side" policy, drawing inspiration from the Soviet Union for economic reconstruction and foreign policy perspectives. However, escalating tensions between the two socialist countries in the early 1960s led to the "Sino-Soviet split." As the Chinese Communist Party engaged in an ideological debate, critiquing the Soviet Union for deviating from the "correct" path of the socialist movement, Chinese leaders felt compelled to forge an independent foreign policy, seeking a path to modernity distinct from both the Soviet Union and the United States. During this process, a realization emerged regarding the insufficient understanding of world history within the country. An illustrative instance occurred on April 14, 1961, when Zhou Yang 周楊 (1907–1989), the deputy director of the Party's Propaganda Department, acknowledged during a meeting that a mistake had been made in discontinuing English and other foreign language education in middle schools. This decision resulted in a populace that knew "too little" about the world, possessing "next to nothing" knowledge about various facets of the world economy, history, and literature. While emphasizing the importance of studying China, Zhou Yang asserted that it was imperative to delve into global knowledge. Spearheading the project to edit national humanities textbooks, he proposed the introduction of new academic areas at universities in urban centers like Beijing and Shanghai, including the study of world history and world economy. Extending beyond the West, he advocated

---

[9] Both terms "area studies" and "global history" did not appear in the discourse of the 1960s and 1970s. Yet a broad range of areas of research and political discussion may serve as prototypes for area studies in China today, such as "foreign studies" (waiguo yanjiu) and "studies of international issues" (guoji wenti yanjiu).

for the exploration of Asia, Africa, and Latin America, not solely in terms of their history but also languages and cultures.[10]

Zhou Yang's speech aptly captures the anxiety among Chinese leaders regarding China's limited knowledge about the world as the nation stepped onto the international stage. During the winter of 1963 to the spring of 1964, Prime Minister Zhou Enlai embarked on a diplomatic tour, visiting ten African countries.[11] Prior to this trip, senior party leaders expressed dissatisfaction with the country's insufficient global understanding.[12] In a party report on December 30, 1963, Mao Zedong voiced his discontent, highlighting the absence of serious research on three major world religions in China, despite their significant global influence. Mao endorsed a petition advocating for the promotion of studies in foreign countries. After this report, the Party Central responded by establishing the "Advisory Committee on International Studies." Under Zhou Enlai's leadership, meetings were convened to formulate a series of measures, including, launching a set of research institutions and reinforcing existing ones, establishing foreign studies organizations at higher education institutes and enhancing the schools and departments of international politics, strengthening research organizations affiliated with foreign embassies, and creating a committee to guide international studies, among other initiatives.[13] These measures underscored the commitment of the Chinese leadership to address the deficit in global knowledge.

By 1964, a network of international studies centers had emerged in China, representing a significant step in the country's engagement with global affairs. Notable establishments included the Center for Soviet and Eastern European Studies (officially founded in 1965) and the Center for Southeast Asian Studies, both initiated by the Party Central's International Liaison Department. The Foreign Ministry established the Center for Indian Studies, while the Chinese Academy of Social Sciences

---

[10] Zhou Yang, *Zhou Yang wenji* [Collected Works by Zhou Yang] (Beijing: Renmin wenxue chubanshe, 1990), 315–316; Chu, *Dangdai Zhongguo zhexue shehui kexue fazhan shi*, 327.

[11] Julia Strauss, "The Past in the Present: Historical and Rhetorical Lineage in China's Relations with Africa," *The China Quarterly*, 199 (September 2009): 781.

[12] Cited from Chu, *Dangdai Zhongguo zhexue shehui kexue fazhan shi*, 327.

[13] Chu, *Dangdai Zhongguo zhexue shehui kexue fazhan shi*, 329–330; Zhonggong zhongyang wenxian yanjiu shi, ed. *Mao Zedong nianpu* [Annotated Chronicle of Mao Zedong] (Beijing: Zhongyang wenxian chubanshe, 1993), vol. 5, 298–299.

created the Center for World Economy and Politics. In addition to these centralized efforts, several prominent universities played a pivotal role in expanding the landscape of international studies. Fudan University, People's University, and Peking University each established departments dedicated to international studies. Fudan focused on the study of Western European and North American capitalism, People's University delved into the history of international communist movements, and Peking University specialized in Asia, Africa, Latin America, and other countries.[14] While the roots of the Chinese Communist Party's research organizations on international studies can be traced back to the Yan'an years, it was during the early 1960s that a nationwide network for international studies was formally established. This development marked a crucial juncture in China's pursuit of a comprehensive understanding of global affairs.[15]

Contemporary scholars recognize the pivotal moment in the promotion of international studies in China during what is now termed "the initial period of the development of area studies in China."[16] However, criticisms abound regarding the quality of research during this era, as subsequent political campaigns and the Cultural Revolution disrupted the development of research agendas within these institutions.[17] Examining the authorship of the pamphlet on studying world history provides a revealing example of these complexities.

The pseudonymous author "Shi Jun" 史軍, translated as "history troops," points to a group of young scholars affiliated with the History Department at Peking University during that time. As of now, individuals such as Fan Daren 范達人 (1935–), Luo Rongqu, Xu Tianxin 徐天新,

---

[14] Chu, *Dangdai Zhongguo zhexue shehui kexue fazhan shi*, 330.

[15] The Central Academy of Research was founded in Yan'an on May 5, 1938. As a prototype for the Chinese Academy of Social Sciences, it included a unit for studies of international issues. Yet its research agenda remained rudimentary. Wen Jize, Li Yan, Jin Ziguang, and Zhai Dingyi, eds., *Yan'an Zhongyang yanjiuyuan huiyilu* [Memoirs about the Central Academy], (Changsha: Hunan renmin chubanshe, 1984), 284–291.

[16] Ren Xiao and Sun Zhiqiang, "Quyu guobie yanjiu de fazhan lichen, qushi he fangxiang: Ren Xiao jiaoshou fangtan" [The history, trend, and direction of the development of area and national studies: an interview with Professor Ren Xiao], *Guoji zhengzhi yanjiu* [International politics studies], no. 1 (2020): 142.

[17] Chu, *Dangdai Zhongguo zhexue shehui kexue fazhan shi*, 330.

and Zhang Peisheng 張培生 are identified as part of this cohort.[18] Under-standing these young historians' trajectories sheds light on the bifurcated legacy of political radicalism in the discipline of history in China.

These young scholars, including Luo Rongqu, were commissioned by the journal to draft the essays in the pamphlet. There are rumors suggesting that Mao himself initiated this idea.[19] In the case of Luo, who was already in the countryside due to his family's unfavorable class standing, he participated in crafting the first essay. However, as the ideo-logical and partisan tone escalated, his contributions were not included in the subsequent essays.[20] During the later years of the Cultural Revolu-tion, Luo faced severe hardships and contemplated suicide. Despite the challenges, he managed to survive and emerged as a prominent historian in the 1980s, advocating for studies on modernization theory.[21]

In contrast to Luo Rongqu's shift away from political radicalism, Fan Daren continued to actively engage in such ideological pursuits. His political activism led to his selection by the Jiang Qing group to compose a series of essays attacking fellow party members and advo-cating hardline ideologies. Evolving from a young scholar, Fan ascended to become the primary contributor to the "Liang Xiao" writing group (homophonous with "two schools"), operating at Peking University and Tsinghua University in the later years of the Cultural Revolution. In the same year that the pamphlet promoting world history studies was published, Fan Daren received the prestigious opportunity to visit Peru and Mexico. He was appointed as a member of the Chinese Academy of Sciences archeologist delegation, a notable honor at a time when few Chinese scholars had the chance to travel abroad. Further recog-nition came with his election as a representative attending the Fourth National Congress.[22] However, the end of the Cultural Revolution brought repercussions for Fan, as he found himself facing consequences

[18] Fan Daren, *Wenge "yubi" chengfu lu* [The Rise and Fall of the Emperor's Scribe during the Cultural Revolution] (Hong Kong: Mingbao chubanshe, 1999), 217.

[19] Fan, *Wenge "yubi" chengfu lu*, 217.

[20] Luo Rongqu, "Qiusuozhai shilu" [Authentic Record from the Qiusuo Hall], in *Qiusuozhe de zuji: Luo Rongqu de xueshu rensheng* [The Footprints of a Seeker: The Academic Life of Luo Rongqu], eds. Lin Beidian and Zhou Yingru (Beijing: Shangwu yinshu dian, 2010), 427.

[21] See Chapter 2 part on Luo.

[22] Fan, *Wenge "yubi" chengfu lu*, 221.

for his association with the "Gang of Four." He endured a year of impris-
onment and was barred from teaching until 1980. As a historian, Fan's
legacy became tainted, and his career bore the mark of the controversies
surrounding his involvement with the radical ideologies of the Cultural
Revolution.[23]

The interplay between scholars and the state has been a significant
theme in modern Chinese intellectual history. In the 1920s, following
the Higher Education reform at Peking University, a new generation
of university professors embraced the identity of academic professionals
committed to promoting objectivism in historical research. Against the
backdrop of the New Culture Movement, leading figures in this generation, such as historian Gu Jiegang 顧頡剛 (1893–1980), adopted a critical
stance toward China's past. They questioned the authenticity of historical
records related to antiquity, employing an evidence-based approach to
scrutinize the past and deconstruct the myth of the long continuity of
Chinese civilization. This approach found widespread acceptance among
Gu's contemporaries.

Fu Sinian 傅斯年 (1896–1950), Gu's roommate at Peking University
and a key figure in the New Culture Movement, assumed a leadership
role in the newly established national research institution, the Institute
of History and Philology at the Academia Sinica (abbreviated as "IHP"),
following an extensive study trip to Europe in 1928. In a famous declaration, Fu asserted that, as a historian, one's duty was to explore history
comprehensively, delving into every corner from "Heaven above to Yellow
Spring below," using hands and feet to uncover historical material.[24] This
perspective reflected a shared value among historians to distance themselves from external influences and prioritize reliance on primary sources
in their scholarly pursuits.

The shifting dynamics of international politics had a significant impact
on the national political landscape and, consequently, the position of
Chinese historians caught between history and politics. As the Japanese
Empire intensified its plans to assert control over Manchuria, Japanese
scholars endorsed this colonial agenda. A prominent figure in this

---

[23] Fan, *Wenge "yubi" chengfu lu*, 201–206.

[24] Fan-sen Wang, *Fu Ssu-nien: A Life in Chinese History and Politics* (Cambridge:
Cambridge University Press, 2000), 73–74. The "Yellow Spring" refers to the hell
according to Chinese religious belief.

movement was the Japanese sinologist and historian Shiratori Kura-
kichi 白鳥庫吉 (1865–1942), who, in his works, deliberately separated
the peoples north of the Great Wall from the Chinese. Utilizing a
linguistic approach, Shiratori argued that both Manchurian and Mongo-
lian languages belonged to the Ural-Altaic linguistic family, asserting no
linguistic ties to the Chinese. Emphasizing these perceived differences,
scholars like Shiratori advocated for the separation of Manchuria from
China.[25] In the early 1930s, Yano Jin'ichi 矢野仁一 (1872–1970), a
professor of Chinese history at the Imperial University of Kyoto, became
a leading voice calling for separating Manchuria from China.[26]

In response to the escalating tensions and the Japanese Kwang-
tung army's takeover of Manchuria following the Mukden Incident of
1931 and Japanese scholars' call for Manchurian independence, Chinese
historians such as Fu Sinian felt compelled to defend China's national
sovereignty through historical justifications. Faced with the challenge of
inadequate military strength to resist foreign aggression, the Nanjing
government appealed to the League of Nations. In response, the League
appointed a five-member Commission, headed by British politician Victor
Bulwer-Lytton, to evaluate the incident. Fu, along with other intellectuals in Peking, delivered a passionate speech urging fellow intellectuals
to employ their knowledge in service of the country. In an expedited
effort to persuade the Lytton Commission that Manchuria had historically been an integral part of China, they decided to compile a five-volume
book.[27] Despite his commitment to academic objectivism, Fu found
himself contributing a volume on the ancient history of Manchuria, a
subject outside his area of expertise. As a result, he made numerous
mistakes with historical facts.[28] The looming crisis of foreign invasions

[25] Pi-ling Yeh, "Jiuyiba shibian hou Zhongguo shixuejie dui Riben 'Man-Meng lun'
zhi bochi: yi *Dongbei shiguang* diyijuan wei zhongxin zhi tantao" [The Chinese History
Field' Confutation on Japan's Manchuria-Mongolia Policy after the Mukden Incident: An
Inquiry Based on The First Volume of *Manchuria in History*], *Guoshiguan xueshu jikan*
(Bulletin of Academia Historia), no. 11 (March 2007): 113.

[26] Wang Fansen, "Sixiangshi yu shenghuoshi you jiaoji ma?—Du 'Fu Sinian dang'an'"
[Are There Overlaps Between History of Ideas and History of Life?: Reading Fu Sinian
Archives], in *Zhongguo jindai sixiang yu xueshu de xipu* [The Genealogy of Modern
Chinese Thought and Scholarship] (Shanghai: Shanghai sanlian shudian, 2018), 540–541.

[27] Yeh, "Jiuyiba shibian hou," 121.

[28] Yeh, "Jiuyiba shibian hou," 131; Wang, "Sixiangshi yu shenghuoshi you jiaoji ma?"
539–540.

and the imperative of national survival had clearly tilted the balance between academic pursuits and political exigencies.[29]

The Nationalist government, led by Chiang Kai-shek, exhibited authoritarian tendencies; however, due to its limited capacity to enforce political control, its influence over Chinese intellectuals remained somewhat subdued. In contrast, the Communist Party, particularly under Mao Zedong's leadership during the Rectification Campaign in Yan'an, explicitly rejected the self-proclaimed intellectual autonomy of the May Fourth generation. Mao openly called upon artists and writers to align their creative work with the interests of the masses. The subsequent political campaigns further reshaped the relationship between the state and intellectuals, spanning from the founding of the People's Republic to the radical years of the Cultural Revolution. This evolving dynamic had an impact on the study of international affairs and world history in China.

From the 1950s to the 1970s, propaganda materials promoting revolutionary radicalism constituted a significant portion of works related to world history and international studies in China. These materials, often lacking vigorous academic research and nuanced historical analysis, were distilled into a black-and-white political narrative. A central theme in these materials was the cultivation of strong anti-imperialist sentiments among the masses.

In 1965, for example, a pamphlet published by China Youth Press recounted a story of American imperialism in China. American image in China, as David Shambaugh has documented, is a highly complex one. On one hand, Chinese educated elites regarded America as the most advanced country in the world, a land of beauty; on the other hand, it was perceived as the foremost enemy due to imperialistic ambitions to invade China.[30] However, during the mid-1960s, the Chinese portrayal of America took a one-sided approach, offering a harsh criticism of America through the lens of imperialism. In the preface, the anonymous editors began by asserting, "American imperialism is not only the No.1 enemy of the people of the world but also the archenemy of the Chinese people." They claimed that the history of American invasion of

---

[29] Focusing on the changes in Gu Jiegang, I also discussed the decline of intellectual autonomy during the Republican period in another essay, see Xin Fan, "The Lost Intellectual Autonomy: State, Society and Historical Writing in Republican China," *Berliner China-Hefte/Chinese History and Society* 43, (2013): 64–76.

[30] Shambaugh, *Beautiful Imperialist*, 3.

China spanned at least 120 years, and American imperialists were accused of committing numerous bloody crimes not only in China but around the world.[31]

Clearly aimed at a younger audience, the book features concise chapters highlighting episodes of American imperialism in China. The first chapter, titled "The Indictments of History," presents four historical encounters. It begins with the USS Brandywine's operations in China in 1844, during which the American navy battleship coerced the Chinese government into signing the Treaty of Wangxia—the first unequal treaty between the two countries. The second episode narrates American citizen Frederick Townsend Ward (1831–1862)'s involvement in foreign corps suppressing the Taiping Rebellion from 1860 to 1862. The third accuses American scholar John Calvin Ferguson (1866–1945) of spying for the Qing government, leading to the death of the revolutionary Zou Rong. The final episode recounts how American entrepreneur Floyd Tangier Smith (1882–1939) joined the Shanghai Volunteer Corps and killed Chinese workers during the May Thirtieth Movement of 1925—a crucial moment in the rise of anti-imperialism in China (Fig. 7.1).

The text goes beyond a mere historical account; after describing Smith's actions, the author adopts a campaign-like language, stating, "This is the ironclad evidence of how American butchers murdered the revolutionary people of China." The author then emotionally engages with the reader, asking rhetorical questions that evoke a sense of collective memory and indignation: "Having seen this piece of indictment, can we forget these bloody scenes? Can we repress the burning hatred in our heart? Can we let our compatriots die in vain? No! No! No! We must always remember these blood debts, seeking total retribution against American imperialism!"[32] This chapter serves as an illustrative example, as the rest of the book follows a similar approach of promoting anti-American sentiments through historical narratives, using emotive language to evoke a sense of national outrage and a call to action against perceived injustices.

From today's professional standards, it is evident that the stories presented in this book were manipulated for political purposes. One

[31] *Mei diguo zhuyi qin Hua zuixing lu* [The Record of Crimes Committed by American Imperialism Invading China] (Beijing: Zhongguo qingnian chubanshe, 1965), 1.
[32] *Mei diguo zhuyi qin Hua zuixing lu*, 7–14.

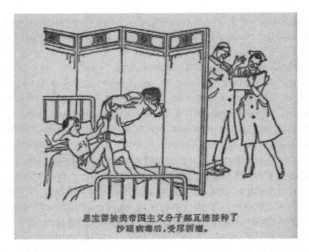

恩宝普被美帝国主义分子郝瓦德接种了
沙眼病毒后,受尽折磨。

Fig. 7.1 Propaganda image of American imperialists conducting biomedical experiments on Chinese people, cited from *Mei diguo zhuyi qin Hua zuixin lu* (Beijing: Zhongguo qingnian chubanshe, 1965), page 50

example from this chapter is an image depicting the story of American doctor Harvey J. Howard (1880–1956) allegedly tested vaccinations on Chinese orphans and subjected them to torture in 1921.[33] Howard served as the head of the Department of Ophthalmology at Union Medical College in Peking during that time and was the former emperor Pu Yi's private doctor. In 1925, Howard was kidnapped by bandits during their visit to Manchuria. They managed to escape after ten months, thanks to Howard's fluency in Chinese, and later published their story, which garnered significant public attention.[34] As an expert in ophthalmology, Howard was acutely aware of the serious situation regarding the spread of trachoma among school children. In a medical report from 1924, he discussed his efforts to prevent the spread of this eye infection disease. Recognizing the poor hygienic conditions in schools, he advocated for the establishment of a national central clinic. However, he was also pragmatic

[33] *Mei diguo zhuyi qin Hua zuixing lu*, 48–50.

[34] Harvey J. Howard, *Ten Weeks with Chinese Bandits* (London: John Lane the Bodley Head Ltd, 1927).

about the lack of public funding support.[35] There is no indication that Howard engaged in any inhumane behaviors aimed at torturing Chinese children.

The shifting dynamics of international relations between China and major powers were reflected in the historical narratives promoted in Maoist China. In 1965, the United States was portrayed as China's number one enemy, but after the Sino-American Rapprochement and the changing global environment, by the 1970s, the Soviet Union replaced the United States as the biggest threat to China. This geopolitical transformation had a direct impact on how the history of Sino-Russian relations was presented. In a pamphlet published in October 1976 by a writers' group based in the Heilongjiang Academy of Social Sciences, adopting the alias Rong Jiang 戎疆 (meaning "defending frontiers"), a revised history of imperial Russia's invasion of China was recounted.[36] Geared toward educating "a broad readership from workers, peasants, and soldiers," the book presented a concise history of relations between imperial Russia and China in a question-and-answer format. Once again, it provided a simplistic narrative labeling Tsarist Russia as "a country that invaded China the earliest, a sly and vicious enemy that took away the most territory from China, was extremely hostile, and had been madly suppressing the Chinese people's revolutionary movements."[37] In this version of history, Russia replaced America as the new number one enemy of China.

The pamphlets on foreign history from the Maoist era, with their highly ideologically charged language, are often not closely examined by historians today. Despite this, their large circulation and emotionally charged tone in promoting revolutionary idealism were appealing to young readers in China during the Cultural Revolution. While these materials may not have significantly influenced the professional writing of world history in China in the years following the Cultural Revolution, it would be a stretch to directly connect them to the origins of global history. However, as we will explore later in this chapter, the strong sentiment of anti-colonialism and anti-imperialism embedded in

[35] Harvey J. Howard, "The Eradication of Trachoma Among School Children in China," *The China Medical Journal 38*, no. 4 (April 1924): 255–270.

[36] Rong Jiang, *Shahuang E'guo shi zenyang qinlue Zhongguo de* [How Tsarist Russia Invaded China] (Beijing: Renmin chubanshe, 1976).

[37] Rong Jiang, *Shahuang E'guo shi zenyang qinlue Zhongguo de*, 1.

these materials remains a significant part of cultural memory. This sentiment has resurfaced among some critics of the West in contemporary China, serving as a noteworthy aspect that continues to shape perspectives on global affairs. The lasting impact of these ideological narratives on cultural memory highlights the complex interplay between historical propaganda and the formation of international relations theory in China.

Despite the revolutionary radicalism, the 1960s and 1970s marked an institutional jump start to international studies in China. Following the Cultural Revolution, many centers previously engaged in "foreign studies" experienced increased institutionalization in the 1980s. Some of them transformed into departments of area studies, such as the Department of Eastern Languages at Peking University and the Institute for the History of Ancient Civilizations at Northeast Normal University in Changchun, focusing on languages and cultures.[38] Some evolved into schools of international studies, like those at Peking University and Tsinghua University, emphasizing international politics. Others transitioned into think tanks, providing policy briefings and political advice. In this transformative process, the CASS played a leading role, establishing eight research centers for international studies, including (Table 7.1),

These institutes cover a broad range of areas, focusing on countries and regions, forming the foundation for area studies in China today.[39]

The rise of area studies is a recent development in China. As a conceptual framework, area studies represent an interdisciplinary approach that focuses on specific geographical regions or culturally defined areas within the social sciences.[40] While some scholars trace its origin back to the European expansion of colonial empires in the early modern era, others connect its rise to the world wars and cold-war politics. The dual roots of China studies in the United States illustrate this dichotomy in the perception of area studies. On the one hand, sinology embodies a centuries-long tradition rooted in the European Enlightenment, with a strong focus on studying China's tradition, language, and culture.[41] On the other hand,

[38] For the Institute for the History of Ancient Civilizations in Changchun, see Fan, *World History and National Identity*, 153–154; 184–190.

[39] Ren and Sun, "Quyu guobie yanjiu de fazhan lichen," 142.

[40] Bert Hoffmann and Andreas Mehler, "Area Studies–Social Research," in *Britannica*, https://www.britannica.com/topic/area-studies.

[41] For a recent survey of this tradition, see the special issue on "Traditions of Sinology" in the *Journal of Chinese History* 7, no. 2 (September 2023): 253–656.

Table 7.1 Eight CASS research centers for international and area studies

Institution Name in the 1980s	Institution Name today
亞洲太平洋研究所 Institute of Asia–Pacific Studies (1988)	亞太與全球戰略研究院 National Institute of International Strategy
西歐研究所 Institute of West European Studies	歐洲研究所 Institute of European Studies
蘇聯東歐研究所 Institute of Soviet and Eastern European Studies	俄羅斯東歐中亞研究所 Institute of Eastern European, Russian, and Central Asian Studies
拉丁美洲研究所 Institute of Latin American Studies	
西亞非洲研究所 Institute of West Asian and African Studies	
日本研究所 Institute of Japanese Studies	
美國研究所 Institute of American Studies	
世界經濟與政治研究所 Institute of World Economics and Politics	

the China Studies that emerged during the Cold War period adopts a more social science approach, examining China as an economic and political entity within the context of international politics, serving the national interests of Western countries[42] (Table 7.2).

Until recently, however, area studies, as a self-claimed subject of scholarly research, did not formally exist in China.[43] Instead, it remained a loose concept encompassing a broad spectrum of studies, including national studies, international studies, foreign languages and cultures, and world history.[44] A rapid increase in the use of area/country-specific

---

[42] Bruce Cumings, "Boundary Displacement: Area Studies and International Studies during and after the Cold War," *Bulletin of Concerned Asian Scholars* 29, no. 1 (1997): 6–26; Zhang Yang, *Lengzhan yu xueshu: Meiguo de Zhongguoxue, 1949–1972* [The Cold War and Academics: Chinese Studies in the United States, 1949–1972] (Beijing: Shehui kexue chubanshe, 2019).

[43] Niu Ke, "Quyu he guoji yanjiu: guanyu lishi he 'yuanli' de sikao—Niu Ke fujiaoshou fangtan" [Area and International Studies: Reflection on History and 'Principles'—An Interview with Associate Professor Niu Ke], *Guoji zhengzhi yanjiu*, no. 5 (2018): 121.

[44] Some scholars point out, this careless use of concepts is prone to causing confusion. Niu Ke, "Quyu he guoji yanjiu," 123n2.

Table 7.2 A survey of occurrences of 區域國別 and 全球史 as subject words in CNKI database (survey conducted on January 4, 2024 and accessed at the University of Cambridge, UK)

studies is evident in a quick survey of journal publications collected in the CNKI database in recent years (refer to the chart on this page). In China, area studies now incorporate an additional dimension that focuses on the in-depth examination of specific foreign countries.

In the new century, subjects in international studies, in general, have experienced rapid development, too. While the earlier stage of growth was spearheaded by national think tanks such as the CASS, new initiatives are now sponsored by the Ministry of Education. Alongside the "eight CASS research centers," Chinese universities have established nine research bases (研究基地) dedicated to international studies(refer to Table 7.3).

Unlike CASS research centers, which are not primarily teaching institutions, the bases at universities also provide standardized undergraduate and postgraduate programs on area studies. These research bases serve as the focus point for the establishment of a second tier and a third tier research centers, each concentrating on more specific regions in international politics. Examples include the School of APEC Studies at Guangxi Nationalities University and the Institute of Southeast Asian Studies at

Table 7.3 Nine university research bases for international and area studies

University Name	Area of focus	University Location
Xiamen (Amoy) University	Southeast Asian Studies	Xiamen, Fujian
Jilin University	Northeast Asian studies	Changchun, Jilin
Fudan University	American studies	Shanghai
East China Normal University	Russian studies	Shanghai
Shanghai Foreign Languages University	Middle Eastern Studies	Shanghai
Renmin University of China	European Studies	Beijing
Sichuan University	Indian Studies	Chengdu, Sichuan
Nankai University	APEC Studies	Tianjin
Ji'nan 暨南 University	Chinese Diaspora Studies	Guangzhou, Guangdong

Yunnan University. With robust state funding support, the development of area studies entered a new stage.[45]

In September 2022, Country and Regional Studies (CRS) (區域國別研究) received formal recognition as a "first-level discipline" (一级学科), solidifying its prominent position within China's academic hierarchy.[46] The recently issued national postgraduate education guidelines further designate CRS as a first-level interdisciplinary subject in graduate education, aligning it with major disciplines such as history, literature, and medical science. As of January 2024, the Ministry of Education has sanctioned 453 education bases (including those in preparation) distributed across 186 higher education institutions nationwide. Over 20,000 teachers are actively engaged in the teaching and research pertaining to CRS topics.[47]

[45] Ren and Sun, "Quyu guobie yanjiu de fazhan lichen," 142–143.

[46] Wang Zhi, "Guoji guanxi xue yu quyu guobie xue de ronghe: jianlun bijiao diqu zhuyi de zuoyong" [The Fusion of International Relations Studies and Area/Country-Specific Studies: Also on the Significance of Comparative Regionalism], *Shijie shehui kexue* [World Social Sciences], no. 5 (2023): 193; for disciplinary classification in China, see "Introduction."

[47] Zhongguo xuewei yu yanjiusheng jiaoyu xuehui [Association of Chinese Graduate Education], "Yanjiusheng jiaoyu xueke zhuanye jianjie jiqi xuewei jiben yaoqiu, [Introduction to the Subjects in Graduate Education and Their Basic Requirements] (abbreviated as "Guidelines") (January 2024): I. https://www.acge.org.cn/encyclopediaFront/enterE ncyclopediaIndex.

In contrast to area studies in Europe and America, research centers in China boldly incorporate the national dimension into their teaching and research alongside the regional focus. The latest graduate education guidelines clearly state CRS's principal goal is to the state demand (國家需求), and list both foreign regions and countries as the primary targets for research.[48] As a result, the official term for this field includes both "regional studies" (區域研究) and "country studies" (國別研究). This distinctive approach suggests that Chinese scholars in area studies are generally less critical of the nation-state framework prevalent in current scholarship with both world history and international studies.[49] This inclination is further evidenced by their recent advocacy for "global history with Chinese characteristics" over the past decade. The trajectory from embracing globalization in the 1980s to celebrating national identity in the second decade of the twenty-first century reflects an ambivalent view toward nationalism in the contemporary development of global history.

As demonstrated in Chapter 2, the rise of global history in China finds its roots in the appreciation of globalization by Chinese historians during the Age of Reform and Opening-up. However, in recent years, universal support for globalization has been rapidly dissipated worldwide. Events such as the rise of Trumpism in America, the choice of Brexit in the United Kingdom, the return to authoritarian politics in China, and the outbreak of the COVID-19 pandemic, along with associated isolationist policy in various countries all seem to indicate the possibility of the end of globalization. While scholars in North America and Western Europe seriously consider the potential for a New Cold War between China and America in the short-term future, scholars in China remain engrossed in debates on the clash of civilizations and the Thucydides Trap when contemplating the long-term course of history. In either scenario, the question arises: What will happen to global history if globalization comes to an end?

With this question in mind, we contend that global history is currently encountering three significant challenges in China, despite the opportunities facilitated by state funding support and widespread interest:

[48] "Guidelines": II. 3.
[49] Niu, "Quyu he guoji yanjiu," 121–122.

The first challenge involves some Chinese scholars advocating for the rejection of globalization. In recent years, there has been a growing aversion to globalization in China, particularly among nationalistic populists and educated elites. Research indicates that, during the COVID-19 pandemic, Chinese youth displayed a strong sense of nationalist sentiments, often harboring high levels of hostility toward foreign nations, especially the United States.[50] For many in China including some prominent scholars, the current globalization movement is perceived as an American-led conspiracy aimed at reinforcing the West's dominance in the world. What was once a passionate embrace of globalization has transformed into outspoken opposition among these intellectuals.

In an influential essay, Jiang Shigong 强世功, a prominent scholar associated with China's "cultural and political conservative" movement, strongly critiques the ongoing globalization process.[51] According to Jiang, in the post-Cold War era, the term "globalization," initially led by the United States, has evolved into a moral judgment. People tend to oversimplify the course, associating "globalization" with positivity, aligned with the principles of Reform and Opening-up, and branding "anti-globalization" (逆全球化) as negative, synonymous with the isolationist policy.

Jiang emphasizes the distinction between "globality" and "globalization" asserting that they are two separate concepts.[52] He argues that "globality" is a sociological concept, whereas "globalization" is a political one. The latter, according to him, implies a struggle for a "universal civilization" where various local civilizations vie for global dominance within the framework of the world imperial order.[53] Jiang contends that, while ancient exchanges embodied "globality," the term

---

[50] Ho Wing-chung, "The Surge of Nationalist Sentiment among Chinese Youth during the COVID-19 Pandemic," *China: An International Journal* 20, no. 4 (November 2022): 1–22.

[51] It is often misleading to place Chinese conservatives within the context of cultural and political conservatism in the West. Yet in this case, Jiang was the Chinese translator of Carl Schmitt's works, and his view was highly influenced by conservative thinkers of Schmitt alike.

[52] Jiang Shigong, "Quanqiuhua yu shijie diguo," *Dushu* [Reading], no. 3 (March 2023); English translation is available as "Globalization and World Empire," *China Watch* 3, no. 11 (March 2023): https://china-cee.eu/2023/03/28/globalization-and-world-empire/.

[53] Jiang, "Quanqiuhua yu shijie diguo," 4.

"globalization" now predominantly refers to Western-dominated global movements, dismissing other forms as "anti-global."

In adopting a civilizing perspective, Jiang contends that despite the inherent globality in all ancient cross-cultural exchanges, globalization has been redefined as a Western-centric ideological construct. Post-Cold War, globalization has been wielded as an ideology, contributing to the establishment of a world empire dominated solely by the United States. Drawing on the ideas of Samuel Huntington and Francis Fukuyama, Jiang describes this ideology as a pursuit of the "end of history" through the imposition of a world empire utilizing the concept of "clashes of civilizations."[54]

Transcending the current discourse on globalization and anti-globalization, Jiang Shigong shifts the focus to question the essence of globalization—probing who propels it and in what manner it progresses. He revisits the classical Marxist critique of capitalism as a global hegemony and incorporates the theory of empire. In this framework, he applauds anti-global forces as inherently anti-imperial, drawing a connection to the roots of the Chinese revolution.

Similar to how Marxist historians during the Mao era framed class struggles as the fundamental global conflict, Jiang decisively characterizes the post-Cold War era as a historical struggle between "globalization" and "anti-globalization." For him, the former seeks to construct a unilateral "world empire," while the latter aspires to forge a multilateral world order. According to Jiang, if the entire post-Cold War history unfolds through America's pursuit of engineering a world empire, China's communist, anti-imperial revolution attains world-historical significance, symbolizing resistance against the emerging world empire. In taking this perspective, Jiang positions China's recent conflicts with the United States within a broader context of world history and civilizations. China's resistance is not merely a manifestation of a national agenda for its ascent; rather, it embodies a global movement rooted in anti-colonial and anti-imperial struggles.[55]

As scholars like Jiang Shigong extol anti-global movements and conceptualize globalization as an imperial agenda, historians in China find themselves compelled to contemplate the ways in which global history,

---

[54] Jiang, "Quanqiuhua yu shijie diguo," 5.
[55] Jiang, "Quanqiuhua yu shijie diguo," 10.

as a historical approach, is entrenched in a cultural hierarchy of knowledge and power between the West and the East.[56] This gives rise to the second challenge that historians in China must confront in their pursuit of global history—namely, how to craft a "global history with Chinese characteristics."

In the opening chapter of this book, I introduced the debate on whether historians could and should write a global history in a Chinese way. Throughout subsequent chapters, I explored how Chinese historians tend to emphasize several aspects in their writing of global history. These include synchronizing "Chinese" historical moments with the world, tracing the translation processes of concepts from the West to China, and making sense of world-historical concepts through historical analogies. Additionally, I delved into various traditions of studying the histories, cultures, languages, and politics of foreign countries through disciplines such as international studies, area studies, foreign studies, world history, and area/country-specific studies. I also discussed the unique sociological structures under which global historians conduct their teaching and research, encompassing national think tanks at the Chinese Academy of Social Sciences, various governmental and party apparatuses, and academic departments further divided into teaching and research units at Chinese universities.

While Chinese historians operate within a distinctive social, cultural, and political environment, I hold the conviction that the fundamental value of global history lies in enabling historians to transcend national and regional frameworks, and engaging in active research agendas to appreciate the globally connected humanity. The answer to whether a national approach should be adopted in writing global history may perhaps be rooted in one's ideological position beyond historical research. After all, global history is never a fully defined field with set-in-stone values and standardized research methods. Its most exciting aspect may indeed reside in its dynamic celebration of connectedness in the collective past of human beings.

While the dynamic nature of global history is enticing to historians like us, it simultaneously poses challenges that global historians must confront. One such challenge is the absence of standardized academic

---

[56] Scholars like Dominic Sachsenmaier argue for a local origin of global historical thinking in China. I echo such an opinion in my own work. At the same time, many scholars still believe that global history is contingent to Chinese historiographical tradition.

"infrastructures" for teaching and researching global history. Global historians in China find themselves wearing multiple hats—they are world historians, national historians, area studies experts, international studies scholars, and even think tank professionals. This fluidity of identity presents both an exhilarating opportunity and a disconcerting challenge.

Amid the rapid ascent of area studies in recent years, there is a growing concern about the potential overshadowing of global history. Many historians in China share the worry that the rise of area studies signifies state influence on academic pursuits, drawing parallels with the situation in the United States.[57] By referencing American academic trends, scholars in China might find themselves aligning their research agendas with national interests. This confluence blurs the once-distinct line between academic pursuits and political considerations, raising concerns about maintaining the integrity of scholarly endeavors within this context.

The rise of the history of great powers serves as a noteworthy example of how world historians engage in the celebration of great-power politics through both teaching and research. In 2003, two world historians, Qi Shirong and Qian Chengdan 錢乘旦, delivered lectures at a Politburo study session of the CCP party central, introducing a historical perspective on the rise and fall of great powers throughout world history. The following year, a twelve-part TV documentary titled "The Rise of the Great Powers" (大國崛起) was broadcast nationally on CCTV. This discourse on the Great Powers gained widespread circulation in Chinese popular and political discussions.

The impact of this discourse became apparent in the summer of 2012 when China and the Philippines clashed over a disputed island in the South China Sea. Chinese spokesperson Fu Ying 傅瑩 openly called for the coexistence of big and small countries, cautioning that the Philippines, being a small country, should not bully China, which is a big country.[58] This perspective starkly contrasts with the discourse of the Republican era, which portrayed China as belonging to the world of *ruoxiao minzu* (weak and small peoples). The contemporary celebration of greatness appears to directly challenge China's historical legacy of anti-colonialism and anti-imperialism.

---

[57] This remains a controversial issue in scholarship. Yet an overwhelming majority of scholars in China hold such an opinion.

[58] https://www.chinanews.com.cn/gn/2012/06-03/3934761.shtml.

Examining past Chinese discourse on global history allows us to gain fresh insights into the global outlook of Chinese leaders. The celebration of "upheaval" (亂) during the Cultural Revolution finds echoes in Xi Jinping's recent rhetoric on change.

Following the Nineteenth Party Congress, Xi has emphasized the current world's status as undergoing "unprecedented changes in a century" (百年未有之大變局). During a talk delivered at the fifth anniversary of the Belt and Road Initiative, he noted,

> In the current world, we are in a period of significant development, great changes, and major adjustments. We need to possess a strategic vision, establish a global perspective, be aware of both risks and concerns, and at the same time, be conscious of historical opportunities. We should strive to navigate through this unprecedented century of great changes, steering our course with determination.[59]

These "great changes" present both challenges and opportunities. Questions arise: What forms the basis of this strategic vision? How is China's global perspective evolving? What do these "risks and concerns" entail, and what constitutes these "opportunities"? To comprehend the nuances in Chinese leaders' political views regarding China's position in the world, one could argue that studying global history is essential. Consequently, global history in China is not merely a significant topic in Chinese historiography and intellectual history but also one with profound implications in international politics.

---

[59] "Bainian weiyou zhi dabianju, zongshuji zhexie zhongyao lunshu zhengkongfakui" [Unprecedented Changes in a Century: These Words by General Secretary Are Startling the Ear and Awakening the Mind], *Qiushi* (August 27, 2021): http://www.qstheory.cn/zhuanqu/2021-08/27/c_1127801606.htm.

BIBLIOGRAPHY

LATE QING JOURNALS AND NEWSPAPERS

Dong-Xi yang kao meiyue tongji zhuan 東西洋考每月統計傳 [Eastern Western Monthly Magazine].
Dongfang zazhi 東方雜誌 [The Eastern Miscellany].
Huatu xinbao 華圖新報 [The Chinese Illustrated News].
Minbao 民報 [People's Journal]
Qingyi Bao 清議報 [The China Discussion].
Xia'er guanzhen 遐邇貫珍 [Chinese Serial].
Xiangxue xinbao 湘學新報 [New Journal for Studies in Hunan].
Xinmin congbao 新民叢報 [New People's Journal]

ARCHIVAL AND PRIMARY SOURCES COLLECTIONS

FRUS: *Foreign Relations of the United States.*
Mao Zedong nianpu [Annotated Chronicle of Mao Zedong]. Beijing: Zhongyang wenxian chubanshe, 1993.
QSXZ: *Qi Shirong xiansheng zhuisilu* [A Collection to Commemorate Mr. Qi Shirong]. Edited by Xu Lan. Beijing: Renmin chubanshe, 2018.
ZMZSC: *Zhonghua minguo zhongyao shiliao chubian–Dui Ri kangzhan shiqi* [The Preliminary Collection of Important Historical Materials from the Republic of China: The War of Resistance Era. First Edition]. Taipei: Zhongguo guomindang zhongyang weiyuanhui dangshi weiyuanhui, 1981.

ZXZSZLHB: *Zhongguo xiandai zhexueshi ziliao huibian* [Collected Documents on the History of Modern Chinese Philosophy]. Edited by Zhong Limeng and Yang Fenglin. Shenyang: Liaoning daxue zhexuexi, 1982.

OTHER PRIMARY SOURCES

Cicero, *De Re Publica*.

Ding, Weiliang [W. A. P. Martin], *Zhongguo gushi gongfan* [International Law in Ancient China]. Translated by Wang Fengzao. Beijing: Tongwen guan, 1884.

Ho, P. S. "International Law and Customs of Ancient China in Time of Peace." *The Chinese Students' Monthly* 11, no. 4 (1916): 238–250.

Huang, Zunxian, *Riben guozhi* [Treatise on Japan]. Guangzhou, 1898.

Joan Robinson Collection, King's College Archive Centre, Cambridge.

Martin, W. A. P. "Traces of International Law in Ancient China." *International Review* 14, (January 1883): 663–77.

———. *A Cycle of Cathay: or China, South and North with Personal Reminiscences*. New York: Fleming H. Revell Company, 1896.

———. *Hanlin Papers: Essays on the History, Philosophy, and Religion on the Chinese*. Shanghai: Kelly & Walsh/The Tientsin Press, 1894.

Mei diguo zhuyi qin Hua zuixing lu [The Record of Crimes Committed by American Imperialism Invading China]. Beijing: Zhongguo qingnian chubanshe, 1965.

Okamoto, Kansuke 岡本監輔. *Wanguo shiji* [History of Myriad Nations]. Shanghai: Shenbao guan, 1879.

Rong, Jiang. *Shahuang E'guo shi zenyang qinlue Zhongguo de* [How Tsarist Russia Invaded China]. Beijing: Renmin chubanshe, 1976.

Shi Jun, *Du yidian shijieshi*. Beijing: Renmin chubanshe, 1973.

Shih Chun, *On Studying Some World History*. Peking: Foreign Languages Press, 1973.

William, Samuel Wells. *An English and Chinese Vocabulary in the Court Dialect* [Ying-Hua yufu lijie]. Macao, 1844.

Wheaton, Henry. *Wanguo gongfa* [Elements of International Law]. Translated by W. A. P. Martin, in *Han'guk kŭndae pŏpche saryo ch'ongsŏ*. Sŏul: Asea Munhwasa, 1981.

SECONDARY SOURCES

"Hanyi shijie xueshu mingzhu congshu" [World Academic Classics in Chinese Translation Series], Commercial Press webpage, https://www.cp.com.cn/han yi40/.

Alitto, Guy. *The Last Confucian: Liang Shu-ming and the Chinese Dilemma of Modernity*. Berkeley: University of California Press, 1986.

Allison, Graham. "The Thucydides Trap: Are the U.S. and China Headed for War?" *The Atlantic* (September 24, 2015). https://www.theatlantic.com/international/archive/2015/09/unitedstates-   china-war-thucydides-trap/406756/.

———. *Destined for War: Can America and China Escape Thucydides' Trap?* New York: Houghton Mifflin Harcourt, 2017.

Aosiwa'erde Sibingele [Oswald Spengler], *Xifang de moluo* [The Decline of the West]. Translated by Qi Shirong, et al. Beijing: Shangwu yinshuguan, 1963.

Barraclough, Geoffrey. *Main Trends in History.* New York: Holms & Meier Publishers, 1979.

Bartsch, Shadi. *Plato Goes to China: The Greek Classics and Chinese Nationalism.* Princeton: Princeton University Press, 2023.

Bayly, C. A. *The Birth of the Modern World.* Oxford: Wiley-Blackwell, 2003.

Beckert, Sven, and Dominic Sachsenmaier, eds. *Global History, Globally: Research and Practice around the World.* London: Bloomsbury, 2018.

Berger, Stefan. "Comparative History and Transnational History." In *Writing History: Theory and Practice*, edited by Stefan Berger, Heiko Feldner, and Kevin Passmore, 292–315. London: Bloomsbury, 2010.

Brook, Timothy. *Mr. Selden's Map of China: The Spice Trade, a Lost Chart & the South China Sea.* London: Profile Books, 2013.

Cao, Juren. *Wo yu wo de shijie* [My World and Me]. Beijing: Renmin chubanshe, 1983.

Cao, Yin. *Chinese Sojourners in Wartime Raj, 1942–45.* Oxford: Oxford University Press, 2022.

Chakrabarty, Dipesh. *Provincializing Europe: Postcolonial Thought and Historical Difference.* Princeton: Princeton University Press, 2008.

Chen, Boyi. *Yinghuan zhilue: Quanqiushi zhong de haiyangshi* [Seeing Across the Oceans: Maritime History in Global History]. Guilin: Lijiang chubanshe, 2024.

Chen, Huaiyu. "The Rise of 'Asian History' in Mainland China in the 1950s: A Global Perspective." *Global Intellectual History* 7, no. 2 (2022): 282–302.

———. *Qinghua yu "yizhan": Meiji jiaoshou de Zhongguo jingyan* [Tsinghua and the "First World War": American Professors' China Experiences]. Hangzhou: Zhejiang chubanshe, 2021.

Chen, Li. *Chinese Law in Imperial Eyes: Sovereignty, Justice, and Transcultural Practice.* New York: Columbia University Press, 2015.

Chen, Qineng. *Jianguo yilai shijieshi yanjiu gaishu* [An Overview of World-historical Studies after the Founding of the People's Republic]. Beijing: Shehui wenxian chubanshe, 1991.

Chiang, Kai-shek. "Guanyu Lugouqiao shijian zhi yanzheng biaoshi" [A Solemn Statement on the Marco Polo Incident] (known as "Lushan speech"). In

Zongtong Jiang gong sixiang yanlun zongji [The Complete Collection of President Mr. Jiang's Thought and Speeches], vol. 14: 582–585. Taipei: Zhongguo guomindang zhongyang weiyuanhui dangshi weiyuanhui, 1984.

Chow, Tse-Tsung. *The May 4th Movement: Intellectual Revolution in Modern China*. Cambridge, MA: Harvard University Press, 1960, 50–51.

Chu, Zhuwu. *Dangdai Zhongguo zhexue shehui kexue fazhan shi (1949–1966)* [History of Contemporary Chinese Philosophy and Social Sciences, 1949–1966]. Beijing: Shehui kexue wenxian chubanshe, 2023.

Cohen, Paul. *Discovering History in China: American Writing on the Recent Chinese Past*. New York: Columbia University Press, 1984.

Conrad, Sebastian, and Dominic Sachsenmaier, eds. *Competing Visions of World Order: Global Moments and Movements, 1880s–1930s*. Palgrave, 2007.

Conrad, Sebastian. *What Is Global History?* Princeton: Princeton University Press, 2017.

Crossley, Pamela. *What Is Global History?* Cambridge: Polity, 2008.

Culp, Robert. "'Weak and Small Peoples' in a 'Europeanizing World': World History Textbooks and Chinese Intellectuals' Perspectives on Global Modernity." In *The Politics of Historical Production in Late Qing and Republican China*, edited by Tze-ki Hon and Rebert Culp, 211–247. Leiden: Brill, 2007.

———. *Articulating Citizenship: Civic Education and Student Politics in Southern China, 1921–1940*. Cambridge, MA: Harvard Asia Center, 2007.

Cumings, Bruce. "Boundary Displacement: Area Studies and International Studies during and after the Cold War." *Bulletin of Concerned Asian Scholars* 29, no. 1 (1997): 6–26.

Day, Jenny. "The War of Textbooks: Educating Children during the Second Sino-Japanese War, 1937–1945." *Twentieth-Century China* 46, no. 2 (2021): 105–129.

———. *Qing Travelers to the Far West: Diplomacy and the Information Order in Late Imperial China*. Cambridge: Cambridge University Press, 2018.

Dirlik, Arif. "Chinese Historians and Marxist Concept of Capitalism," *Modern China* 8, no.1 (1982): 105–131.

Duan, Wanhan, Gu Hansong, and Chen Bixiang, eds. *Shijie wuqian nian* [The World in Five Thousand Years]. Beijing: Shaonian ertong chubanshe, 1991.

Duara, Prasenjit. *Rescuing History from the Nation: Questioning Narratives of Modern China*. Chicago: The University of Chicago Press, 1995.

Evasdottir, Erika. *Obedient Autonomy: Chinese Intellectuals and the Achievement of Orderly Life*. Vancouver: University of British Columbia, 2004.

Fan, Daren. *Wenge "yubi" chengfu lu* [The Rise and Fall of the Emperor's Scribe During the Cultural Revolution]. Hong Kong: Mingbao chubanshe, 1999.

Fan, Xin. "Historical Analogies, Historia Magistra Vitae." In *Bloomsbury History: Theory and Method Articles*. London: Bloomsbury Publishing, 2021. https://doi.org/10.5040/9781350970885.074.

————. "The Anger of Ping-Ti Ho: The Chinese Nationalism of a Double Exile." *Storia Della Storiografia* (History of Historiography) 69, no. 1 (2016): 147–160.

————. "The Lost Intellectual Autonomy: State, Society and Historical Writing in Republican China." *Berliner China-Hefte/Chinese History and Society* 43 (2013): 64–76.

————. "The Making of the Zhanguo Ce Clique: The Politicization of History Knowledge in Wartime China." In *The Engaged Historian: Perspectives on the Intersections of Politics, Activism and the Historical Profession*, edited by Stefan Berger, 136–150. New York: Berghahn Books, 2019.

————. *World History and National Identity in China: The Twentieth Century.* Cambridge: Cambridge University Press, 2021.

Fang, Weigui. "'Anxingqi' yu gainianshi: jianlun Dong-Ya zhuanxingqi gainian yanjiu" [The "Saddle Period" and the History of Concepts]. *Dong-Ya guannianshi jikan* [East Asian Journal of History of Concepts], no. 1 (December 2011): 85–116.

————. "'Yihui,' 'minzhu,' 'gonghe' gainian zai Xifang yu Zhongguo de chuanbian" [The Transformation of Concepts "Parliament," "Democracy," and "Republic" in China and the West], *Ershiyi shiji* [The Twenty-first Century] 58, no. 2 (April 2000): 49–61.

Fedasiuk, Ryan. "The China Scholarship Council: An Overview." *CSET Issue Brief*. Washington, DC: Center for Security and Emerging Technology at Georgetown University, July 2020.

Feng, Tianyu. *"Fengjian" kaolun* [Re-examining "Feudalism"]. Beijing: Zhongguo shehui kexue chubanshe, 2010.

Fischer, David Hackett. *Historians' Fallacies: Toward a Logic of Historical Thought*. New York: Harper and Row, 1970.

Foucault, Michel. *Power/Knowledge: Selected Interviews & Other Writings, 1972–1977*. New York: Pantheon Books, 1980.

Fredman, Zach. *The Tormented Alliance: American Servicemen and the Occupation of China, 1941–1949*. Chapel Hill: University of North Carolina Press, 2022.

Fukuyama, Francis. *The End of History and the Last Man*. New York: Free Press, 1992.

Furth, Charlotte. "Intellectual Change: From the Reform Movement to the May Fourth Movement, 1895–1920." In *An Intellectual History of Modern China*, edited by Merle Goldman and Leo Ou-fan Lee, 322–405. Cambridge: Cambridge University Press, 2002.

Gasster, Michael. "Reform and Revolution in China's Political Modernization." In *China in Revolution: The First Phase 1900–1913*, edited by Mary Wright, 67–96. New Haven: Yale University Press, 1968.

Ge, Zhaoguang. "Sixiangshi weihe zai dangdai Zhongguo ruci zhongyao" [Why is Intellectual so Important in Contemporary China?]. *Aisixiang* [The Love for Intellectual Thought] (December 2021), cited from *Wenhuibao*, https://www.aisixiang.com/data/130011.html.

———. "The Evolution of a World Consciousness in Traditional Chinese Historiography." *Global Intellectual History* 7, no. 2 (2022): 207–225.

Getachow, Adom. *Worldmaking after Empire: The Rise and Fall of Self-Determination*. Princeton University Press, 2019.

Goldstein, Martin. *American Foreign Policy: Drift or Decision*. Wilmington, Delaware: Scholarly Resources Inc., 1984.

Goody, Jacky. *The Theft of History*. Cambridge: Cambridge University Press, 2007.

Grieder, Jerome. *Hu Shih and the Chinese Renaissance: Liberalism in the Chinese Revolution*. Cambridge, MA: Harvard University Press, 1970.

Gries, Peter. *China's New Nationalism: Pride, Politics, and Diplomacy*. Berkeley: University of California Press, 2004.

Guo, Songtao. *Lundun yu Bali riji* [London and Paris Diaries]. Edited by Zhong Shuhe. Changsha: Yuelu chubanshe, 1984.

Han, Yongli. "Zhongguo xuezhe guanyu Zhongguo kangzhan zai dierci shijie dazhan zhong diwei yanjiu shuping" [A Review of Chinese Scholars' Study the Role of China's War of Resistance in the Second World War]. *Wuhan daxue xuebao* [Wuhan University Journal (Humanity Sciences)] 59, no. 4 (July 2006): 481–485.

Haneda, Masashi, "Japanese Perspectives on 'Global History'." *Asian Review of World Histories* 3, no. 2 (July 2015): 219–234.

Harrison, Henrietta. *The Perils of Interpreting: The Extraordinary Lives of Two Translators between Qing China and the British Empire*. Princeton: Princeton University Press, 2021.

He, Bingsong. "Zhongguo gudai guoji fa" [International Law in Ancient China]. *Fazheng xuebao* [Journal of Law and Politics] (1920): 5–13.

He, Yan. "Yu Kaisi jiangyan: cong quanqiushi de jiaodu kan Wusi Yundong" [Talk by Klaus Mühlhan: Rethink the May Fourth Movement Through Global History]. *Wenhui bao* (May 5, 2014): https://www.whb.cn/zhuzhan/guandian/20140505/6316.html.

Ho, Wing-chung. "The Surge of Nationalist Sentiment among Chinese Youth during the COVID-19 Pandemic." *China: An International Journal* 20, no. 4 (November 2022): 1–22.

Hoffmann, Bert, and Andreas Mehler, "Area Studies–Social Research." In *Britannica*, https://www.britannica.com/topic/area-studies.

Howard, Harvey J. "The Eradication of Trachoma among School Children in China." *The China Medical Journal* 38, no. 4 (April 1924): 255–270.

————. *Ten Weeks with Chinese Bandits*. London: John Lane the Bodley Head Ltd, 1927.

Hu, Hanmin. "Hu Hanmin zizhuan" [Autobiography by Hu Hanmin]. In *Geming wenxian* [Documents on the Chinese Revolution], edited by Zhongguo guomindang zhongyang dangshi shiliao bianzhuan weiyuanhui, Series 3. Taipei: Zhongyang wenwu gongyingshe, 1965.

Huang, Chin-shing [Huang Jinxing], "Cong pubian shi dao shijie shi he quanqiu shi—yi Lanke shixue wei fenxi shidian" [From Universal History to World History and Global History–Ranke's Universal History as the Departure Point for Understanding the Current Issues of World History]. *Beijing daxue xuebao (Zhexue shehui kexue ban)* [Journal of Peking University (Philosophy and Social Sciences)] 54, no. 2 (March 2017): 54–67.

Huang, Grace. *Chiang Kai-shek's Politics of Shame: Leadership, Legacy, and National Identity in China*. Cambridge, MA: Harvard University Press, 2021.

Huters, Theodore. *Bringing the World Home: Appropriating the West in Late Qing and Early Republican China*. Honolulu: University of Hawai'i Press, 2005.

Iggers, Georg, Q. Edward Wang, and Supriya Mukherjee. *A Global History of Modern Historiography*. London: Routledge, 2013.

Jenco, Leigh. *Changing Referents: Learning Across Space and Time in China and the West*. Oxford University Press, 2015.

Jiang, Shigong. "Quanqiuhua yu shijie diguo." *Dushu* [Reading], no. 3 (March 2023): 3–11; English translation is available as "Globalization and World Empire." *China Watch* 3, no. 11 (March 2023): https://china-cee.eu/2023/03/28/globalization-and-world-empire/.

Jin, Qiu. *The Culture of Power: The Lin Biao Incident in the Cultural Revolution*. Stanford: Stanford University Press, 1999.

Jin, Yao. "Dongfang guojifa puxi de chongxin faxian" [The Eastern International Law Pedigree], *Shehui kexue qianyan* [Advances in Social Sciences] 7, no. 8 (2018): 1164–1170.

Johnson, Ian. *Sparks: China's Underground Historians and their Battle for the Future*. Oxford: Oxford University Press, 2023.

Karl, Rebecca. *Staging the World: Chinese Nationalism at the Turn of the Twentieth Century*. Durham: Duke University Press, 2002.

————. *The Magic of Concepts: History and the Economic in Twentieth-Century China*. Durham: Duke University Press, 2017.

Khong, Yuen Foong. *Analogies at War: Korea, Munich, Dien Bien Phu, and the Vietnam Decisions of 1965*. Princeton: Princeton University Press, 1992.

Kishimoto, Mio. "Gurōbaru hisutorī ron to 'Kariforunia gakuha'" [Global History Theory and the "California School"]. *Shisō* [Thought], no. 1127 (2018): 80–100.

Kocka, Jürgen. "Comparison and Beyond." *History and Theory* 42, No. 1 (February 2003): 39–44.

Kushner, Barak. *Men to Devils, Devils to Men: Japanese War Crimes and Chinese Justice.* Cambridge, MA: Harvard University Press, 2015.

Lackner, Michael, Iwo Amelung, and Joachim Kurz, eds. *New Terms for New Ideas: Western Knowledge and Lexical Change in Late Imperial China.* Leiden: Brill, 2001.

Landes, David. *Revolution in Time: Clocks and the Making of the Modern World.* Cambridge, MA: Harvard University Press, 2000 [1983].

Lean, Eugenia. *Vernacular Industrialism in China: Local Innovation and Translated Technologies in the Making of a Cosmetics Empire, 1900–1940.* New York: Columbia University Press, 2020.

Lei, Haizong. *Zhongguo wenhua yu Zhongguo de bing* [Chinese Cultural and Chinese Military]. Beijing: Shangwu yinshuguan, 2014.

Li, Bozhong. *Jiangnan de zaoqi gongyehua, 1550–1850* [Early Industrialization in the Yangzi Delta]. Beijing: Shehui kexue wenxian chubanshe, 2000.

Li, Hongtu. "Quanqiu sixiangshi: chongsi xiandai quanqiu zhixu de sixiang qiyuan" [Global Intellectual History: Reexamining the Intellectual Origins of the Modern World Order]. *Huadong shifan daxue xuebao* [Journal of East China Normal University] 52, no.5 (2020): 3–10.

Li, Huaiyin. *Reinventing Modern China: Imagination and Authenticity in Chinese Historical Writing.* Honolulu: University of Hawaii Press, 2013.

Li, Jianming. *Lishi xuejia de xiuyang he jiyi* [Historians' Education and Their Craft]. Shanghai: Shanghai sanlian shudian, 2007.

Li, Jing. "Ge Zhaoguang: Quanqiushi shi bici lianxi de lishi" [Ge Zhaoguang: Global History is a History of Connectedness]. *Nanfang renwu zhoukan* [People in the South Weekly], no. 12 (April 28, 2023): https://www.infzm.com/contents/248149?source=131.

Li, Laifu [Leif Littrup]. "Juyou Zhongguo tese de shijieshi" [The World History with Chinese Characteristics]. Translated by Li Jianrong, *Wuhan daxue xuebao* [Journal of Wuhan University (Philosophy and Social Sciences Edition)], no. 4 (1993): 19–26.

Li, Longqing. "Yingjie xinshiji chonggou shijie lishi xinkuangjia" [Embracing a New Framework for Reconstructing World History]. *Huazhong shifan daxue xuebao* [Journal of Central China Normal University (Humanities and Social Sciences edition)] 39, no. 4 (2000): 118–122.

Li, Xiaoqian. *Xifang shixue zai Zhongguo de chuanbo, 1882–1949* [The Spread of Western Historiography in China, 1882–1949]. Shanghai: Huadong shifan daxue chubanshe, 2007.

Lippert, Wolfgang. *Entstehung und Funktion einiger chinesischer marxistischer Termini: Der lexikalisch-begriffliche Aspekt der Rezeption des Marxismus in Japan und China.* Wiesbaden: F. Steiner, 1979.

Littrup, Leif. "World History with Chinese Characteristics." *Culture and History* 5. Suppl. (1989): 39–63.

Liu, Jiahe, and Chen Xin, "Lishi bijiao chulun: bijiao yanjiu de yiban luoji" [A Preliminary Analysis of Historical Comparison: General Logic in Comparative studies]. *Beijing shifan daxue xuebao* [Journal of Beijing Normal University (Social Science Edition)], no.5 (2005): 67–73.

Liu, Jiahe. "Lishi de bijiao yanjiu yu shijie lishi" [Comparative Studies in History and World History]. *Beijing shifan daxue xuebao* [Journal of Beijing Normal University (Social Science Edition)], no. 5 (1995): 46–51.

Liu, Lydia. *The Clash of Empires: The Invention of China in Modern World Making*. Cambridge, MA: Harvard University Press, 2004.

———. *Translingual Practice: Literature, National Culture, and Translated Modernity—China, 1900–1937*. Stanford University Press, 1995.

Liu, Simu, Wang Zhende, Hou Chengde, and Ma Xinmin, "Zhongguo kangri zhanzheng jiqi zai di'erci shijie dazhan zhong de diwei he zuoyong" [China's War of Resistance and its Role and Contribution in the Second World War]. *Shijie lishi* [World history], no. 4 (1980): 5–13.

Liu, Xiaofeng. "Ouzhou wenming de 'ziyou kongjian' yu xiandai Zhongguo: du Shimite *dadi de fa* zhaji" [The "Free Space" for European Civilization and Modern China: Notes on Reading Schmitt' *Der Nomos der Erde*]. *Sixiang pinglun* [RUC Perspectives], no. 4 (2018): 67 pages.

Liu, Xincheng, "The Global View of History in China." *Journal of World History* 23, no. 3 (September 2012): 491–511.

———. "Quanqiu shiguan zai Zhongguo" [The Global View of History in China]. *Lishi yanjiu* [Historical Research], no. 6 (December 2011): 180–187.

Lu, Jiandong. *Chen Yinke de zuihou ershi nian* [The Last Twenty Years in Chen Yinke's life]. Beijing: Sanlian shudian, 1995.

Luo Rongquan. "Huiyi Luo Rongqu dage" [Remembering My Big Bother Luo Rongqu]. *Zhuanji wenxue* [Biography] 88, no. 1 (2006): 81–96.

———. "New Perspectives on Historical Development and the Course of Modernization in East Asia." Translated by Guo Wu, *Chinese Studies in History* 43, no.1 (Fall 2009): 17–27.

———. *Qiusuozhe de zuji: Luo Rongqu de xueshu rensheng* [The Footprints of a Seeker: The Academic Life of Luo Rongqu]. Edited by Lin Beidian and Zhou Yingru. Beijing: Shangwu yinshu dian, 2010.

Luo, Zhitian. "Beifa qianhou Qinghua yu Beida de shixue" [Historical Studies at Tsinghua (University) and Peking University around the period of the Northern Expedition]. *Qinghua daxue xuebao (zhexue shehui kexue ban)* [Journal of Tsinghua University (Philosophy and Social Sciences Edition)] 31, no. 6 (2016): 9–11.

Ma, Guang. *Rupture, Evolution, and Continuity: The Shandong Peninsular in East Asian Maritime History during the Yuan-Ming Transition*. Wiesbaden: Harrassowitz, 2021.

MacKinnon, Stephen. *Wuhan, 1938: War, Refugees, and the Making of Modern China*. Berkeley: University of California Press, 2008.

Manela, Erez. *The Wilsonian Moment: Self-Determination and the International Origins of Anticolonial Nationalism*. Oxford: Oxford University Press, 2007.

Manning, Patrick. *Navigating World History: Historians Create a Global Past*. New York: Palgrave Macmillan, 2003.

Martin, Dorothea. *The Making of a Sino-Marxist World View: Perceptions and Interpretations of World History in the People's Republic of China*. Armonk, NY: M. E. Sharpe, 1990.

Martineau, Anne-Charlotte. "Overcoming Eurocentrism?: Global History and the *Oxford Handbook of the History of International Law*." *The European Journal of International Law* 25, no. 1 (February 2014): 329–336.

Matten, Marc A., and Yang Zhao, *Chinese Students and their PhD Education in the United States (1919–1945)*. Erlangen: FAU University Press, 2023. https://open.fau.de/handle/openfau/30267.

Mitter, Rana. "State-building After Disaster: Jiang Tingfu and the Reconstruction of Post-World War II China, 1943–1949." *Comparative Studies in Society and History* 61, no. 1 (2019): 176–206.

———. *Forgotten Ally: China's World War II, 1937–1945*. Boston: Houghton Mifflin Harcourt, 2013.

Mülhahn, Klaus. *Making China Modern: From the Great Qing to Xi Jinping*. Cambridge, MA: Harvard University Press, 2019.

Niu, Ke. "Quyu he guoji yanjiu: guanyu lishi he 'yuanli' de sikao—Niu Ke fujiaoshou fangtan" [Area and International Studies: Reflection on History and 'Principles'—An Interview with Associate Professor Niu Ke]. *Guoji zhengzhi yanjiu* [International Politics Studies], no. 5 (2018): 120–160.

Novak, Peter. *That Noble Dream: The "Objectivity Question" and the American Historical Profession*. Cambridge: Cambridge University Press, 1988.

Oberheim, Eric and Paul Hoyningen-Huene, "The Incommensurability of Scientific Theories." *The Stanford Encyclopedia of Philosophy* (Fall 2018 Edition), edited by Edward Zalta, https://plato.stanford.edu/entries/incommensurability/.

Ogura, Kin'ichi. *Kinsei Yōroppa no higashi to nishi* 近世ヨーロッパの東と西 [Eastern and Western Europe in Early Modernity]. Tokyo: Yamakawa shuppansha, 2004.

Pantsov, Alexander. *Victorious in Defeat: The Life and Times of Chiang Kai-shek, 1887–1975*. New Heaven: Yale University Press, 2023.

Papelitzky, Elke. *Writing World History in Late Ming China and the Perception of Maritime Asia*. Wiesbaden: Harrassowitz, 2020.

Peng, Minghui. *Taiwan shixue de Zhongguo chanjie* [The Chinese Complex in Taiwanese Historiography]. Taipei: Maitian chubanshe, 2001.

Peng, Xiaopu. "Xilun *Zouding xuetang zhangcheng* zhong youguan waiguo wenshi jiaoxue de fangce" [On the Rules Regarding Foreign History and Literature Education in the *Memorial on Regulations on School Curricula*]. *Guoli Taiwan shifan daxue lishi xuebao* [History Journal of National Taiwan Normal University] 17, (June 1989): 241–285.

Perdue, Peter. "A Single Entity." *London Review of Books* 43, no. 10 (May 20, 2021).

Qi, Shirong, ed. *Shijie shi* [World History]. Beijing: Gaodeng jiaoyu chubanshe, 2006–2007.

———. "Guanyu kaizhan shijie xiandaishi yanjiu de jige wenti" [Several Questions Concerning the Unfolding of World-Historical Studies]. *Lishi jiaoxue wenti* [Issues of Historical Pedagogy], no. 2 (March 1988): 1–10.

———. "Guanyu zai shijie shi jiaoxue zhong jinxing aiguo zhuyi sixiang jiaoyu de jidian yijian" [Several Suggestions on How to Implement Patriotic Education in World-historical Pedagogy]. *Guangming ribao* [Guangming Daily] (July 28, 1951).

———. "Zhongguo kangri zhanzheng zai di'erci shijie dazhan zhong de diwei he zuoyong" [The Role and Contribution of China's Anti-Japanese War of Resistance in the Second World War]. *Lishi yanjiu* [Historical Research], no. 4 (1985): 118–133.

———. *Shixue wujiang* [Five Lectures on Historiography]. Beijing: Renmin chubanshe, 2017.

Qian, Mu. *Zhongguo lishi yanjiu fa* [Methods to Study Chinese History]. Beijing: Jiuzhou chubanshe, 2019.

Rahav, Shakhar. "Beyond Beijing: May Fourth as a National and International Movement." *Journal of Modern Chinese History* 13, no. 2 (January 2019): 325–331.

Rawski, Evelyn. "Reenvisioning the Qing: The Significance of the Qing Period in Chinese History." *Journal of Asian Studies* 55, no. 4 (1996): 829–850.

Reed, Christopher. *Gutenberg in Shanghai: Chinese Print Capitalism, 1876–1937*. Vancouver: University of British Columbia Press, 2004.

Reinhardt, Anne. *Navigating Semi-Colonialism: Shipping, Sovereignty, and Nation Building in China, 1860–1937*. Cambridge, MA: Harvard Asia Center, 2018.

Ren, Xiao and Sun Zhiqiang. "Quyu guobie yanjiu de fazhan lichen, qushi he fangxiang: Ren Xiao jiaoshou fangtan" [The History, Trend, and Direction of the Development of Area and National Studies: An Interview with Professor Ren Xiao]. *Guoji zhengzhi yanjiu* [International Politics Studies], no. 1 (2020): 134–160.

Sachsenmaier, Dominic. *Global Entanglements of a Man Who Never Traveled: A Seventeenth-Century Chinese Christian and his Conflicted Worlds*. New York: Columbia University Press, 2018.

———. *Global Perspectives on Global History: Theories and Approaches in a Connected World*. Cambridge: Cambridge University Press, 2011.

Schmitt, Carl. *The* Nomos *of the Earth in the International Law of the* Jus Publicum Europaeum. Translated by G. L. Ulmen. New York: Telos Press, 2006.

Schwartz, Benjamin. *The World of Thought in Ancient China*. Cambridge, MA: Harvard University Press, 1989.

Seaton, Philip. *Japan's Contested War Memories: The "Memory Rifts" in Historical Consciousness of World War II*. Routledge, 2007.

Shambaugh, David. *Beautiful Imperialist: China Perceives America, 1972–1990*. Princeton: Princeton University Press, 1993.

Shen, Guowei. *Xiyu wanghuan: Zhong-Ri jindai yuyan jiaosheshi* [New Language Boomerang: The History of Linguistic Exchanges between China and Japan in Modern Times]. Beijing: Shehui kexue wenxian chubanshe, 2020.

Shen, Wanying. "Jiawuzhan qian *Wanguo shiji* zai Zhongguo de chuanbo yu liubian" [The Spread and Evolution of *Wanguo shiji* in China before the Sino-Japanese War]. In *Yazhou yu shijie* [Asia and the World]. Edited by Li Xuetao and Shen Guowei, vol. 4: 198–208. Beijing: Shehui kexue wenxian chubanshe, December 2021.

Shiner, Larry. "Reading Foucault: Anti-Method and the Genealogy of Power-Knowledge." *History and Theory* 21, no.3 (1982): 382–398.

Smith, Craig. *Chinese Asianism: 1894–1945*. Cambridge, MA: Harvard Asia Center, 2021.

Fogel, Joshua, ed. Special issue on "Traditions of Sinology." *Journal of Chinese History* 7, no. 2 (September 2023): 253–656.

Strauss, Julia. "The Past in the Present: Historical and Rhetorical Lineage in China's Relations with Africa." *The China Quarterly*, 199 (September 2009): 777–795.

Sun, Jiang. "Quanqiu bentuhua de gainianshi" [A Global History of Localized Concepts] (book series launch speech at Nanjing University). *Pengpai xinwen* [The Paper News] (13 June 2023), https://m.thepaper.cn/newsDetail_forward_23461626.

Svarverud, Rune. *International Law as World Order in Late Imperial China: Translation, Reception and Discourse, 1847–1911*. Leiden: Brill, 2007.

Tam, Gina Anne. *Dialect and Nationalism in China, 1860–1960*. Cambridge: Cambridge University Press, 2020.

Tanaka, Stefan. *Japan's Orient: Rendering Pasts into History*. Berkeley: University of California Press, 1993.

Tsu, Jing. *Kingdom of Characters: A Tale of Language, Obsession, and Genius in Modern China*. London: Penguin, 2022.

U, Eddy. *Creating the Intellectual: Chinese Communism and the Rise of a Classification*. Berkeley: University of California Press, 2019.

van de Ven, Hans. *China at War: Triumph and Tragedy in the Emergence of the New China, 1937–1952*. Profile Books, 2017.

———. *War and Nationalism in China, 1925–1945*. London: Routledge, 2002.

van Dongen, Els. *Realistic Revolution: Contesting Chinese History, Culture, and Politics after 1989*. Cambridge: Cambridge University Press, 2019.

Veg, Sebastian. *Minjian: The Rise of China's Grassroots Intellectuals*. New York: Columbia University, 2019.

Vries, Peer. "The California School and Beyond: How to Study the Great Divergence?" *History Compass* 8, no. 7 (July 2010): 730–751.

Wagner, Rudolf. "Reconstructing the May Fourth Movement: The Role of Communication, Propaganda, and International Actors." *Journal of Transcultural Studies* 12, no. 2 Supplement (October 2021): 6–44.

Wang, Fan-sen. *Fu Ssu-nien: A Life in Chinese History and Politics*. Cambridge: Cambridge University Press, 2000.

Wang, Fansen. *Zhongguo jindai sixiang yu xueshu de xipu* [The Genealogy of Modern Chinese Thought and Scholarship]. Shanghai: Shanghai sanlian shudian, 2018.

Wang, Hui. "Contemporary Chinese Thought and the Question of Modernity." Translated by Rebecca Karl, *Social Text* 55 (1998): 9–44.

———. "Dangdai Zhongguo de sixiang zhuangkuang yu xiandaixing wenti." *Tianya* 5, (1997): 133–150.

Wang, Jing. *High Culture Fever: Politics, Aesthetics, and Ideology in Deng's China*. Berkeley: University of California Press, 1996.

Wang, Lixin. "Quanqiu shi yanjiu yu guoji lilun chuangxin de keneng gongxian" [On Global Historical Studies' Possible Contribution to Innovations in IR Theories]. *Zhongguo shehui kexue bao* [Chinese Social Sciences Newspaper], (November 10, 2022).

Wang, Q Edward. *Inventing China through History: The May Fourth Approach to Historiography*. Albany: State University of New York Press, 2001.

———. "Between Marxism and Nationalism: Chinese Historiography and the Soviet Influence, 1949–1963." *Journal of Contemporary China* 9, issue 23 (August 2000): 95–111.

———. "World History on a Par with Chinese History? China's Search for World Power in Three Stages." *Global Intellectual History* 7, no. 2 (2022): 303–324.

———. "Worldviews in Twentieth-Century Chinese Historiography." *Global Intellectual History* 7, no. 2 (2022): 201–206.

Wang, Xiaoqiu. *Jindai Zhong-Ri wenhua jiaoliushi* [The History of Modern Cultural Exchanges between China and Japan]. Beijing: Zhonghua shuju, 2000.

Wang, Zhi. "Guoji guanxi xue yu quyu guobie xue de ronghe: jianlun bijiao diqu zhuyi de zuoyong" [The Fusion of International Relations Studies and Area/Country-specific Studies: Also on the Significance of Comparative Regionalism]. *Shijie shehui kexue* [World Social Sciences], no. 5 (2023): 192–209+247.

Wei, Shuge. *News under Fire: China's Propaganda against Japan in the English-Language Press, 1928–1941*. Hong Kong: Hong Kong University Press, 2017.

Wen, Jize, Li Yan, Jin Ziguang, and Zhai Dingyi, eds. *Yan'an Zhongyang yanjiuyuan huiyilu* [Memoirs about the Central Academy]. Changsha: Hunan renmin chubanshe, 1984.

Weston, Timothy. *The Power of Position: Beijing University, Intellectuals, and Chinese Political Culture, 1898–1929*. Berkeley: University of California Press, 2004.

Whatmore, Richard. *What Is Intellectual History?* Cambridge: Polity Press, 2015.

Wu, Shellen. *Birth of the Geopolitical Age: Global Frontiers and the Making of Modern China*. Stanford: Stanford University Press, 2023.

Wu, Xiaoqun. "Women zhen de xuyao 'quanqiu shiguan' ma?" [Do We Really Need a "Global View of History"?]. *Xueshu yanjiu* [Academic Research], no. 1 (2005): 22–25.

Wu, Yinhua. "Lishi leibi de leixing he yaoqiu" [The Categorization of and Prerequisites for Historical Analogy], *Jianghan luntan* [Jianghan Tribune], no. 9 (June 1982): 32–35.

Wu, Yujin, and Qi Shirong, eds. *Shijie shi* [World History]. Beijing: Gaodeng jiaoyu chubanshe, 1992–1994.

Xie, Kankan. "Ambivalent Fatherland: The Chinese National Salvation Movement in Malaya and Java, 1937–41." *Journal of Southeast Asian Studies* 52, no. 4 (2021): 677–700.

Xing, Ke. "Wan Qing zhi Minguo shiqi Zhonguo 'Shijieshi' shuxie" [The Writing of 'World History' from Late Qing to the Republican Period]. *Xueshu yanjiu* [Academic Research], no. 5 (2015): 113–120.

Xing, Sally Chengji. "Pacific Crossings: The China Foundation and the Negotiated Translation of American Science to China, 1913–1949." PhD diss., Columbia University, 2023.

Xu, Lan. "Xin Zhongguo 70 nian shijieshi xueke de huigu yu zhanwang" [Retrospect and Outlook on the 70 Years of World History in New China]. *Guangming ribao* (August 26, 2019), http://www.qstheory.cn/llwx/2019-08/26/c_1124922041.htm.

Xu, Luo. "Reconstructing World History in the People's Republic of China Since the 1980s." *Journal of World History* 18, no. 3 (September 2007): 325–350.

Xue, Fucheng. *Chushi Ying-Fa-Bi-Yi siguo riji* [Diaries of Mission to Britain, France, Belgium, and Italy]. Changsha: Yuelu chubanshe, 1984.

Yan, Xuetong. *Ancient Chinese Thought, Modern Chinese Power.* Princeton: Princeton University Press, 2013.

Yang, Yu. *Quanqiu shixueshi: cong 18 shiji dao dangdai* [Global Historiography: From the 18th Century to the Present]. Beijing: Peking University Press, 2011.

Yeh, Pi-ling. "Jiuyiba shibian hou Zhongguo shixuejie dui Riben 'Man-Meng lun' zhi bochi: yi *Dongbei shiguang* diyijuan wei zhongxin zhi tantao" [The Chinese History Field' Confutation on Japan's Manchuria-Mongolia Policy After the Mukden Incident: An Inquiry Based on The First Volume of *Manchuria in History*]. *Guoshiguan xueshu jikan* (Bulletin of Academia Historia), no. 11 (March 2007): 105–142.

Yu, Pei, and Zhou Rongyao, eds. *Zhongguo shijie lishi xue 30 nian* [The Thirty Years of Chinese World History Studies (sic)]. Beijing: Zhongguo shehui kexue chubanshe, 2008.

Zarrow, Peter. *After Empire: The Conceptual Transformation of the Chinese State, 1885–1924.* Stanford: Stanford University Press, 2012.

———. *Educating China: Knowledge, Society, and Textbooks in a Modernizing World, 1902–1937.* Cambridge: Cambridge University Press, 2015.

Zeng, Tao. "Jindai Zhonguo de guojifa fuhui lun" [The Hermeneutical Theory of International Law in Modern China]. *Fashi xuekan* [Journal of the History of Law] 11, no. 2 (2007): 217–239.

Zhang, Yibo. "'Sa'er pubian shi' de Zhongguo lishi jiangou yu Ouzhou jindai xueshu zhuanxing" [Construction of Chinese History in Sale's *Universal History* and Modern Academic Transformation in Europe]. *Jianghai xuekan* [Jianghai Journal], no. 2 (2022): 172–184.

Zhang, Xiaoming, "Quanqiu shi yu guoji guanxi yanjiu de rongtong yu hujian" [The Fusion of and Mutual Lessons between Global History and Studies of International Relations]. *Zhongguo shehui kexue bao* [Chinese Social Sciences Newspaper], (November 10, 2022).

Zhang, Xupeng, "Quanqiu shi yu minzu xushi: Zhongguo tese de quanqiu shi heyi keneng" [Global History and National Narrative: The Possibility of a Global History with Chinese Characteristics]. *Lishi yanjiu* [Historical Research], no. 1 (2020): 155–173.

Zhang, Yang. *Lengzhan yu xueshu: Meiguo de Zhongguoxue, 1949–1972* [The Cold War and Academics: Chinese Studies in the United States, 1949–1972]. Beijing: Shehui kexue chubanshe, 2019.

Zheng, Guanying. *Zheng Guanying wenji* [Collected Essays by Zheng Guanying]. Edited by Xia Dongyun. Shanghai: Shanghai renmin chubanshe, 1982.

Zhong, Weimin. *Chaye yu yapian: shijiu shiji jingji quanqiuhua zhong de Zhongguo* [Tea and Opium: China in the Nineteenth Century Economic Globalization]. Beijing: Zhonghua shuju, 2010.

Zhong, Yurou. *Chinese Grammatology: Script Revolution and Literary Modernity, 1916–1958.* New York: Columbia University Press, 2019.

Zhou, Lisheng, and Zhou Yanpei. "Zhongguo gongchandang guanyu minzu fuxing de huayu biaoda" [The Chinese Community Party's Discourse on the Rejuvenation of the Chinese Nation]. *Renmin wang* [People's Net] (March 16, 2022), http://theory.people.com.cn/n1/2022/0316/c40531-32376508.html.

Zhou, Yang. *Zhou Yang wenji* [Collected Works by Zhou Yang]. Beijing: Renmin wenxue chubanshe, 1990.

Zou, Rong. *Geming Jun* [Revolutionary Army]. In *Xinhai geming qian shinianjian shilun xuanji* [The Selected Works on the Debates During the Decade Before the 1911 Revolution], edited by Zhang Zhan and Wang Renzhi. Beijing: Salian shudian, 1960.

Zou, Zhenhuan. *Xifang chuanjiaoshi yu wanqing xishi dongjian: yi 1815 zhi 1900 nian xifang lishii yizhu de chuanbo yu yingxiang wei zhongxin* [Western Missionaries and the Eastern Spread of Western Historiography: The Spread and Impact of the Translated Historical Works from the West from 1815 to 1900 as the Center]. Shanghai: Shanghai guji chubanshe, 2008.

INDEX

Printed by Printforce, United Kingdom